D0775301

HUMAN PREDATORS

How to Recognize, Avoid, and Defend Yourself against Liars, Cheaters, Manipulators, and Abusers

John Shimer & Christian Shimer

bookhouse
PUBLISHING

bookhouse
PUBLISHING

2950 Newmarket St., Suite 101-358 | Bellingham, WA 98226
Ph: 206.226.3588 | www.bookhouserules.com

10 9 8 7 6 5 4 3 2 1

Printed in the United States of America

Library of Congress Control Number: 2022908818

ISBN: 978-1-952483-43-1 (Paperback)
ISBN: 978-1-952483-44-8 (eBook)
ISBN: 978-1-952483-45-5 (Audiobook)

Editor: Julie Scandora
Cover design: Laura Zugzda
Book design: Melissa Vail Coffman

HUMAN PREDATOR

*Anyone who consistently acts without conscience
to dominate others using fear, psychological manipulation,
trickery, or violence (sometimes known as an asshole)*

THE TOP 12 DEVIANT BEHAVIORS OF HUMAN PREDATORS

1. Compulsively lie, gaslight, and distort reality.

2. Ignore rules and laws.

3. Constantly test and violate the boundaries of others.

4. Lack empathy, ignore other people's feelings, or exhibit inappropriate emotional reactions to other people's pain.

5. Operate under a zero-sum game mentality—I win / you lose.

6. Use embarrassment, intimidation, emotional blackmail, or violence to control and manipulate others.

7. Keep those around them on an emotional roller coaster (I hate you; I love you) to keep them off balance.

8. Dominate others yet are always playing the victim.

9. Never apologize, never take responsibility, always deny, blame, and confuse.

10. Create chaos and conflict rather than reduce them.

11. Can't take criticism; are vengeful, punitive, and ruthless.

12. Are addicted to drugs, alcohol, power, violence, sex, publicity, money, or other high-risk activities.

DISCLAIMER

The authors do not suggest readers consider themselves qualified to label people in any way after reading this book. If you encounter someone you believe fits the description of a human predator, your only smart move is to put distance between you and that person.

CONTENTS

SECTION 1: **Be Afraid. Be Very Afraid!** 1

SECTION 2: **Prey Animal, Know Thyself** 19
How You Signal to Human Predators You Are Vulnerable
and Theirs for the Taking

SECTION 3: **Nine BIG Personality Traits of Human Predators.** 77
Meet the Mr. Hyde behind Every Dr. Jekyll

SECTION 4: **The Art of War against Human Predators** 195
How to Stay off the Menu of Human Predators Seeking
Fresh Meat for Their Twisted Agendas

RED-FLAG WARNINGS OF HUMAN PREDATORS 303

"

Most humans are on a quest to connect.
Not connecting causes discomfort and sometimes great pain.
Through camaraderie, family, friendship, love,
we seek personal affirmation and a sense of belonging.
We are often lost without these connections.
Unless, of course, we connect with a human predator.
When that happens,
we experience far greater pain
than is ever experienced by being alone.

"

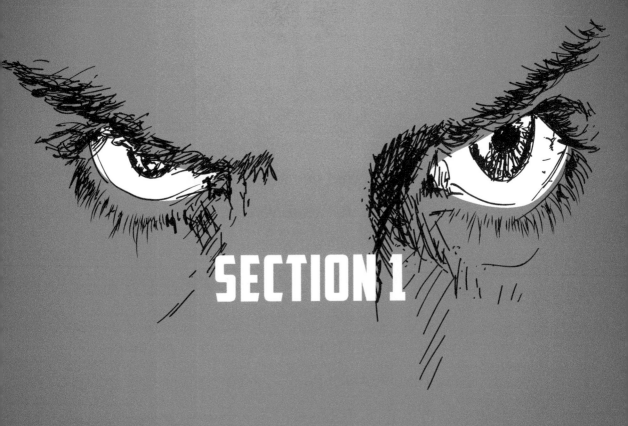

SECTION 1

"

There're two types of fear.

There's the kind that keeps you alive

And the kind that keeps you from living.

Here you will learn about both.

Here you will learn how to use both to keep you safe.

Here you will learn how to protect yourself.

Here you will learn the true nature of human predators.

Here you will learn how to prepare yourself

To deal with their insidious, manipulatory abuse.

"

BE AFRAID! BE VERY AFRAID!

HAVE YOU EVER HAD SOMEONE zip into your parking space before you could get into it and then flip you the bird? Ever had a supervisor at work make a pass at you or coworkers go out of their way to make you look bad to the boss? Do you know people who constantly put you down to feel good about themselves? Ever had an ex-spouse lie to try to get custody of your children? Have you ever been threatened by a bully, had your reputation ruined by a constant gossiper, or been victimized by a cyber-troll trashing your online reputation?

If you answered yes to any of these questions, you can honestly say you have had personal experience with a human predator. Your own label for these people might be *asshole* (or worse), but you are about to learn that the label of *asshole* is actually blinding you to the full potential for harm these people represent. Instead of merely gritting your teeth and seething internally with frustration at their offenses against you, it's important to comprehend that all these people are dangerous, destructive human predators who represent a hundred shades of grey in terms of abusive, manipulative behaviors designed to bring them delight at your expense.

A human predator is anyone who consistently acts without conscience to dominate others using fear, psychological manipulation, trickery, or violence. Have you yet met anyone who fits this definition? Have you been the one preyed upon by someone who behaves this way? Did you feel victimized? Do you still feel victimized? Do you fear meeting more people like the one(s) who preyed on you in the past? Would you like to avoid an encounter with human predators on the rest of your journey through life? Then keep reading this book!

My first entanglement with a human predator didn't occur until I was out of college. I was only twenty-four years old, and I got my ass kicked. A bank I worked for in Tucson, Arizona, knew I had been trained in professional fundraising with the United Way of America and asked me to take a leave of absence from my duties as a bank management trainee to direct a fundraising campaign to raise one hundred thousand dollars in just six weeks to save the reputation of a prominent bank executive serving as chairman of the campaign. Because they hadn't raised a dime, I thought I would receive a rapid promotion if I showed them how to achieve success. But when I used my skills in fundraising to bring in that money on time so the Arizona Kidney Foundation could open the nation's first outpatient kidney dialysis center, I was *terminated* by the bank. I was

> **RED FLAG #5:** Because they have no empathy, human predators do not catch a yawn when you yawn. You can be in a room with five people and yawn, and everyone will start yawning except the one who has no empathy.

completely traumatized by this turn of events and deeply emotionally wounded by the insane behavior of my employment supervisor who was outraged because I received so many accolades from top management in such a short time. His final words to me during my exit interview were, "I just don't think you will be happy being a banker." There appeared on his face a sly, sick grin as he delivered this message to me, and his eyes were as cold and unblinking as a wolf's. It was as if he were experiencing a dark pleasure that only he understood.

The first thing I did was hit the books to try to understand what had happened and why I felt so crushed by the experience. I read every book I could find on the topic of difficult people, but in 1968/69, there wasn't much available. Furthermore, I was sure that what I had encountered was something far worse than a difficult person.

By age forty, my experience and knowledge had expanded enormously, my self-confidence was once again flying high, and the expression *human predator* had become an integral part of my vocabulary. I had become a very successful fundraising consultant to nonprofit organizations and was in high demand for my services organizing major objective fundraising campaigns. More importantly, I was getting quite adept at spotting the early warning signs and red flags of human predators on the prowl and hunting for me. When I found myself face-to-face with one of these beasts of the human jungle, my skills at outsmarting them were firmly part of my defense system . . . a skill set I will teach you in this book.

The information in this book about human predators isn't found anywhere else. Yet, without this information, no one can be expected to successfully navigate the ocean of humans we interact with and mutually depend on for our very lives. Both my son (my co-author) and I have long wondered why a basic course on the predatory behaviors and practices of humans towards other humans has never been created and taught (starting in high school). How in the world can anyone be expected to lead a happy, peaceful, and successful life on planet Earth without knowing what is taught here (without knowing how to navigate a world riddled with assholes)?

Psychologists and psychiatrists use a variety of clinical labels to identify people who act consistently towards others without empathy, compassion, or conscience. These professionals will howl and scream at anyone using the expression *human predator* (or the street term, *asshole*) to describe such a manipulator.

With all due respect to the healers among us who do so much to help humans suffering from mental and emotional disorders (and who are frequently as thoroughly manipulated by human predators as you or I), I am not bound by their professional restrictions and can present hard realities to you from the position of a human prey animal, the self-same type of person who is the victim of human predators. Yes, I am a human prey animal, and my purposes in this book are to say exactly what no one will say and to give my readers the ability to see what they must see to avoid becoming jerked around by one human predatory actor after another for the rest of their lives.

Our goal in writing this book (even with the cover art) is to stimulate a primal response so you will conclude, "I'd better have a look at this because I may be on some predator's menu." By reading this book, you will (at the very least) master the knowledge of what to look out for and how to take evasive action from those trying to harm you!

THE REAL-LIFE MONSTERS YOU WERE NEVER TOLD ABOUT

It's a jungle out there!

The jungle I'm talking about is made up of more than eight billion people who populate planet Earth. Among them are countless human predators on the hunt. The remainder (the majority—the rest of us) are their human prey animals. Even if you don't think of yourself that way, the human predators do.

What's worse is you can't see the predatory humans as they graze invisibly among the human herd! They remain undetected to you because they look just like ordinary people you pass on the street every day. Some of them may reside in your home, might be members of your extended family, possibly wield power over you as an employer, or perhaps perform their nasty deeds as a professional advisor or colleague. If not a member of an affinity group, these predators may be found among people you admire as personal heroes, including celebrities, media personalities, and so-called humanitarians. Many occupy positions of great power or authority in your community. In fact, some of them are (right this minute) taking advantage of the public trust they've been given by voters. (We call these people *politicians*.) And it doesn't matter what political party you belong to, the political landscape is teeming with human predators.

Over a lifetime, I discovered there are legions of human predators walking among us and sometimes (sadly) they are walking right next to us (marriage partners). And now they show up all over the internet. Currently there is a rise in predatory behavior in our culture and around the world. Tectonic economic changes, the COVID-19 pandemic, and the anonymity enticement of the internet are causing people who weren't previously predatory to become that way. If predatory behavior becomes culturally acceptable, the majority of a society can become abusive predators (think of Hitler's Germany as just one example). Could this happen in our society? What might push us in that direction? Perhaps another issue like slavery? How about the current battle over voting rights? Even now, due to divisive political issues, inflation, and climate change, those who were already prone to be predatory feel freer to come out into the light to act out their abuses. **These people can ruin your financial life, trash your emotional life, and drive you to have suicidal thoughts, and they can do this without ever breaking a law.**

FACING THE TRUTH

Some of these people are born without the same brain-wiring as you and me, and no matter what circumstances they are born under, they are destined to become predatory. Natural-born human predators are referred to by psychologists and psychiatrists as sociopaths, psychopaths, narcissists, borderline personalities, anti-social personalities, high-conflict personalities, and a variety of other personality disorders. All these people have one thing in common: they are very difficult to be with for long because of the toll they take on the rest of us.

Many other human predators are created through substance abuse addictions. I'm talking about alcohol, prescription pharmaceuticals, street drugs, or over-the-counter medications that dull their conscience, destroy an addict's moral compass, and cause them to act exactly like natural-born human predators whose brain wiring is genetically twisted from birth. If you think I'm referring to the down-and-out, homeless wretch who can be found living on the streets of Anytown, USA, I am not. I'm talking about those who are high-functioning substance abusers who seem to be (on the surface, at least) as normal as you or me but whose abuse of their chosen substance is constantly progressing, escalating, and eating away at or killing brain cells while these people occupy highly responsible employment in society.

Then, too, the addiction predator doesn't have to be hooked on a substance to develop predatory tendencies. An addiction of any type (behavioral addictions, thought addictions, or drama addictions) can create the same predatory tendencies as in substance abusers. What are those behaviors? Here is a good starter list:

1. Total focus on getting whatever feeds their addiction
2. Loss of empathy for the needs or wants of others
3. Loss of compassion
4. Manipulation and lying
5. Deafness to appeals to give up their addiction

On top of predators genetically wired from birth and those formed from addiction, emotional and physical trauma suffered in childhood or in adulthood often create predatory humans. Trauma rewires the brain and can totally change previously normal people into very serious human predators of all types.

And finally, cultural dogma addictions are huge contributors to human predatory thinking and behaviors. Carefully taught to children from the time they are capable of learning, extreme biases promoted by societies around the world shut down critical thinking and merciful actions when it comes to a society's sworn enemies and to people who embrace different ways of thinking, non-mainstream religious beliefs, or have different skin color. These cultural dogma addictions are so persistent and intensely held that even attempting to discuss them civilly with those who hold them is a high-risk gamble that typically disintegrates into adversarial standoffs.

Of course, in addition to the human predators in the jungle, there are human prey animals (people with a healthy conscience, which predators seek to take advantage of). Remember, it's not about seeing yourself as a prey animal; it's about understanding that is how they see YOU.

I suspect you (like me) are fully capable of forming warm, caring, loving relationships and have a clear sense of the difference between right and wrong. So you may find it hard to accept there are people out there not like you, people who don't care about right and wrong and only want to take advantage of you. Human predators are indeed wandering the jungle, and you will benefit tremendously from learning how to protect yourself from them, even if you have never met anyone who is predatory.

Let's begin your education by shining a light on the four major contributors to creating humans who find personal fulfillment from messing up your life in some twisted way.

NATURAL-BORN HUMAN PREDATORS

Those who are natural-born predators have brains wired to be predatory from birth (like Ted Bundy and Bernie Madoff). These people have been studied by science sufficiently to tell us their genetics are clearly different. Their genetic profile creates clear and distinguishable brain anomalies that can easily be exposed with a PET scan. For example, the amygdala in the brains of natural-born predators is deformed from birth. The amygdala is one of two almond-shaped clusters of nuclei located deep and medially within the temporal lobes of the brain's cerebrum. Shown to perform a primary role in the processing of memory, decision-making, and emotional responses (including fear, anxiety, and aggression), the amygdalae are considered part of the limbic system. Think of this part of the brain as the traffic control tower for all information coming into the brain where the proper emotional runway is assigned to that information. If broken or dysfunctional due to a genetic defect, the result is that no emotions are assigned to any information coming in or going out of the predator's brain.

Those with this deficit can still present themselves in emotional ways, but this is always a performance, a skilled representation of what they have learned with their cold empathy by studying others. There is no sincerity behind emotional displays or seeming acts of empathy and kindness by these predators, only cold, calculated use of feigned behaviors so they get their way.

By the way, these natural-born predators are terrific soldiers in wartime. They kill without hesitation and have no fear of battle. But if they become your nation's leader, they are destined to be more like Adolph Hitler, Mussolini, or Idi Amin.

Natural-born human predators can't be cured. They can sometimes be influenced to modify their behavior, and that's what psychiatrists and clinical psychologists attempt to do for these people. But a natural-born human predator's underlying genetic code, which created his or her unique brain structure, does not change.

SUBSTANCE ABUSERS

Estimates for the number of people with substance abuse addictions are insanely high. According to Defining the Addiction Treatment Gap, "Drug use is on the rise in this country and 23.5 million Americans are addicted to alcohol and drugs. That's approximately one in every 10 Americans over the age of 12." Simply put, this estimate tells us 10 percent of Americans over the age of twelve suffer from substance abuse addictions.

According to the American Addiction Centers, of the total of all those addicted to substances (legal or illegal), only 11 percent ever present for treatment. Of course, the 89 percent not presenting for treatment have little hope of being cured, and this means their brains are slowly (sometimes rapidly) being altered and degraded by their drug of choice.

The loss of a sense of right and wrong is one of the first brain functions to be shut down, and from that flows all kinds of predatory behaviors you will learn about in this book.

THOUGHT ADDICTIONS
(Including Drama Addictions and Behavioral Addictions)

Below is a list of addictions outside substance abuse that permeate modern society. Each one of the addictions on this list is known as a *thought addiction*. Thought addictions emerge when anyone allows one specific purpose to become his or her all-consuming reason for existing.

1. Money-making
2. Power and influence
3. Religion
4. Gambling
5. Sex
6. Internet surfing
7. Shopping
8. Hoarding
9. Videogame playing
10. Plastic surgery
11. Binge eating
12. Thrill seeking
13. Black-and-white thinking
14. Blaming
15. Catastrophizing
16. Minimizing and maximizing
17. Fortune-telling/jumping to conclusions
18. Labelling
19. Mind-reading (falsely believing you know what others think)
20. Overgeneralizing

21. Selective interpretation
22. Personalization (everything that happens is about you)
23. Emotional reasoning
24. Over-responsibility (everything is your fault)
25. Stalking
26. Internet pornography
27. Co-dependency

This list of thought addictions only scratches the surface. And, yes, thought addictions also shut down an individual's sense of right and wrong, and this is clearly evidenced if you stand between something (or someone) that a thought addict wants or needs. Even worse predatory behavior is displayed by thought addicts if you *have* something he or she wants or needs. Experts claim that thought addictions are one thousand times more powerful and influential than substance abuse addictions. Yet because thoughts are invisible, how will you ever know with any certainty that someone suffers from a thought addiction or not? More importantly, how will you know if someone's thought addiction will make him or her a predator because this is not always what happens with thought addictions.

Thought addictions can express in very strange ways. Hoarding, addiction to being ill, eating disorders, drama addictions of all types, and even cultural dogma addictions are great examples. Most of these addictions present as repetitive dramas these addicts play out in everyday life at home, at work, and now on the internet.

Of course, we all engage in attention-seeking behaviors at times to meet our psychological needs. But if you are a person who regularly gossips, exaggerates, gets into pointless arguments, or stirs up problems for others, it's very possible you have a thought addiction.

Now, if your addiction becomes amplified to a point where it becomes your only reason for getting up every day or your primary purpose in life, then your personal drama has taken over your life and it operates on your brain almost exactly as if you were addicted to opiates. Your sense of psychological well-being and pleasure reaches an apex only when you can pull off your drama using other people as key actors to play out roles that leave them feeling damaged, harmed, or deflated.

For example, one of the thought addicts you will learn about here is the high-conflict addict, a predator who is purposely highly divisive with everyone so he or she can either dominate others or watch from the sidelines as the divided parties go to war with one another. It turns out these people are frequently given leadership roles in society and are seldom seen as addicts. Sadly, the high-conflict personality pops up everywhere.

Occasionally, some drama addictions involve not other people but our electronic devices. The excessive or constant viewing of television, our cell phones, the internet, and even the news can be expressions of drama addictions. With thirty seconds of downtime, who can resist going to his or her cell phone? How about a Facebook addiction? It happens to many people.

Are there victims of these addictions? Indeed, there are. The loss of time with key people in the lives of these addicts leads to bad relationships and the loss of relationships. Like the hoarder who retreats deeper and deeper into a personal mountain range of stuff, those addicted to their phones and to chasing online websites lose all touch with themselves as well.

Seldom, if ever, do these electronic device addicts and thought addicts ever come to the attention of professional therapists. But they can affect your life in ways that are nasty and consequential. And complicating this type of addiction is the lack of therapies to treat them effectively. Once people's brain chemistry changes so dramatically that their addictive thoughts and behaviors become the only trigger of adrenaline or feel-good brain chemicals for them, rewiring their brains is nearly impossible.

TRAUMA VICTIM PREDATORS

Think of anyone suffering from post-traumatic stress disorder (PTSD). About 3.5 percent of Americans have PTSD in a given year. Yet a large segment of those not diagnosed with PTSD experience traumatic stress events, becoming seriously damaged, and go on to become predatory humans. The vast majority of these predatory people never come to the attention of professional therapists.

Even those with clinically diagnosed cases of PTSD are seldom treated properly or fully. Because these men and women can be situationally triggered by sounds, lights, words, or tone of voice from others, they can suffer terrifying flashbacks that instantly make them dangerous predators to those within striking distance. Police officers, firemen, first-responders, victims of criminal violence, adult survivors of childhood sexual abuse or violence, and war veterans are a few well-known examples. If these supremely important role players in society who are responsible for the safety and well-being of every citizen aren't professionally attended to and helped after they are traumatized, they can and often do become predatory. Even with the best medications and therapy, those trying to recover from major traumas face a lifelong struggle with triggering events that send them into miserable mental states, causing dangerous behaviors, wild mood swings, depression, suicidal ideation, and drug use.

CULTURAL DOGMA ADDICTIONS

Cultural dogmas have been likened to a drug that is free and fed to everyone on the planet in one way or another. When anyone attempts to challenge a cultural dogma, those holding the dogmatic belief will instantly go into survival/attack mode. Some of us will become stone-cold killers in the face of such an attack. Societies around the world are guilty of encouraging their cultural dogma addictions, and that tends to make them invisible as a form of addiction to the society that fosters them. Forget about seeing cultural dogma addictions as requiring therapy. Humans are so blind to how their cultural dogma addictions cost their own society they are unable to connect the dots to the impacts those addictions have on healthcare, mental healthcare, law enforcement, and military preparedness.

In this way cultural dogma addictions are different from thought addictions as most thought addictions are seen by societies around the world as deviant, dangerous, and destructive (either self-destructive or destructive to the interests and well-being of others).

A great example of cultural dogma addictions is citizens of nations in the Middle East and their beliefs about their perceived enemies in Israel and their resulting thoughts and actions towards Jews. The citizens of Israel are just as addicted to cultural dogmas toward the citizens of Muslim nations. These cultural-dogma addictions have persisted for thousands of years in the Middle East and result in all types of predatory behaviors. Not so easy to look at are some of our own cultural-dogma addictions right here in the United States. How about our addiction to white superiority and white privilege? How much predatory behavior towards dark-skinned people has occurred because of this cultural dogma?

> **RED FLAG #11:** Human predators build you up and praise you everlastingly when you are loyal, but they tear you to pieces if you ever disagree with them. Creating this contrast of emotional highs and lows makes you desperate to win back their favor when they are displeased with you.

Each year around the world, these cultural dogma addictions cause massive loss of life, non-lethal injuries, and mental health problems. Yet altering cultural dogmas in even small ways is extremely difficult. One need think only about how hard and how long women in the United States had to fight for the right to vote or are still struggling to achieve equality of pay in the workplace. These are merely two examples, and yet they are poignant because they hint at how cultural dogma addictions permeate life, persist, and create so much suffering. The human cost in grief and pain from cultural dogma addictions is incalculable.

In this book, the subject of cultural dogma addictions will not be addressed further, even though they are the drivers of enormous amounts of human predation.

Bottom line? Whether you encounter a naturally born human predator or someone who is a predator due to trauma, addiction, or cultural dogmas, these humans are all difficult and dangerous, and when triggered by the right cues, they see you as prey if you are within their sphere of influence. Even if the word *prey* only means you become an objectified tool for someone's twisted agenda, you are never a whole person in the human predator's eyes. Such people will use you in any way they need to get their high, their payoff, their supply.

A STREET-SMART HANDBOOK FOR DEALING WITH HUMAN PREDATORS

This book is your street-smart guide to the normal-looking, real-life monsters that no one told you to watch out for as you make your way through the human jungle. **Yes, some of them commit criminal acts, but most you will learn about here are intent on committing non-jailable offenses against you designed to mess you up emotionally, to take away your ability to earn a living, to violate your body, to waste your time, to annoy you endlessly, to entangle you in weird psychological dramas, to create chaos and hostility between you and others, to enrage you just for the fun of watching you melt down or behave irrationally, and to drive you crazy and even make you suicidal.**

These human predators are all around you. They are coming for you, and you won't be able to see them without the knowledge presented in this book. Even if your current thinking about human predators is at odds with what you read here, you have nothing to lose by at least learning of your own prey weaknesses and what drives and motivates predators to manipulate and victimize people. Sooner or later, you will need the practical advice taught in this book on how to avoid predatory humans (or to extract yourself from those who have managed to get their claws into you). If right now you are trying to deal with or fend off a human predator, this book will help you understand what's happening, how to protect and free yourself, and how to make yourself less attractive to these kinds of people once you get yourself free.

By the end of this book, you will be able to see the abusive behavior patterns of those wanting you to be on their menu (whether they want you rare, medium rare, or well done), and you will finally have the knowledge that can empower you to safely navigate these human landmines, avoid their abuse, and maintain a life of peace, joy, empathy, and compassion—none of which these people ever experience.

To best protect yourself against human predators, your education must begin with understanding your own prey weaknesses—weaknesses we all share. There is no victim shaming in this book. You will only learn how to make yourself less yummy to those who come hunting you. After all, those predators I'm warning you about are looking for signals that you are a prey animal. What exactly are predators wanting to see from you to decide they should stalk or attack you? The only way you will know the answer to this question is to read section 2 that follows.

"

*Pathological abusers gain
internal energy from the
conflict and chaos they create
in the lives of their victims.
The survivors are left
emotionally drained and
struggle to regain the quality of
life they once easily enjoyed.*

—Shannon Thomas

"

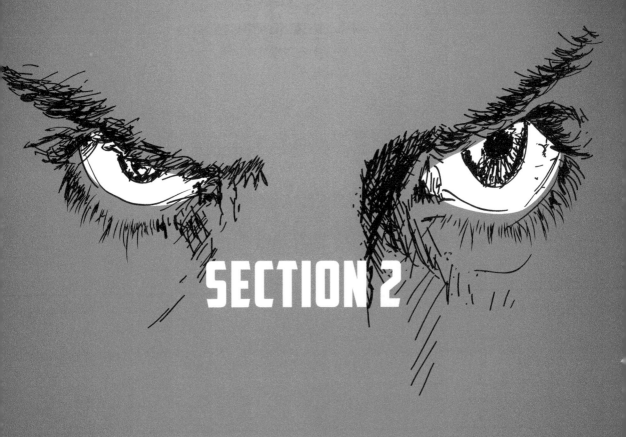

SECTION 2

"

Good people are
A MAGNET TO HUMAN PREDATORS.
If you are a sensitive, kind individual,
Especially one possessing a high capacity for empathy,
HUMAN PREDATORS WILL BE CIRCLING.
Be aware of it.
Learn to see the red flags.
THEY ARE ALWAYS THERE.

"

PREY ANIMAL, KNOW THYSELF

How You Signal to Human Predators
You Are Vulnerable and Theirs for the Taking

H AVE YOU OCCASIONALLY FOUND YOURSELF needing to hit an ATM machine late at night or in the wee hours of the morning? Even when the area around the ATM machine is well lit, you probably found yourself on high alert for potential muggers. Actually, I just returned from an early morning raid on my bank's ATM machine. Driving there, I could swear a car was following me, and I kept a sharp eye on my rearview mirror until that car turned off. "Stay calm and alert," I told myself. It was 5:00 a.m., and the dark of night hadn't receded one inch to the sun that would be breaking the horizon in about sixty minutes. As I left my car and approached the cash-stocked robot securely embedded in the outside wall of the bank building, a stiff wind was blowing. This caused the hairs on the back of my neck to stand straight up. Why? Because the wind in the trees made it difficult to hear approaching footsteps of bandits who might be hidden in shadow until that machine disgorged the five hundred dollars I was there to withdraw.

Did I feel like prey at that moment? Absolutely! My brain and nervous system fully registered the creepiness that is normal when we feel highly vulnerable to physical predatory attack. In that moment, I felt my animal self go on full alert as adrenaline was released within my veins. That was twenty minutes ago, and the adrenaline is still coursing through my body, even though I'm safely back in my home. Are these animal reactions to potential threats of attack outmoded and useless in the world we live in as highly evolved modern humans? Hell NO! And in this section, I'm going to tell you why we still need them—maybe more than ever.

THE EVOLUTION OF THE PREDATOR-PREY RELATIONSHIP

Primitive humans were looking over their shoulders for four-legged predators all the time. Millions of years ago until thousands of years ago, the intent to kill was primarily to survive and nourish the body. Back then life was truly about eating or being eaten every day, and our bodies and brains evolved in every way over millions of years to deal with this reality. Trust me, nothing about the savage elements of the human brain has changed. We are still highly savage creatures with all our wars, territoriality, and sword-rattling (except now ICBMs have replaced swords). However, in the periodic absence of world wars and our best attempts at social cooperation, modern humans need to be on alert for much different kinds of predators.

In highly dense, urban societies where survival is based on social contracts of cooperation and the rule of law, predators are humans seeking to use those laws and social conventions against you to get their hands on your money or your body or your psyche (and sometimes all three). In fact, a huge number of modern-day human predators are seeking to carry out twisted psychological dramas that involve you playing a starring role. Additionally, there is a small percentage of these extremely twisted humans who actually hunt and kill other humans for sport.

If any of these initial observations don't resonate with your personal view of modern human populations, stick with me as I walk you through this little shop of horrors where the worst of human beings will be fully, unashamedly on display for you to see, but not always the ones you typically think of as predators. **Here, in addition to those you are willing to identify openly as dangerous criminals, you are going to learn about the predators who commit crimes against the emotions of others, crimes against the spirit, and crimes against your ability to earn a living through honest, ethical, hard work.**

Contrary to our linear-thinking brain's tendency to search out the similarities we share with other humans, you will discover in this book (maybe for the first time) how each human brain is its own little galaxy of wiring and chemistry, no two alike. And as those brains progress through the years (through every stage of life), each of us evolves uniquely and in nearly unpredictable ways. While the stages of our lives have modestly predictable themes, the wide variety of idiosyncratic expressions during each life stage approach infinity as well.

How big a stretch is it for you to wrap your thinking around this idea? Experience has taught me that we don't want to look at the world this way. It's too complex. It's inconvenient. It's all too messy and unmanageable. Our comfort zone is found in searching for ways we are like one another so we can validate a few simple navigational values we hold sacred. The human brain is poorly designed to manage the

> **RED FLAG #15:** At all costs, human predators set up their lives so they aren't directly accountable to anyone at work, at home, or in any way that might bring down criticism on them.

tumultuous turbulence of infinity or the innumerable human expressions we are exposed to on our life's journey. Yes, we openly admit to our infinite facial differences, but embracing the idea that our brains are as different as our faces is off-putting and violates our universal need for simplicity and certainty.

Now add to this complexity the idea that some of the people you meet will be looking at you as their next mark to be used and manipulated for some twisted purpose. Clearly this idea violates the natural tendency we have to see others as like us or as we want them to be for us. Yet we resist seeing (even blind ourselves to seeing) human predators because, as we construct our inner, mental galaxy of reality, we don't create a category for wolves in sheep's clothing. Also because we navigate our lives with our personal constructs of reality, we are very poor at fact-finding when it comes to other people. And if you have never been taught to look for the red-flag warnings of human predators or the core personality characteristics that drive human predators (no matter what their presenting personalities are), you are the most vulnerable of human prey animals.

We all (and by *all*, I mean every human being on the planet) tend to project onto others the qualities we want them to possess. And this tendency we all have blinds us to low-profile, modern-day human predators on the hunt. Of course, all predators try to be low-profile, but human predators can blend in so well with human prey animals they almost seem to have a cloak of invisibility. And our denial that human predators roam freely in our company makes their invisibility even more effective.

Let's look at some examples of the shocks our brains can experience when we fail to see the other as potential predator, even those who seem so friendly and good to be around when we first know them.

Have you ever worked for someone you came to label (secretly) an asshole? What characteristics led you to employ this label? Think about your answer while I describe two assholes you might find in the workplace.

Boss #1 – The Sexual Predator

When you started working for this man, he was the sweetest, most sensitive person you had ever met. Others in his field respected him as a hardball attorney who knew how to win in jury trials by employing courtroom theatrics that were legendary. His command of the law was described as encyclopedic. Yes, he worked you like a slave and often had you stay late toiling on a brief to help him get ready for an extremely rushed deadline. Well, of course, he stayed late too and worked with you, often right across the table from you. You noticed he had a private bar in his office during the second time you worked late with him on one of those legal briefs. Now, three months into this job, he was hitting the sauce fairly often during those late-night sessions, but he didn't seem to get drunk or out of control. In fact, he became even more solicitous towards you, more friendly, courteous, and kind. But last week, he changed places at the table, and instead of sitting across from you at the giant conference room worktable, he took up a position right next to you so you could share documents you were working on together. He offered you drinks from his bar, but you are a teetotaler and politely refused his offer. After one excellent catch on your part tonight, your big-shot attorney/boss placed his hand on your thigh as he thanked you. Suddenly alarm bells went off in your head! A line had been crossed! You know this. You feel this. And you want to run. But can you run and still have a job tomorrow?

Boss #2 – The Psycho Game-Player Predator

You have worked for five years moving up the ladder of your company's enterprise with smashing success. The woman CEO of the firm has recently retired, and your new CEO (actually the man you will report to) has been on the job two weeks when he calls you into his office along with another manager. The CEO knows you both run separate sales divisions of the firm, and after some idle small talk about current events, he gets right down to business. Looking you straight in the eye, the new CEO (let's name him Satan) asks you why your division's sales are running 20 percent less than the other manager's division. In your mind you are flabbergasted because you know your division's product sales jumped by 30 percent last year to reach new records. Besides, your division sells tractors around the world. The other manager's division sells lawnmowers. Has there ever been an example of comparing apples to oranges that is better than this? You think, "Hell NO!" So, you are wondering how to respond without pissing off the new CEO. After all, he has a dead-serious look in his eye and doesn't appear to be kidding around. Quickly you come back with a question, "Are you aware that my division's sales brought in eight billion dollars last year, while my highly respected colleague here brought in only two billion dollars in sales revenue in the same period?"

The color in Satan's face turns red with rage. "Are you saying you can't compete any longer?" he responds, lips tight with anger. Then he turns to the other man and confronts him. Satan says coolly, "Your colleague here sounds like he's kicking your ass with growing revenue for this firm. Why are your sales proceeds so low?"

Now you are really confused. The first attack was sent your way. Now he's attacking the other manager with your ammunition. You think, "What the hell is going on here? What kind of mind game is our new CEO playing?"

While all these questions run through your mind, Satan stands up behind his desk and declares, "Both of you get out of my office until you are able to come back in here with answers to the questions I posed to each of you. When you return, I will be judge and jury as you two face off against one another. And, gentlemen, I expect you both to be fully prepared to defend your answers. Do not return here until you are ready to do battle. And I expect your face-off in no more than ten days from now!"

What are the chances you will still be working at this firm ten days from now? The more important question is this—Why would you want to?

Marriage partners can be assholes, too. And when a marriage partner turns against you, your potential losses are more than financial. Your entire psychological existence can be threatened, your soul can be sucked out of you, and the will to go on can be destroyed. Could this happen to you? Not if you are forewarned about how marriage partners can turn into human predators and you heed these warnings. Following are two examples.

MARRIAGE PARTNER #1 – THE CRAZY-MAKER PREDATOR

The announcement came after nearly nine years of marriage. Actually, it was presented as a suggestion bordering on a demand, made casually on a sunny Sunday afternoon at a public park while watching your two children at play (ages six and eight, a girl and a boy): "If either one of us ever has an affair, let's not tell each other."

When you heard your wife speak these words, a bottomless pit formed in your stomach. Yesterday you had spent the entire day moving your family into the first home you had ever purchased, and it was a symbol of achievement, commitment, and unity that you and she had been working for since the birth of your first child. However, when the day for moving in arrived, she had clearly stated she wouldn't help. She decided to take the kids to the park that day, and you literally did all the work moving out of your apartment with a rental truck and special dollies for large items. It was muscle-tiring, back-breaking work. In your mind, you rationalized that your wife would be thrilled to live in this beautiful home located in the glorious foothills overlooking the city. It was brand new, and you had purchased it at a screaming-low price because an economic downturn in the nation created a buyer's market.

So now it was Sunday, and you were growing feverish with anger after your wife's casual suggestion. "Is she having an affair? Is that the real reason she didn't want to help with the move? Does she no longer love me?" You resolved to get the children off to bed and securely tucked in for the night before confronting her, which you did at about ten that evening. Surprisingly, when confronted, she openly admitted it.

"How long?" you asked.

"Six months," she responded with total coolness.

"What the hell are you doing? Do you not get that we are parents of two young children and your behavior could ruin our marriage and our family?"

She was silent for many minutes before responding. "This is really all your fault! I was only nineteen when we married. I had never had a chance to explore the sexual side of who I am. If you hadn't married me so young, none of this would have happened. I thought you would understand. And if it makes you feel better, I'm not interested in divorce. Go ahead and have an affair yourself. It won't bother me. It's just sex."

You are now in a state of shock. Checking yourself into a mental hospital to keep from killing your wife (or yourself) is one option you are entertaining. The other option is strangling her with your bare hands. She was emotionless when she spoke just now. No affect whatsoever. What kind of person tells her husband these things and then tells him it's all his fault? After her recitation of these revelations, she walked out of the room and started getting ready for bed. The bed you sleep in together. What are the chances you will sleep on the couch tonight, insane with rage and in a state of psychotic confusion? And where does this rabbit hole go from here? Will you find your way out of it ever? Wait, is that the Mad Hatter just up ahead? Or is it your own reflection in a mirror?

Marriage Partner #2 – The Narcissist Predator

You were thirty-five when first you met the actor in a Hollywood hangout. The minute he walked in, you spotted him, and your eyes followed him like an eagle as he sauntered to the bar and ordered a drink. You were the aggressor that night. Having come to this famous watering hole in Tinseltown with your closest girlfriend, the two of you planned the attack together. Pulling out a pen and a small scrap of paper from your purse, you jotted down a few words and then boldly walked over to the bar where the actor was drinking alone. Sitting down next to him, you ordered a drink for yourself and then slipped the small piece of paper along the bar to a position right in front of him. He casually picked it up, unfolded the paper you had so cleverly creased, and read the note. It asked, "Married, divorced, or single?" And that's how you started a whirlwind romance that ended with a classic Hollywood wedding. It was epic, dramatic, over-the-top with guests from the Hollywood A list, B list, and C list.

Of course, you were totally blinded by your hormones to any oddities he displayed, ones that gave your girlfriends the creeps. Everywhere you went from the day you met him, he showed up too. Even when you went to play tennis with your friends, someway he knew exactly where you would be, and he made an appearance. Friends said this was not normal. You chalked it up to his absolute adoration of you.

Now, looking back at the last sixteen years, you find yourself profoundly disoriented and exhausted by the relationship. No matter how hard you have tried to please this man, he criticizes you endlessly. But when it comes to your requests of him, he has no empathy for your needs. His demands of you are always primary in his mind. And he seems lost in a fantasy world of his own self-importance in the world. He claims he is a great actor, one of the greatest who ever lived. For this reason, he wants nothing to do with your friends as they are beneath him. He wants only to ever find company with the elite of Hollywood, the A-list people. When he auditions and gets rejected, he goes into a rage, all of which he displays only at home.

You have a five-year-old daughter, and you know you have to protect her from the man she calls her father. Is divorce an option? You gave up your own career to become this man's helpmate. How might you pick up the pieces of your professional life and become financially self-sufficient? Is that a fantasy? You know your husband won't give you a dime in divorce court without mounting a World War III legal defense. You, on the other hand, have not one red cent. He owns you. And he knows this. Suicidal thoughts creep into your mind. But, no, you won't give him the satisfaction! You will find a way. You WILL find a way! But life has never been more frightening. "What kind of freak is this man?" you question. And then you realize you must seek professional help. Either you learn more about what you are dealing with, or you will go to an early grave. It's time to find a coach who can guide you out of this nightmare.

Occasionally your next-door neighbor can be an asshole. The problem is you can't divorce a neighbor or resign, although moving is always an option. But is it really? Think about what you would do, or how you might counsel friends who found they were living next door to these people.

Neighbor #1 – The Paranoid Psycho-Ward Escapee Next Door

Since the beginning of the COVID-19 pandemic, citizens across the United States have been on the move for a lot of different reasons. Certainly, one is to get away from high-density urban environments that are deteriorating from lack of law enforcement and controversy regarding masking-up to help defeat COVID-19. Where I live, high in the mountains of Idaho (Sun Valley, to be specific), the influx of former city dwellers has been somewhat of a stampede. Housing and raw land sales have skyrocketed here, as have prices. More than once, it's crossed my mind as to whether these people have a clue what kind of new neighbors they will encounter.

The Smiths, a former Los Angeles family of three (and not their real name), purchased a home here in May as soon as their daughter's school schedule allowed them time to go house-hunting. The place they bought was fully unoccupied by the owner, so moving in quickly and setting up house was a breeze. However, once the property closed escrow, the seller disclosed verbally that the Smiths might not like the neighbors who own the property slightly uphill and directly behind them. Apparently, they had been known to cause trouble. Could this explain why the owner didn't occupy the house?

RED FLAG #10: Human predators will say things to friends and colleagues like "If you were a true friend, you would do (BLANK) for me." This is called friendship shaming.

The family's two side neighbors also dropped by and had harsh words about the family living up behind them. Because that neighbor's house was uphill from the Smiths' new purchase, they noticed how the people living there had a direct view of their house and into their new backyard. Still, after two months, nothing occurred, and there was no interaction between the Smith family and their backyard neighbor. But on August 1 of 2021, things changed.

One night about two o'clock, the adult members of the Smith family woke up to the sound of their front doorbell ringing. With a video feed that displays on their cell phones, they could see a man standing barefoot in his pajamas on their porch and pounding hard on their front door. Their first thought? The man must be drunk! Then the man started screaming. He demanded they come out and face him because he was going to kick their ass, fuck them up, and worse. After three minutes, the pajama man left the porch and started walking around the outside of the house. Mr. Smith hurried downstairs to make sure all the doors and windows were secure while his wife called the police.

Before the police arrived, which takes a little longer here than in Los Angeles because our law enforcement infrastructure is overwhelmed by all the new people moving in, a sunlight-bright spotlight was beamed from the neighbor's house behind them directly into the backyard of the Smiths' home. They had never seen anything like this and were stunned to see how the spotlight filled their entire home with its megawatt beam.

When the police arrived, they could see the home they were looking for instantly as it was bathed in a halo of light, which appeared to be coming from the neighbor's house behind the caller's home. After a quick explanation of what the Smiths had seen on their phones (and recorded), the cops went to the home with the spotlight to get that neighbor's scoop on things. It turned out the neighbor living behind the Smiths' new residence was the one on their porch threatening them with a good ass-kicking. In fact, when the psycho behind the Smiths' home had walked around their house, he apparently had jumped the fence and then manually turned on the giant spotlight.

As the backyard neighbor met with police officers, he claimed that earlier in the evening he had seen Mr. Smith come into his own backyard with nothing on but boxer shorts and claimed (loudly) that Mr. Smith was trying to expose himself to the psycho's family. He claimed he had videos of all this, but the ones he showed the police were all peeping-Tom-type scenes of the Smith family inside their own home doing totally normal things. Nothing inappropriate or scandalous. Basically, the psycho had been filming the Smiths since they moved in and expected the police to grasp how reasonable this was, instead of a huge breach of privacy.

Mr. and Mrs. Smith were briefed about all this and were devastated. Sadly, the filming had been accomplished from inside the psycho's home by taking advantage of the height difference of the two homes and the angle of the Smiths' venetian blinds. No trespassing had occurred to obtain the film, so no criminal charges could be filed.

This story has a happy ending, unlike the next one. On August 16, 2021, the backyard, psycho neighbor put his home up for sale, and it sold in three days. On September 1, the psycho and his family walked away with a huge profit, and new neighbors moved into the former psycho ward at the end of September. But what would you have done, or counseled the Smith family to do, if the psycho-ward escapee had not given us this happy ending?

Neighbor #2 – The Cat Murderer Next Door

While attending college, I worked as a child guidance counselor to blind children in Jacksonville, Illinois. After graduation, I stayed through the summer in Jacksonville, continuing this work while renting an upstairs apartment just off the town square until I began my graduate studies in social work in St. Louis, Missouri. The lady who lived below me had a son who attended Illinois Central College but returned home each summer. Early into the three months I lived in Jacksonville before heading for St. Louis, the young man decided to adopt a stray cat (a kitten actually), but his mother wouldn't allow the cat inside the house, so the boy kept the little fluff ball outside. Sadly, the kitty would show up at my door every morning before I went to work looking half-starved and meowing. Concerned the boy wasn't giving her regular meals, I started leaving food in a bowl outside my front door. Then I bought a huge bag of cat food and a bowl and left them at the front door of my neighbor's apartment below. The next morning both were found outside my front door, returned. This all happened in early June.

Continuing to feed the cat regularly so she wouldn't starve, one morning in late July, I found the cat crying at my front door and, unlike previous days, acting like she wanted to come inside. I let her in and noticed she was pregnant and was close to full term. She stayed only a short time the first day but then wanted in after the breakfast I gave her each morning, so I made a little corner with towels for her, and she'd stay for about twenty minutes each day on her little towel bed before I kicked her out on leaving for work. After a week of this, she showed up at my door one evening and cried until I let her in. Curled up in her corner with the towels, she gave birth to three babies. Believing the boy and his mom below should be notified, I went to their apartment but was told by the mother their cat was a boy, so the mother cat and babies couldn't possibly be theirs.

Knowing I couldn't keep the mother kitten and her babies, I posted flyers all over the apartment complex and on every lamp post and telephone post within a two-block area. Apparently, her son saw one of the flyers and was furious at his mom. So she called the police on me and told them I stole her cat. When the officers arrived at my front door with the lady in tow from down below, I explained that indeed the cat wasn't mine, but I had gone to my neighbor (the lady right in front of me) and reported the cat and her babies, yet the woman lied to the police, claiming she had never met me or even seen me before.

Happily returning the momma cat and her newborns to their rightful owner, feeling confused and angry at the same time, I wondered what cataclysmic end this would come to when the boy returned to college, which he did in late August. Sure enough, two days after her son was gone, I took my trash to the dumpster behind the apartment and heard meowing. When I opened the dumpster, the meowing was much louder and coming from a box deep under a lot of other garbage bags. Retrieving that box was a stinky affair, but worth it. Inside that box, I found the momma cat and her three babies looking starved and dehydrated. I rushed them to a veterinarian, but sadly, one of the babies died on the way. The momma cat and her two remaining babies were saved and then transferred to a shelter where they were adopted by real cat lovers.

> **RED FLAG #27:** Human predators often take credit for the achievements of others, thereby making themselves look like the hero when they are, in fact, the chaos-maker.

Two weeks after this horror show, I drove to St. Louis to attend graduate school at the George Warren Brown School of Social Work, a part of Washington University. In spite of my graduate studies, I never comprehended the deviancy of people who could behave so despicably. To me, these people couldn't be human, and on some level, I understood this even back then. Oh sure, I learned lots of fancy names for those who act without conscience, but the asshole label was still my favorite name for all of them.

All the assholes in the stories above are human predators. The word *asshole* is not a scientific term. Neither is the expression *human predator*; nor is it even a professional label in the field of psychiatry or psychology. For that reason, it has to be used here with caution and full disclosure about its invention as a term of art in this book. But I'm guessing you will find it an apt expression in describing the full range of behaviors and personality traits this book talks about. So I'll use *human predator* throughout, instead of expressions like *bad actor* or *asshole*, although I hope you will forgive me if occasionally I slip up and use epithets. Sometimes I simply can't help myself.

One question itching your curiosity is probably "What causes people to be human predators?" Let's look at this question next.

WHAT CAUSES SOMEONE TO BE A HUMAN PREDATOR, AND WHAT IS NORMAL ANYWAY?

In a nutshell, a combination of faulty brain wiring at birth (genetic in origin) and addictions and trauma scars create human predators with personalities operating in ways considered abnormal by people who see themselves as normal. While these causes were covered in section 1, allow me to repeat three key messages that you must hold firmly in mind as you grow your understanding and defenses against human predators.

1. *Some are born with their brains wired to be predatory.* These people have been studied by science sufficiently to tell us that their genetics are clearly different and they have a high profile of warrior genes. Their genetic profile also creates clear and distinguishable brain anomalies that can easily be exposed with a PET scan, meaning you can't see

natural-born predatory humans by any outward appearance they present. But if you learn how to look for and see them, on the outside, these people display similar characteristics. They are often narcissistic, they have zero empathy for others, they have no conscience, and they are great at acting like normal people to keep from being seen for what they are inside. Human predators will also lie with no indications they are telling untruths, no micro-expression giveaways, no body language tells, and no eye movements that typically give away lying behavior of any kind.

2. *Some human predators are created by traumatic experiences.* Trauma rewires the human brain. Exactly how this happens is poorly understood, and therein lies a huge problem. How in the world might you see human predators who have absorbed emotional or physical trauma during childhood, like abuse or early-life abandonment? How about traumas experienced as adults? Yes, it's also true that both emotional traumas and physical traumas can cause adults to start presenting predatory thoughts and behaviors. And you will almost never see the predatory behaviors coming when around these people.

3. *Substance-abuse addicts and those addicted to thoughts or dramas can easily escape detection as human predators.* Substance abusers can be high-functioning individuals and often are, so forget about looking for the down-and-out, drug-addled wrecks of human beings living in cardboard boxes in some downtown urban center. The dangerous substance abusers are people occupying the corporate suites of business organizations, as well as middle management and junior management positions in businesses across America. Also remember that thought addictions (which, earlier I noted, experts claim are one thousand times more powerful and influential than substance abuse addictions) are everywhere among us, and huge numbers of these addicts present as normal in almost every way until they decide you have something they want.

WHAT IS NORMAL? WHAT IS DEVIANCY?

Although the goal of this book is not to make you an expert on the causes of predatory behavior, I fully understand the natural curiosity to give this question importance. Part of us wants to know if we should have empathy and compassion for human predators.

If my response to your urge to have empathy and compassion for others is an absolute no regarding human predators, I run the risk of offending your emotional sensibilities. So the best response about your possible concern for predators is that when they are committing their predatory behaviors, they have no conscience whatsoever and don't care a bit about the people they harm. Either they were born with no conscience, or their conscience has been shut down or turned off by their addictions or by the traumas that have rewired their brains. This means your best response to predatory behavior is to take the defensive actions you will learn about in section 4 of this book.

RED FLAG #16: Human predators offer evasive answers when confronted or even probed casually for information about themselves. If they feel you are accusing them, they will respond with counterattacks, putting YOU on the defensive. Behind this ploy to distract you or change the subject, look for a denial of anything they are accused of doing.

Another part of us wants to know if human predators ever feel guilt about the way they behave. Here, again, if I respond with an absolute no, there is a danger your sense of justice will be offended. You might find it inconceivable that anyone committing a series of predatory acts against you can go through life not registering any awareness of having done something morally abhorrent. What kind of justice is that? But if we go down the rabbit hole of debating whether ours is a just world, we will never find our way out. The best path forward is to examine your personal definition of what it means to be normal.

Even *normalcy* is somewhat of an illusion and a word few agree on. Why is that? Because we each have our personal definition of *normal*, and those definitions always have built into them definable bottom lines, or tolerances. We each can explain, when pressed to do so, what behaviors we believe society should tolerate and those we believe should be sanctioned. However, seldom (if ever) are these definitions identical for any two individuals.

Our laws are an attempt to put in writing a social contract that creates limits to what the majority will and won't allow. So perhaps our laws are the closest we can come to common ground for discussing normal versus predatory behavior. Still, in truth, there is no such thing as normal. In fact, *predator* is an easier word for large numbers of people to agree on, not that there is ever universality in agreement about what predatory behavior is, but consensus is more easily achieved in identifying a predator than defining a normal or abnormal person.

The expression *human predator* as defined in the beginning of this book is anyone who consistently acts without conscience to dominate others using fear, psychological manipulation, trickery, or violence. What kinds of people fit this definition? I'm guessing you will agree the following satisfy it:

1. Serial killers
2. Murderers
3. Muggers
4. Bank robbers
5. Thieves
6. Rapists
7. White-collar criminals
8. Pedophiles
9. Stalkers
10. Human traffickers

Usually there is little pushback from anyone when it comes to this top-ten list. So let's move to the next tier down, the second ten types of people with deviant behaviors:

1. Psychopaths who commit crimes of all types
2. Sociopaths – those with no empathy and no conscience
3. Prostitutes
4. Pimps
5. Adult internet trolls seeking to entrap children for sex
6. Spouse abusers or batterers
7. Crime syndicate leaders and their members
8. Street gangs
9. Drug addicts
10. Drug pushers

Did you find any on this list you would object to calling *human predators*? How about prostitutes? Some of them have no other way to make money, no education, no vocational training, nothing. But they potentially create conditions for sexually transmitted diseases to spread and mutate, and these diseases are an existential threat to the human race where prostitution exists. So, if threatening others with harm in any way is predatory behavior, then prostitutes are creating threats to the health of all, and this makes them predators. Right? Or perhaps you disagree.

What is amazing to me is how few people object to another item on the above list—sociopaths. There seems to be a general consensus that those who navigate their lives without empathy for others and no conscience do deserve to be included on this list of human predators. Yet one must ask why. There are no laws on the books of governments of any jurisdiction that make being a sociopath a crime. And you can't be sent to a mental hospital if diagnosed by a professional therapist (psychologist or psychiatrist) as being a sociopath. This brings up the question, "What is it about sociopaths we all recognize as deviant?" and leads to another: "Why do we seek sociopaths as people to befriend and bring close to us?"

Let's explore these questions together in section 3 of this book. Right now, it's supremely important to examine your vulnerabilities to sociopathic behaviors, all of which make you extremely available as prey. These are the four vulnerabilities we'll examine now:

- Projection and the need for certainty
- Ego stroking
- The follower impulse
- Your hopes and dreams

VULNERABILITY #1 – PROJECTION AND THE NEED FOR CERTAINTY

Human predators count on the brain's inability to think about everyone we meet as a unique intellectual and emotional galaxy unlike anyone else we have ever met or known. Stated another way, these predators count on each of us seeing people as we want to see them—fitting into a personality slot we've created for them in our personally constructed version of reality. And because few of us create a character profile for human predators in our personal worldview, all predators have to do is display a personality type we are familiar with. As we check off the matching boxes in our heads for "acceptable," into a slot they go. Just writing this gives me chills because I am no different from you. Everywhere I go, this default trait of my brain causes me to assign character traits to people I meet for the first time. And even though I have known someone for years, I almost always fail to connect in the present moment with that person's being somewhat different or altered from the last time I was with him or her. That means I frequently misjudge where people are emotionally and what their current agenda is when they come into my presence. I'm talking about people I know really well or believe I know really well.

This flaw in human intellect and emotional judgment is truly our greatest vulnerability to human predators. Logically, we know that every day everyone is changing in little ways. I would also have you consider that sometimes the changes in people we know extremely well are dramatic because of trauma they experienced since the last time we saw them.

How does the projection of our personal worldview onto anyone and everyone get us into trouble? Let's look at a common example:

Projection and the Need for Certainty
Example #1 – The Door-to-Door Salesman

Several days ago, a young man in his mid-thirties knocked on the door of our home in Sun Valley, Idaho. Upon opening the door, I noticed he was very nice looking and was wearing a vest that is typically worn by those working on construction sites with reflectors that help make them highly visible. Around his neck was an official-looking lanyard with an identification card, laminated and very clearly displaying what looked like a permit with a number. As he talked to me about our roof (which does need replacing as it is made of expensive wood shakes that are twenty-one years old), he was extremely articulate. He stood far enough away that my personal boundaries felt honored. And I gave him extra points for going door-to-door on a battery-powered scooter—an expensive one. His pitch was that, because of the fire danger in our area and because of a recent law making it illegal to repair a shake roof in our county, our homeowner's insurance policy was required to pay the full cost of a new roof. All he wanted was my phone number so a certified roof inspector could call and make an appointment to examine the roof. If the roof inspector certified the roof needed replacement, we could use his report to approach our insurance company. I said he was welcome to have his inspector call, and I gave him my personal cell phone number.

But the call never came.

Several days went by, and then the same young man showed up at our front door again. This time he expressed surprise that I identified him (I greeted him by name), and then he said he recognized me as well. This is when I started hearing alarm bells in my head and caution lights began flashing yellow. Still, like Sherlock Holmes, I pressed on to gather additional information. Had his inspector called as agreed, I was prepared to give him the name and number of our general contractor, the man who had built our home and has meticulously taken care of it for twenty-one years. But no and instead, the man canvasing our neighborhood was now back, and when I informed him that his inspector never called, he quickly called the roof inspector and got him on the phone. At that point it was six on a Friday evening, and the inspector wanted to come right over. This request I refused. We were just sitting down for dinner, and the sun was fading slightly. I suggested the inspector come the following day.

When he arrived on Saturday, I gave him the news that no one touches our home unless he or she is under the direction and supervision of our general contractor. I gave him our contractor's business card with contact information. That's when he asked if he could at least climb up and look over the roof. "No," said I. He then began to argue that our contractor would want a piece of the action and this would raise our costs. "We are good with that," I offered. "We are also happy to pay full costs for the roof replacement, with or without the insurance company's participation." This information completely stunned the inspector. He just stood there looking at me as if he couldn't believe what I had said.

The scam was to hook into another universal weakness of the human brain—to want something for nothing. My wife and I learned long ago that there is truly no such thing. We always pay full price for anything we buy, purchase only from those whose credentials have been thoroughly vetted, and give bonuses to all who work for us over and above the costs of construction or service repairs. This practice has created a reputation with the trades people and skilled laborers in our community allowing us to obtain service even when they are swamped with work.

Once the roofing inspector left, we started making calls to check out these people. Although we knew our general contractor would do this if contacted by them, our own investigation verified the two men were indeed running a scam. The con is concluded when they get a signed contract and a 50 percent up-front, good-faith payment from the client. In this case, that would have been forty thousand dollars. Then these scam artists disappear. Is this a crime? It's certainly against the law. These con artists are very clever about not getting caught, however. They have several teams that move swiftly into small communities, score as many marks as possible in a small window of time, and then disappear.

It also occurred to me that this team was checking my mental alertness. Fortunately, both my wife and I are still mentally sharp. But being in my late seventies is another vulnerability as many of my similar-age friends are suffering from memory problems. Scam artists look for cognitive decline in elderly people all the time, and when found, senior citizens often become easy prey.

Tellingly, and to the point of disclosing my own desire to see others as I wish to see them, I really found myself wanting to trust the young man who made the two visits to our home. He had successfully checked off many of the boxes I have in my head for trusting others. He was quite handsome, dressed appropriately for his line of work, articulate, and entertaining (he had a sense of humor), and he spoke with authority, showing

> **RED FLAG #1:** Human predators will try to isolate you from friends and loved ones. Their purpose is to be the only voice you ever hear so they can better control you.

no micro-expressions in his face that typically tip me off when someone is lying. He received extra points for showing me he was environmentally sensitive by riding a battery-powered scooter around our neighborhood instead of a big, gas-guzzling truck. When he returned the second time feigning unfamiliarity, I deduced he was either stupid or checking my memory (thus checking my vulnerability).

In the end, everything he and his grifter friend did was highly choreographed. I was the potential mark and might have become prey had my wife and I not sensed something was off and planned with our contractor a careful defensive action.

Perhaps the above example is too extreme to show how projection repeatedly trips us up. Let's look at a more everyday example.

Projection and the Need for Certainty
Example #2 – The Pregnant Waitress

Several years ago, my wife and I had sat down to enjoy a delightful early lunch out when approached by a waitress who clearly appeared pregnant. The young lady, perhaps in her early thirties, was brusque and tedious when first interacting with us. We both have learned to suspend initial judgments and reactions to all difficult first encounters as you never know when someone is just barely holding it together. Life is hard, and the burden carried by others is always invisible to even the most observant.

Talking about the many moods a woman goes through when pregnant, we discussed thawing techniques as an empathetic couple.

"Best to let her be whoever she needs to be," I suggested.

"You may be right, but when she returns for our order, I'm going to see if I can break the ice," responded my wife.

The need of empaths to express caring for others can lift people up, but it can also be an unwelcome intrusion that provokes a hostile response. Without crystal-clear signs that empathy or compassion or both are being requested, it's best to remain quiet and just observe. I didn't see anything crystal clear from the young woman's vibe taking our order except anger. I also thought I saw a hardness that invited nothing from anyone. Yet I yielded to the superior intuition women have that allows them to see the cues from other women, cues that I (as a man) often miss.

The second encounter with our waitress was no less cold. As she asked about our readiness to order, my wife gave her luncheon choice as pleasantly as a person can ask, and then it was my turn. I smiled as I tried to make eye contact with the waitress while making my request. When I ended, not only had I failed to make eye contact, but our waitress wasn't even going to repeat the orders for confirmation.

Then my wife asked in a caring manner, "When is the baby due?"

That's when eye contact was finally made. Our waitress looked straight at my wife and asked, "Is someone pregnant?"

My wife turned beet red with embarrassment. To this day I don't know how she kept from dropping her jaw, displaying that wide-open-mouth look you see only when someone is completely mortified. I know my wife was dying inside while attempting to think of a quick and appropriate response. But no! She could think of nothing to say and was drowning in her shame.

Letting my wife boil in her own stew for what seemed like the longest minute ever recorded, the waitress finally turned on her heels and walked away. To this day, my wife refuses to mention a woman's pregnancy unless the topic is first brought up by the woman herself.

Had my wife truly misread the waitress? Yes, I think so. My wife's need to relieve her own discomfort as an empath in this situation had blinded her to the "do not disturb" vibe of the waitress. That kind of misplaced projection can happen to anyone.

We know from studies of human psychology that humans don't feel comfortable with uncertainty and seek a haven of internal certainty as quickly as possible. My wife was merely expressing her uncertainty through projection. Whenever our own internal uncertainty leads to inappropriate action, the results can be mortifying.

All humans cling to their anchored beliefs as navigational tools for making their way in life. For this reason, you can count on them to nearly always act on those core beliefs (projection in action). And human predators know this. Because sustained indecision and ambiguity are uncomfortable, human predators will often purposely create internal discomfort in their potential marks. Sometimes they use the "slammed door in your face" ploy to do this. They may say something like, "You are just not at the right place in your life for this business opportunity." The potential mark, typically offended, will try to quickly discharge his or her internal discomfort of being rejected by arguing that he or she is indeed at the right place in life and interested, even *super* interested. Bingo! The bait has been taken.

When incoming evidence contradicts our core beliefs, humans tend to dig in deeper to hold onto those beliefs. Why? Because we want life to be more simple than it really is. Life is always (and at all times) complex, however. If that complexity breaks through our brain's carefully constructed, simple reality, we fight back. Sometimes we fight vehemently, emotionally, and with dogged hostility.

Frequently when fighting back, we ask others to consider the views of someone claiming to be an expert. We do this to persuade those who are treading on our core values to see things our way. But do people who claim to be experts have a better grasp than anyone else of the initial conditions, variables, and functions of a personal situation we are facing (more on this later)?

This is what I did in the example above involving the waitress. I, too, was uncomfortable with the perceived pain and suffering of the supposedly pregnant waitress. My core belief is that we should all do whatever we can to relieve the pain and suffering we encounter in this world. Yet the pregnant waitress didn't strike me as open to relief of her pain, so I took no action (as I've learned to do when I am in doubt but still feeling uncomfortable). However, I did defer to my wife as an authority on women. You can see how that turned out. After my wife's so-called intervention, the waitress (who had shown passive hostility before the intervention) became a predator who was determined to get even. She wasn't turned into a Class AAA predator, but she was now actively hostile and ready to embarrass her customer.

This is an exceedingly valuable insight, and if I can persuade you to embrace it, you can begin learning to pause when uncertain, instead of defaulting to a rigid, brittle, false certitude that most give into all too quickly. Yes, this will probably leave you feeling uncomfortable for a while, but the story of the pregnant waitress shows clearly what can happen when you don't put your discomfort on pause. If you offend others needlessly, you will trigger the predator/prey relationship.

What I'm also telling you is that, while we all want certainty, absolute certainty is *never* possible because in most cases (1) many variables are invisible, (2) the functions of those invisible variables are unknown, and (3) the solutions (the predicted path and the predicted outcomes) depend entirely on initial conditions, which can change, and even small alterations can completely alter the outcome.

This is why we often find ourselves making wrong-headed decisions and taking actions with full bullheaded force that have unpleasant consequences. It all comes down to the assumptions we make. And we all make assumptions when we form our decisions. Yet if we pause and examine our assumptions carefully before acting, we usually experience better results.

Now, let's return to the waitress in the example I shared and ask a question I'm hoping you noticed was never answered. "Was the waitress pregnant?" Or was she simply overweight and we incorrectly assumed she was pregnant?

Think about these questions. She never denied she was pregnant. Instead, she simply returned my wife's question with a question of her own—Is someone pregnant?—and didn't tell us if she was pregnant or not. Her response was a hostile way of telling my wife to back off, butt out, and leave her alone. Yet my wife was mortified because she interpreted the waitress's response as a denial of her pregnancy. Was that interpretation correct?

Two weeks after the event, I returned to that restaurant alone to have lunch and to snoop. A different waitress helped me with my order, and the "pregnant waitress" was nowhere in sight. Would it surprise you that I discovered the young woman who nearly caused my wife a heart attack had given birth and was no longer working at the restaurant? To this day, I haven't shared this information with my darling wife. I'd rather leave her with the lesson I'm trying to teach you.

Your greatest vulnerability to human predators of all types is projecting your worldview onto others and signaling to them your core beliefs and your deepest personal needs. If you do this repeatedly, the potential predator will pounce or, at the very least, offer you bait that appeals to your core beliefs and deepest needs.

The bottom line is this—you need to learn how to observe others very carefully, very methodically. Additionally, you must hold in check your knee-jerk behaviors, actions, and reactions that are triggered by the bait predators dangle in front of your beliefs and views of the world. Further, while it's perfectly OK to cling fast to your beliefs, acting on them without knowing the hidden agendas of those offering you bait is bound to get you hooked.

The objective here is not to make you paranoid about everyone you meet. Instead, the objective is to encourage you to approach everyone with better observational skills, deep thought, and the will to gather more evidence of what you are seeing in everyone. Making assumptions about people and their agendas is always high risk.

Was the pregnant waitress a human predator? Yes and no! She was clearly an angry woman who was employed in the hospitality industry. That alone does not compute. She not only gave off an extremely angry vibe, but also, when she had an opportunity to lower her icy demeanor, she chose instead to offend and embarrass her customer. At that point she was determined to get her pound of flesh from my wife's psyche. We don't know why she was so angry that day. Yet without doubt, she clearly extended no invitation to help relieve her anger. And this is

> **RED FLAG #9:** Human predators use emotional blackmail—a technique that makes you believe if you do X, you are a great friend, girlfriend, daughter, wife, colleague, etc. But if you do Y, you are unattractive, bad, dumb, etc.

important! It's important because my wife placed her internal discomfort above the real-world facts signaling there wasn't the slightest interest in us by the waitress.

What I have described in the waitress, and in my wife's behavior, is a form of circumstantial narcissism. Both women were so committed to their own worldview in that moment neither one had any real interest in the other (which is the most common form of using others simply to meet our own needs). **If we aren't reading the signals people give off, we are failing to see them as real people (or as real people seeking to exact a price from us).** When we act on our own needs only, we are using others as tools to reinforce our personal beliefs and personal objectives. This is what the great philosopher Martin Buber called an *I-it relationship*.

In I-it relationships, we are simply using people as tools to accomplish a personal interest or a personal goal. And whenever we do this, we are all being a little predatory and a little blind.

There is one remaining question that deserves more attention. "Are we all somewhat predatory?" The answer is yes, but to qualify as a true human predator, you must be someone who consistently and without conscience seeks to dominate others. Furthermore, human predators use fear, manipulation, trickery, and violence in their drive to dominate others. For all these reasons, you are cautioned to draw a gigantic distinction between those who commit a one-off predatory act and those who fit the full-on, in-your-face definition of a human predator given in this book. **And for heaven's sake, never resort to calling anyone a human predator or calling them any of the street names that appeal to you.** Trust me when I tell you, if you accuse a real human predator of being one, that individual will up the ante to violent confrontation so fast you won't know what hit you.

OK, the point has been made, and you can chew on these observations while we look at other potential blind spots.

What is your second greatest vulnerability to human predators? Those who live for (and get off on) the personal joy of dominating you in some way will frequently strike on several levels where you may have weaknesses as they try to hook you. So I want you to think for a moment about how well you know your own personality. What additional blind spots might keep you from seeing someone sneaking up on you fully intent on finding your weaknesses? How about your ego?

VULNERABILITY #2 – EGO STROKING

While projection is caused by casting your worldview onto others, based on your beliefs, social conventions, or emotional discomfort, ego vulnerability is caused by others who master the skill of stroking your psyche in ways that stimulate a positive response. Let's immediately look at an example.

Ego Stroking
Example #1 – The Honey-Pot Trap

Imagine an extremely attractive person of your favorite sex (at any venue you might find yourself) walks up to you out of the clear blue and invites you to have a private conversation. Even though you are already engaged in a rather intense discussion with others when the invitation is extended, would you say yes, or would you turn down this invitation without hesitation?

Most of us would at least be tempted by such a request. Let's also imagine you are enough tempted to give five minutes of your time to this lovely soul.

In chatting, you discover that he or she, in addition to being easy on your eyes, seems to have a radar to tune into topics of extreme interest to you. Before you realize how much time has passed, five minutes become twenty minutes, and you discover yourself smiling and laughing and really enjoying yourself. The problem is you have a firm commitment to meet your closest friend in another ten minutes, but the drive to that engagement is fifteen minutes away. Breaking away is hard, but you pull yourself together and quickly exchange phone numbers so you can continue chatting this person up later.

While driving to meet your best friend, you can't get this new acquaintance out of your head. It's as if you have known each other forever, and this person seems so into you, really gets you. He or she said things you loved hearing, and yet you two have just met. It's like magic has suddenly occurred in your life, and you want more of it! Right?

What's going on here? Can this be real? And will you call this person the first chance you have to continue getting to know him or her? Think carefully and honestly before you answer.

Almost everyone releases a huge rush of hormones under the circumstances described here. All five of the feel-good brain chemicals (dopamine, serotonin, endorphins, norepinephrine, oxytocin) will immediately be released by most people who experience such a magic moment. And when these two things happen simultaneously, there is no way your brain will allow you to doubt the good intentions of that wonderful person with whom you just spent twenty minutes.

The name I've given for this kind of human experience is the *charisma effect.*

THE CHARISMA EFFECT DEFINED

The charisma effect is people's reaction to an individual, event, or even material object that makes them view that person or thing in a highly positive light. This happens by their psyches triggering the release of one or more of the five feel-good brain chemicals (see full presentation below). Under the influence of the charisma effect, you feel (experience) fascination, awe, ecstasy, euphoria, love, and even adoration of the source of that stimulus. People often elicit the charisma effect with their amazing good looks, their tone of voice, the way they pay attention to you, how they make eye contact with you, or a talent in common with you. When Hollywood producers and directors want to evaluate the star power of an actor's charisma, they give screen tests and then use focus groups to help measure the degree and depth that many people say they are transfixed by the actor's on-screen persona.

RED FLAG #23: Anyone with whom you must work, live, or have a professional relationship and who is constantly self-referential is a warning you are dealing with a human predator. Being self-referential means frequently using *I*, *me*, *my*, and *mine* and always steering the conversation back to himself or herself in whatever way possible.

The use of the charisma effect to produce feelings of awe and astonishment, reverence and love/admiration go back in time to at least the Egyptian pharaohs who spent enormous amounts of their nation's treasure and the toil, sweat, and tears of their subjects to build pyramids, monuments, and tombs. Since those ancient efforts to trigger the charisma effect in their subjects, every religion on Earth has employed these exact same tactics to alter the brain chemistry of their followers and true believers. However, no one person (or religion) has universal appeal to the psyches of all humans.

Here, our goal is to help you become fully aware of how predatory individuals use the charisma effect to dominate you as they carry out their nefarious agendas. Frequently, though, the charisma effect is triggered by people who come into your sphere of influence with absolutely no agenda involving you. Let's begin growing your awareness of how people can change your brain chemistry instantaneously when they have absolutely no intention or desire to do so.

Recently my wife and I were having dinner with another couple at a restaurant we really like, but the two women in our party were supremely unhappy about the placement of our table. After about ten minutes of back-and-forth between the women, their verbal complaints stopped immediately when a celebrity was escorted by the host to the table right next to ours.

The celebrity's name is David Foster, the well-known music producer who lives in Los Angeles. I didn't recognize him at first, but my wife and her lifelong girlfriend instantly identified Mr. Foster and his wife. Suddenly the two women at our table changed their tune. Their posture shifted (they sat up, spines ramrod straight). They talked like two giddy schoolgirls and kept glancing over at the table where Mr. Foster was sitting with his lovely, young, pregnant wife.

Most surprising to me were the stories they started sharing about Mr. Foster and all the people he had made famous. And if you haven't guessed, the complaints about where our table was placed in the restaurant were substituted by talk of providence and destiny. The two women at my table now regarded its placement in that restaurant as extremely favorable, and for them the evening became memorable—all because a famous person, who doesn't even know their names, was seated at the table next to ours.

This sudden change in attitude was affected by the close encounter these two women had in that moment with a celebrity. While the charisma effect may be triggered by a variety of stimuli that will be illustrated in this book, this particular close encounter with David Foster, if illustrating nothing else, reveals how my wife and her girlfriend underwent a monumental change in brain chemistry that occurred instantly when they saw Mr. Foster and his wife seated at the table next to ours. Similar changes occur in the brains of everyone when we assign higher status to the people around us.

It's worthy of note that neither my wife nor her friend honestly knows anything deeply intimate about David Foster. He could secretly be a serial killer as yet unidentified by law enforcement (he isn't, by the way). More likely, of course, is that the last thing Mr. Foster wanted that evening was to be recognized for his celebrity status. He most likely wanted a quiet night out with his wife to relax and be himself. That's why he requested a table outdoors as far away from other people as possible. Had either of the women at my table lost control and approached David Foster for an autograph, they almost certainly would have robbed him of the simple pleasures he was seeking. And I think I would have thrown up with disgust and embarrassment.

What do you think would have happened had Mr. Foster turned around and said hello to my wife and her friend? I probably would have had to call 911.

What biological changes do you think occurred inside the brains of my wife and her girlfriend when David Foster and his wife were seated at the table next to us?

Perhaps this is the best place to stop and take care of some housekeeping chores, so you have a deeper understanding about the five feel-good brain chemicals identified above that play such an important role in our overall happiness and sense of well-being.

Playing the Brain-Chemical Game

The human brain has five known (and fairly well-understood) pleasure and mood-boosting chemicals that strongly influence our attitudes and actions, and **if you are going to become even a tiny bit better at understanding your vulnerability to ego stroking, you need to know a little about how these five chemicals work:**

- **Serotonin** modulates mood; improves cognition reward, learning, and memory; and assists with a large number of physiological processes. People who are depressed often have low levels of serotonin. However, serotonin's feel-good effects in the brain could be considered its starring role in the body.

- **Dopamine** is the motivation-and-reward brain chemical. On a given day, if you feel motivated and ready to tackle your list of projects after a workout, you can thank dopamine. Dopamine gives us the motivation to achieve something of value or makes us feel rewarded on the inside.

- **Endorphins** are the ultimate feel-good chemicals. You've heard people talk about runner's high, the feeling of bliss and oneness with the world that comes after running a while. Also, endorphins help relieve pain. Endorphins also help calm fear and anxiety, thereby making you feel more tranquil and at peace with yourself.

- **Norepinephrine** is ramped up by your two small adrenal glands above your kidneys, as well as by your brain. When more norepinephrine flows into your bloodstream, you become more alert and focused. Norepinephrine also boosts memory retrieval, so you become better at recalling information stored in your brain. When something really positive happens, like stroking your ego, norepinephrine anchors that experience in your memory for easy retrieval.

- **Oxytocin** is sometime called the *love hormone* because oxytocin levels increase during sex. It is also associated with empathy, trust, and relationship-building. Oxytocin is a hormone that is produced in the hypothalamus and then transported to and secreted by the pituitary gland. Oxytocin is the reason advertising agencies often connect their products with sexually implied, or even sexually explicit, images. These illustrations trigger the release of oxytocin, and discovering this has led to the advertising meme *sex sells*.

All these brain chemicals play a huge role in driving our behaviors. Too much or too little in any one of these brain chemicals leads to behaviors that are hard to explain, difficult, repetitive, obsessive, deviant, compulsive, and even violent.

The charisma effect describes the brain-chemistry bath that occurs when a person triggers any one or more of the five above-named mood-influencing chemicals in another or others. The activating person can be famous, like a celebrity, Stephen King, or the Dalai Lama. Or the person can be a non-celebrity, common citizen like the love in our life. When we fall in love, and here I am talking about romantic love, our brains are bathed in all five chemicals, and any time we are near our beloved, these good brain chemicals are released again. Also, it's worth noting that beautiful women and movie-star-handsome men can trigger the charisma effect just by walking into a room. This response, combined with a small amount of ego stroking from these comely people, creates vulnerabilities that can quickly turn you into prey.

To anchor this vulnerability in your mind, I will share that I spend my winter months living at a platinum-rated country club in Southern California. I have watched brilliant, extremely wealthy men in their senior years fall prey to beautiful young women who knew exactly how to take advantage of this vulnerability. It's not only the twenty- to forty-something men and women who find their egos and the chemical magic of the human brain causing them to stop thinking critically and become victims of human predators with no morals, no conscience, and no qualms about using this vulnerability to set up others for a big heartbreak or worse.

VULNERABILITY #3 – THE FOLLOWER IMPULSE

Let's begin this discussion with a little humor. There is a story, perhaps mythical and perhaps not, of a seeker of truth who devoted two decades of his life looking in the Amazonian jungles for a crystal that was supposedly worshipped by ancient native tribes because it spoke only the truth.

High atop a prominent cliff, placed upon a stone-carved altar, and surrounded by waterfalls that plunged one thousand feet into the river below, the crystal sat gleaming in the sun, hidden far from modern humanity by hundreds of miles of dangerous forests and dense vegetation. Many had sought this treasure but had failed. "At long last," cried the man as he approached the crystal with awe, "I shall finally know the truth about everything!" Sitting in a position of meditation and reverence while waiting for the crystal to speak, the man heard its first words: "All the problems you have in life are due to your own weaknesses." Whereupon the great seeker of truth became enraged, leaped to a full standing position, and shouted at the crystal, "You fucking fake! You don't know me at all!" Then he picked up the crystal and threw it into the waterfalls while watching it sparkle and shine from the sun's rays as it plunged into the raging river, never to be seen or heard from again.

Sharing this little parable has a two-fold purpose. First, I'm reminding you that this section is meant only to focus on the natural human weaknesses that predators are looking for when they hunt for prey. Not for a second, however, should you conclude from these offerings that you are the cause of any problems that are created when a predator gets his or her claws into you. Much more will be said about this in section 4 when you will learn about how to avoid or break away from human predator engagement.

The second purpose for sharing the above parable is to reveal the universal need humans have for confirmation of their beliefs and actions. The shorthand label for this need is *confirmation bias*. In 2016, Michael Lewis wrote an astonishingly successful book about two social scientists from Israel who spent more than twenty years of their brilliant lives conducting social psychology experiments that demonstrated how our brains default to seek out confirmation of our beliefs (our biases) on all levels of thinking. Most importantly, the two scientists, Amos Tversky and Daniel Kahneman, demonstrated convincingly how we all vigorously (often irrationally) protect our core beliefs with bias confirmation when those beliefs are confronted or offended. Why is this revelation so important to know when discussing the follower impulse as a vulnerability?

A human predator knows that large numbers of potential prey share certain core beliefs, and by appealing to these beliefs in specific ways, he or she will gain immediate entrée into the hearts and minds of large groups. Here's an example for you to think about:

The Follower Impulse
Example #1 – The Faith Healer

The audience of several thousand had gathered at a major venue in downtown San Francisco for what promised to be a night of spectacular healing miracles. A susurration of excited voices prophesized a knowing certainty that the preacher had been chosen by God to heal through the laying on of hands. Only two men in the audience were non-believers, and even they were moved by the energy in the great hall filled with the hopeful, the sick, the suffering. Most of the physical ailments of attendees were invisible to the naked eye. Some had canes, so you could tell they were mobility challenged. Many were senior citizens, and some were small children whose parents had brought them, hoping for a miracle cure. There was no charge for entering the hall. Later, however, an opportunity to make an offering was given to audience members after the Holy Spirit had descended in full force through the man with hair the color of black shoe polish, teeth as white as light bulbs, and voice that managed to be screeching, nasal, and guttural at the same time.

> **RED FLAG #53:** Human predators listen to your hopes and dreams and concerns to make you feel understood, but then they tell you the only way forward to make your dreams come true is through them.

None of these showmanship ploys would be impressive to James Randi, one of the unbelievers in attendance. Known across the nation as "The Amazing Randi," one of America's renowned magicians for several decades, he had retired and turned his considerable talents, intellect, experience, and knowhow as a magician into debunking frauds, fakes, and charlatans. He knew that to appear bigger than life you had to tell a big lie that people wanted desperately to hear, appear bigger than life on the outside, and use tricks that allowed you to do things considered inexplicable to the common man (the audience in this case).

Peter Popoff was a charlatan, and James Randi was in attendance that night to observe and try to see through the curtain of fakery Popoff was employing to fleece the flock of faithful sheep whose needs for healing were not only real but also sometimes so serious that their lives were on the line.

When Popoff entered the theater, he didn't stand above the people in his audience but walked right out into the aisles and proclaimed, "God is touching hurting people around the world! It's such a joy to share the reality of his saving power, healing power, and grace! Amen!" The audience replied with an enthusiastic "Amen!" With this as the only introduction, Popoff went straight to work. As if hearing the voice of the Holy Spirit whispering in his ear, Popoff hesitatingly called out the name of an audience member and asked her to stand and join him up front. The believer, now thrilled with everlasting joy to be one of the chosen that night, made her way to stand near Popoff. During the believer's walk (or sometimes a dance by others later selected) to the front, Popoff questioningly called out her affliction as if wanting the chosen one to affirm his miraculous diagnosis. Once finger-touch close, he screamed at the evil spirit that possessed the woman, "Begone! Leave this body!" Then placing his hands to the supplicant's forehead, the preacher shouted, "Heal in the name of the Holy Spirit."

As the performance went on and Popoff called others up, he also used other commands for the affliction to shrink or become invisible or even for the immobile to walk. Using the power of his arms and hands, he then pushed hard against the supplicants' foreheads, and they would fall backwards into the arms of big, strong men who were standing beside them, prepared to catch the now-healed bodies.

The audience whooped and hollered, "Alleluia! Oh, Jesus," and the energy in the room rose to fever pitch. Approximately one hour into this healing extravaganza, huge plastic garbage containers were brought out, and Popoff asked able-bodied audience members to escort these containers around the hall, up and down the aisles, and pass them through every row to collect offerings in gratitude to God for the work of the Holy Spirit. In truth, the money collected would go directly to Popoff and his wife, Elizabeth. The monthly gross of these offerings totaled one million dollars.

Randi suspected he knew exactly how this fraud was being perpetrated. Through a private investigator, special radio-wave detection equipment was secreted into the auditorium two weeks later just minutes before another of Popoff's healing sessions in the same auditorium. There was no guarantee a radio frequency could be discovered that allowed someone offstage to feed Popoff the information he seemed to be receiving from the Holy Spirit, so this entire effort was a high-risk gamble. However, if successful, recording equipment also inserted with the cache of high-tech equipment would capture this feed. The private investigator, costumed as a security guard, planted the supersensitive radio wave detection equipment himself by simply walking in the back door of the auditorium.

Randi was seated in the audience on the night this strategy was employed. With a minuscule radio receiver that fit almost undetectably inside his ear like a hearing aid, he was hopeful he would hear the Holy Spirit speak to Popoff. Randi's friend, the other non-believer in attendance at the performance two weeks earlier, had noticed the same type of receiver in Popoff's ear when he passed close by. You and I never would have noticed this receiver had we not known what to look for, but both Randi and his friend did know. Like all audience members, in the lobby earlier in the evening before the show began, they had been asked to fill out information cards with personal details about their desire to be healed. Clearly this was how names and health conditions were identified by Popoff and the Holy Spirit. The only missing link was the method of transmission.

Not only did the equipment detect the radio frequency, but also Randi discovered that night something he hadn't guessed—the Holy Spirit was a woman whose voice sounded eerily like Popoff's wife, Elizabeth. The recording equipment the private detective had planted worked brilliantly, and Randi revealed this entire ruse several weeks later to the *Late Night with Johnny Carson* television audience. While millions watched and heard everything, the secret audio recording was played simultaneously with a video recording of Popoff giving his performance. The synchronization was perfect for completely exposing the scam.

Do you think this revelation shut down Peter Popoff and his act? While Popoff immediately declared bankruptcy to stave off lawsuits from former audience members, twenty-five years later, Peter and Elizabeth Popoff were still scamming the faithful out of millions—but now Popoff was preaching debt relief. You read that right! While the specifics changed over time, Popoff's message was now that God wants us to be affluent and debt-free and Popoff is a prophet sent by God to help people transform their lives from poverty to affluence.

All those who ever attended Peter Popoff's shows were seeking a strong leader to solve their problems. Whether their problems were caused by serious sickness or deep debt, each person felt overwhelmed and wanted desperately to find a personal savior. This resulted in a three-step process for roping them in:

1. Their extreme need for help set them up to become prey for a predator like Popoff.

2. The predator (Popoff) used the charisma effect to get people in his audiences to believe whatever he told them as the gospel truth by telling his followers exactly what they wanted to hear—that God knew their problems (in health or money matters).

3. Popoff then claimed to have been sent by God to deliver them from those problems.

These three steps checked off the boxes in the heads of every attendee that Popoff might truly be the leader they sought. To seal the deal, Popoff followed up with what appeared to be direct contact with the Holy Spirit, and this trick whipped his audience into a state of passionate, irrational fervor.

If you declare that the audience members attending his rallies deserved what they got for being so gullible, let's look at a far less drastic example together and see how each of us gets manipulated on a regular basis to embrace a leader we know almost nothing about but who promises to solve what we perceive to be overwhelming problems that will be or are afflicting us.

THE FOLLOWER IMPULSE
EXAMPLE #2 – THE POLITICIAN

Hailing from a wealthy East Coast family, the candidate for president and his beautiful wife had taken the nation by storm. This was his first run for the presidency, and it was a high-risk bet. Part of his strategy was using his considerable wealth to barnstorm around the country, holding public rallies, and speaking directly to a burgeoning horde of followers. No one who had been in politics long gave him a real chance of winning, and he was doubtful, as well. Still, he pressed on, believing his messages were very much what the voters wanted to hear. Rumors abounded about his extramarital dalliances, but no one believed someone with such a gorgeous wife would do anything like that. Whisper campaigns with unsubstantiated, salacious accusations were just one of the prices a candidate for president had to pay. The only smart thing to do was never address them. Besides, the national electorate had so many other serious issues on its mind. He knew exactly how to appeal to those concerns when he got in front of a microphone. And the results spoke eloquently with recent polls revealing a huge spurt upwards in popularity.

The old guard was worried about those numbers. Neither liberals nor conservatives had ever seen such passionate, vocal followers. Voters were coming out of the shadows, it seemed, for this charismatic man who somehow had the ability to say the right things in the right way for his legions of supporters. His messages offered a whole new way of looking at America's future and the nation's relationship to the rest of the world.

But in the eyes of professional politicians, the new candidate's leadership style was anti-establishment in every way. Yet while he spoke clearly of ideas unpopular in Washington, DC, the passion of his followers came close in fervor to that for a religious prophet. And because everyone in the DC establishment could count, they knew the final tally of votes would be close and the Electoral College was where this race would be decided. More troubling was how the emergence of a new voting block might also change the congressional races. If this candidate's groundswell of support swept into office a majority in the House and Senate, no telling how this would alter the political landscape in America.

RED FLAG #39: When human predators engage in lying, they can do so without any of the tells of people who have a conscience.

Who would you guess this politician was as described above? If you said Donald Trump, you are easily forgiven for offering the wrong answer. The right answer is John F. Kennedy. And when he ran for president, he did offer a new vision of America and its potential place in the world. He was married to a beautiful woman, Jackie Kennedy, and he was rumored to have had many affairs during his marriage. Of course, there was no internet in the early sixties, and news traveled slowly compared to the speed of information dissemination today. John Kennedy also brought to this nation a vision of international connectedness that was radical and inspiring to younger voters. Those messages resonated with the new generation of college-aged young people so well that the number of youthful voters passionately following Kennedy shook the establishment to its core. The contingency of old-guard, establishment politicians was all about America first. Ideas like the Peace Corps, landing on the moon, and his New Frontier domestic policies seemed over-the-top crazy to the generation that had fought in World War II and was then embroiled in a heated Cold War with the former Soviet Union.

Because the United States Constitution established a republic, the nation's founders created the world's largest stage for human predators to take advantage of the follower impulse. **The predators in election campaigns tell gigantic lies they know voters want to hear, they present as larger-than-life figures (with lots of help from the mainstream media), and they employ psychological tricks and sleight-of-hand fakery to wow their supporters**. These psychological tricks include (1) putting down their political adversaries in ways that make opponents look smaller and less trustworthy, (2) using trustworthy citizens to go door-to-door to encourage other citizens to vote for the candidate, (3) never admitting to any of the (false or true) accusations made against them, thereby maintaining their larger-than-life personas, (4) spending millions on saturation advertising campaigns so their names are always in your face and on your mind, and (5) hiring private polling companies to conduct polls that are slanted just enough to inflate how popular each candidate seems to be with voters. This is, by no means, an exhaustive list of the often-dirty tricks used by politicians to increase voter actions in their favor.

RED FLAG #41: Human predators take risks that endanger others. They have a reckless disregard for safety of self or the safety of others as indicated by being indifferent to or rationalizing having hurt, mistreated, or stolen from another. This trait is called shamelessness.

Clearly there are elected representatives who are super-honest, hard-working advocates on behalf of their constituents. You can probably identify several. But the ones who use the political stage the way Peter Popoff used the religious stage for his personal gain are human predators exactly like Popoff, and you are best served knowing this. How else will you be able to protect yourself?

Do you, or does any citizen of our great nation, deserve to be scammed by predatory politicians? No, we don't deserve that! But it happens.

The core themes of predatory behavior explaining how politicians win campaigns and treat their political opponents and political enemies have not changed much since the early days of our democracy. Since then, we have created more powerful ways to hunt (newspapers, television news programs, the internet) and take people down.

Most importantly, ask yourself objectively, "Would political predators succeed at all if you and I did not have a follower impulse?" Even though we know little about their true character or state of mind, we become followers of and vote for our favorite candidates all the time. Don't be embarrassed if you have an aha moment in answering this question. Millions of years of genetic programing went into creating the follower impulse in human DNA. Ancient tribal members following a chief was a great model for primitive humans banding together to battle the threats all around them. Today we continue to elect a commander-in-chief every four years. And as tribal members who are descendants of ancient humans, we need to perceive our nation's chief as a good and decent, strong and mighty leader who represents our interests. Even with this evolutionary artifact fully operative in modern times, evolution does continue, however.

Please consider another truth that evolution is expressing in humans. Critical thinking, the process of digging deep for facts and then objectively and logically thinking for oneself, has also been growing as a human trait. You can see its emergence in the written records of ancient history by studying the Athenian Greeks. Most of you reading this book are familiar with names like Socrates, Aristotle, and Plato. But there are so many more from this period that have left us a treasure-trove of thinking for themselves and who, by their examples, showed us how to question everything, including our own thoughts, assumptions, and conclusions. The ancient Greek aphorism "know thyself" was the first of three maxims inscribed in the forecourt of the Temple of Apollo at Delphi. The other two maxims were "nothing to excess" and "surety brings ruin." My observation is that humans still haven't universally internalized these three maxims, at least not at the level of our genetic code. Yet I am hopeful about humans' ability to grasp that critical thinking about modern-day predators can save their lives, their livelihoods, and their sanity. And as you will discover in section 4 of this book, **critical thinking is your most powerful weapon when it comes to avoiding human predators.**

VULNERABILITY #4 – YOUR HOPES AND DREAMS

Throughout my adult life, I have encouraged everyone in my sphere of influence to be in touch with his or her hopes and dreams, pursue those dreams with hard work and diligence, and make those dreams come true. From my perspective, a life lived without dreams so personally powerful that they get you up and out of bed at the crack of dawn each day to pursue them is no life at all. But now I must warn you about how human predators will use your dreams to divert your good and decent dream-to-reality energy in ways designed to make their own dreams come true and leave you with absolutely nothing except a broken spirit. So buckle up!

YOUR HOPES AND DREAMS
EXAMPLE #1 – THE CON ARTIST

"I never took anything from anybody. Those people gave me their money either of their own free will or out of greed."

The words above were never spoken by anybody (that I know of). Yet these two sentences are exactly what con artists would tell you if you were able to stop them from denying what they really did to those who trusted them. Since people have been in existence, there have been those willing to cheat others out of their possessions, especially money. Many of these con artists have managed to establish their reputations in the popular imagination through tapping into the hopes and dreams of the innocent. One name stands out in modern times above all others: Bernie Madoff.

In total, Bernie Madoff made off with 64.8 billion dollars, and he wasn't caught until 2008, although many highly intelligent financial experts were suspicious of his investments as far back as 1999. Madoff died in prison on April 14, 2021. Do you remember reading of his death? Probably not because the world was still in the throes of fighting a pandemic and rational people were doing all they could to get vaccinated against COVID-19. Who had time to check up on Bernie Madoff's health?

His clients were men and women of modest means, as well as of enormous wealth. In fact, several of the largest investment banks on Wall Street don't want you to know they were also taken by Madoff. Fearing lawsuits for libel, I won't name those banks here. But they were all taken by the six-step formula below, which works very successfully on almost everyone who must invest money to build retirement assets.

You see, retirement is the dream that Madoff tapped into to take advantage of his victims. It's a dream sold to us by every financial planner, insurance company, investment company, and bank (whether large or small), as well as the American Association of Retired People, Wall Street investment houses (including online-only brokerage firms), and our parents and grandparents. The dream, in simple summary, states you are to (1) work like crazy your entire adult life, (2) save as much as 20 percent of your income, (3) invest it wisely so it grows to some huge amount of money, and then (4) when you are sixty-five to seventy, begin to enjoy the golden years. Forget about the fact that nearly 70 percent of the labor force lives paycheck to paycheck and can't save a dime. Forget about the fact that investing has enormous risks. And especially forget that a significant percentage of the population dies before they reach retirement age.

Bernie Madoff didn't forget any of this. He lived by six simple rules:

- Promise and provide a guaranteed 11 percent return (compounded annually) on all money invested with him.
- Make sure your monthly statements to clients show the return provided, but keep the details of your investments as opaque as possible.
- Make sure your potential clients have the opportunity to talk with other famous clients who are thrilled with your results.
- Maintain a sense of exclusivity. Occasionally, turn clients away, at least initially, so they want all the more to be accepted into your club.
- Take all the investment money your clients give you, even if it's all the money they have.
- Keep your successful investment formula a proprietary secret, no matter how hard potential clients or existing clients press you to disclose how you are managing to beat everyone else in the investment industry year in and year out.

How did the ever-in-control Bernie manage to fool everyone except the few math savants who did the simple computations that should have exposed him? He paid out the 11 percent compounded annually as promised to his existing clients using new money that new clients gave him month after month after month. He never invested any money at all. This is called a Ponzi scheme, named after Charles Ponzi, who used this same fraudulent scheme in the 1920s. Ponzi was not the first to employ this notorious fraud. It's just that Ponzi received so much worldwide press coverage when the con came crashing down that his name became forever attached to this "rob Peter to pay Paul" criminal operation.

What finally brought Madoff down was the financial crises of 2007 and 2008, which robbed him of the ability to bring in new clients to pay the redemptions demanded by old clients as the market turned south. His own sons turned him in, claiming they didn't know their father was running a Ponzi scheme. Personally, I believe they did know, and as human predators often do to one another, they turned on each other. It was an epic battle of predator versus predator, and that is what brought down the biggest human predator ever in the world of investing.

My wife and I were victims of Madoff indirectly through a highly-thought-of major Wall Street investment bank. Only a small fraction of 1 percent of our wealth was lost by the big bank that managed our investments, and I won't identify that bank. However, many Ponzi schemes are presently active around the world, and most of the men and women behind them will never be caught. Including Bernie Madoff's story as an example of how Ponzi-scheme actors steal the dreams of their victims is probably the only swing I will ever get at the jaws of these predators. Yes, this story on Madoff is personal!

Above I listed those enterprises that promote the dream of saving and investing for retirement. Can you imagine how many billions are spent on marketing this dream by these actors? There is one major promotor of the retirement dream I did not mention in the list above. That actor is the United States government.

Without a doubt, the federal government recognizes how difficult it is to set money aside for retirement. This is why the Social Security tax was created. Since the government knows most people won't (or can't) save enough, it takes the money out of your paycheck and places it in a gigantic trust fund so the money will be available to provide you a minimum income once you retire. But there is a problem with this system, one you or I could easily make regarding our own retirement funding needs.

What if, when you are eligible to receive income payments from the Social Security Trust, there isn't enough money in the trust to pay you? How will you be any better off than Bernie Madoff's former clients?

To make this situation worse, this nation's Central Bank insists on implementing monetary policies that cause inflation. Essentially this means the dollars earned by your hard work now are less valuable every single year that passes. Thus, it is more expensive to live every year. By the time you reach retirement age, how much of a life will you be able to afford with inflation eating away at the value of the Social Security payments coming to you? In a very real way, the entire system is built on a promise the government never intends to keep, that promise being Social Security income for retirement will, at the very least, afford you a financial floor so you will never have to be old and destitute. Ask any of Bernie Madoff's former clients who are now old and destitute because of his unkept promises how that feels and then answer the question—"Is Social Security itself a Ponzi scheme of sorts?"

Right now, the situation has deteriorated to the point that every dollar paid out to retirement-age citizens comes from the money paid into the Social Security trust fund from those who work to pay into the fund. Isn't that exactly what Bernie Madoff and family were doing? You decide!

Your Hopes and Dreams
Example #2 – The Yoga Guru

Today it's known to students of yoga as Hot Yoga. To the thirty-seven million people practicing yoga in the United States, it was previously known as Bikram Yoga. Why the name change?

Bikram Choudhury was born in 1944 in Calcutta, British India. He claimed he won the National India Yoga Championship three years in a row when he was a teenager. However, the first national yoga competition in India took place in 1974, several years after Bikram had left the country. Did Bikram lie? Was Bikram a lying, sociopathic human predator?

One thing Bikram Choudhury did not lie about is the twenty-six yoga poses he pieced together from the repertoire of five hundred ones taught by the great yoga guru in India named Bishnu Charan Ghosh. Though Bikram did falsely claim to have been a pupil of Ghosh for years, this is still not an earth-shaking lie. Earth-shaking lies are ones that steal the very souls of people for selfish purposes. And Bikram did exactly that with his other lies. Let me tell you how.

After his emigration to the United States in 1971, Bikram began to teach yoga to support himself. His style of instruction was a huge red flag, or it should have been to those who paid handsomely to join his classes in Los Angeles. He was rude and insulting to his students, bragged constantly of the celebrities he had instructed, and berated anyone attending his classes who was overweight. Nevertheless, Bikram yoga (the twenty-six positions he taught) expanded rapidly across the United States.

By the 1990s, Bikram Choudhury was famous enough to launch a training institute for those who wanted to become instructors in his unique style of yoga. Those who attended his nine-week training program paid handsomely for the privilege. The cost in terms of money, however, was not the only price extracted from his students. Bikram was constantly roaming the classroom placing his hands all over the most beautiful female pupils as he "corrected" their postures. Dressed only in a skimpy thong himself, Bikram would frequently approach the female students from behind and slide up "thong to yoga tights" close to them and move up and down, in and out as if in coital ecstasy. Was any of this illegal? No! As long as no one objected, Bikram was simply living out his America dream.

Would you believe this predatory behavior made Bikram Choudhury rich and famous? In fact, he became so rich and so famous that superstars hired him at ungodly prices to be their personal instructor. No names will be revealed here because the claims about who Bikram tutored can never be trusted. Furthermore, it just doesn't matter, does it? The man became supremely wealthy and amassed a collection of twenty-two luxury cars that included a dozen Rolls-Royces, five Bentleys, and a rare 1969 Murena 429 GT. Bikram loved those cars. He loved them almost as much as the forced sexual favors he bullied out of his most prized mentees. How exactly did he pull this off?

Knowing the laws of the United States would not protect him, Mr. Choudhury cleverly founded a school in India for his most superior students. All young, amazingly beautiful women (because, wouldn't you know it, Bikram was homophobic), these chosen ones were given full-ride scholarships to the superior classes held in India. All their expenses were paid. The girls were flown to India first-class, had a suite at the finest hotels, and had all their meals covered by Mr. Choudhury himself. This was a dream come true for these young women. Well, it was a dream until they arrived in India to discover that they *and* Bikram were booked into the same suite. That's when the dream became a nightmare.

Where is Bikram today? Curious you should ask.

After he was successfully sued in 2013 by a small group of his victims and a judgment against him for $7.5 million was awarded this brave group of plaintiffs by the court, Bikram did a disappearing act and has never paid. In 2020 it was reported he was hiding out in Mexico, on the run from Mexican authorities for not paying his $180,000 bill at the Princess Mundo Imperial Hotel. The hotel confiscated Bikram's passport, so getting out of Mexico may be somewhat of a problem for him now. But if you see a dark-skinned, partially balding man, wearing only a skimpy thong walking down Hollywood Boulevard anytime soon, don't offer him a ride, OK?

While Bikram Choudhury failed to prey on as many people as Bernie Madoff, he committed real crimes as well as moral crimes throughout his adult life. Taking advantage of his position as yoga teacher, Bikram Choudhury traumatized many women who came to him with the dream of dramatically improving their lives. Many human predators who steal the dreams of others in non-criminal ways eventually turn to crime out of desperation as their character flaws bring the world down around them.

Those who have positions of enormous power over others can silence the voices of their victims through legal maneuvers used by high-powered attorneys who specialize in cleaning up the messes of human predators so they don't get convicted and go to jail. Even good and decent people who gain positions of enormous power over others are frequently tempted by that power to use it for selfish purposes. Those who give into this temptation become human predators. In section 3, you are going to learn how to see when powerful people cross the line separating leadership and abuse.

Before wrapping up this explanation of how your hopes and dreams can be used against you by human predators, I want to share one more story.

Your Hopes and Dreams
Example #3 – The Audition Scam

Sam and Glenn were standouts in the high school drama club, and their work together on stage and off created a fun, synergistic friendship. While the most talented teenagers seldom achieve stardom, there is no want of passionate effort and hard work put forward by talented dreamers to climb Hollywood's success ladder. These two young up-and-comers thought they were smarter than most about the pitfalls and detours on the road to become members of Tinseltown's elite. They weren't. The future-focused duo had dreams of turning their talents into careers, dreams that were fueled more by optimism than by wisdom. Eager to launch their climb to the top, they began looking for opportunities when suddenly an opportunity found them.

The advertisement in the Sunday paper read, "Want to Start a Career in Radio Broadcasting?" Within minutes of reading this auspicious full-page pitch-line, the two teens were on the phone assessing the merits of responding to the ad. One especially succulent tease in the persuasive promo was the "get your own radio show" line. Without doubt, those paying the big bucks for this full-page display ad were in search of new talent. And the auditions were in Hollywood, believe it or not, with a specific deadline to respond and only three days of actual on-site appointments available. No fee was being charged, but there was a processing cost of one thousand dollars per person. This money would be used to package the studio recording, along with a professionally prepared resume for the handful of actual radio stations that had hired the studio to screen talent.

On arriving in Hollywood, a trip paid for out of their own pockets, Sam and Glenn found the recording studio and went through the hour-long paper parade of form-filling, in-depth-background assessment for resume purposes. Everyone working at the studio seemed professional and congenial. Surely this was a reputable team of highly skilled talent scouts. No one could mistake them for anything else.

The in-studio recording was just as slick. While the next applicant filled out his or her paperwork, Glenn and Sam each had their one-hour session in the recording studio with a sound engineer. Both young men displayed that day their astounding gift of gab, quick wits, and marvelous humor. They were naturals. And the sound engineer and others on the talent scout team descended on both of them to tell them so as they left the studio. The superlatives were confidence building, and the promises about next steps were pointed, detailed, and definitive.

Both of these young men were nineteen years old. And together, their excitement could not have been more real than the entire nation's enthrall-ment with Christa McAuliffe's selection to become the first civilian on the spaceship *Challenger* that blasted off on that same day.

The tragedy of the *Challenger* proved to be an omen for Sam and Glenn. On returning home and telling all their friends they had just blasted off into the world of broadcast radio, day after day went by with no word from the studio in Hollywood. Could the studio have lost their phone num-bers? Maybe, but both teens had the studio phone number. Repeated calls received no answers, not even an answering machine. After two weeks of calling, they received a recorded message from the phone company that the number had been disconnected and was no longer in service. Like the *Challenger*, the dream of these two would-be broadcasters had blown up. And both young men ate bitter that day for the first time in their lives.

They ate bitter because human predators had turned their dreams of lemonade into lemons. It would not be the last time.

Do you think Glenn and Sam should have seen the con coming at them from a mile away? Or would you be of the opinion, as am I, that teaching about human predators and the weaknesses we have to them should be taught in high school? As it turns out, many years on, I discovered these two teens actually considered the world of broadcast media only one of many possibilities for applying their prodigious talents until someone planted a big signpost in the Sunday edition of the *Arizona Republic* pointing to a shortcut to make this particular dream come true. At that point, this latent dream of theirs became an immediate, top-priority dream for these two young men, both of whom were seduced by the shortcut. **How many of you reading this book have a latent dream that you gave up on the way to becoming a responsible adult, parent, and spouse?** Do you think your dream can't be tapped into by human predators now, all these years later? How about shortcuts? Are you vulnerable to offers of shortcuts that bait you into surfacing those latent dreams?

Then too, of course, there are your top-priority passionate dreams—the ones that drive you every day. Are you immune to seductive offers by scam artists to open doors, get you to the front of the line, or introduce you to rainmakers who can launch you? Or do you have both feet planted firmly on the ground by certain knowledge that to get where you are going takes hard work, sacrifice, and most importantly, time. You see, time is always the enemy of the impatient. And **every human predator knows the lure of immediate gratification is irresistible to all but those most grounded in reality.**

Should you never tell your dreams to others? Of course not! Just pick carefully. And if you see any of the red flags you will learn about in section 3 (and listed at the end of the book), for goodness' sake, follow the instructions in section 4 to shed the blood-sucking assholes (I mean human predators) who are out to steal your dreams and destroy your faith in yourself.

OK, are we done here? Have I truly exposed you to the four weaknesses you have to being turned into prey by human predators? Of course,

I won't ever know the answers you give to these questions. But God knows, I have tried to warn you, alert you, and protect you from four of the big ones! Only you will be able to look back one day and say, "Hey, that book I read years ago on human predators saved me a lot of heartache. Let me tell you a story you won't believe."

SUMMARY

This second section has been devoted to help you know yourself a little better and specifically to protect yourself from human predators. The point is not to stop being wonderful you; the point is to be aware of you enough to know how you may be inviting someone to take advantage of you. To be forewarned is truly to be forearmed, especially if **your weaknesses are exactly what human predators are hoping to use against you.**

Remember that many of what a predator considers weaknesses are simply the normal, everyday ways you create what makes you wonderful! Their goal, however, is to use your good traits against you. Our goal is to allow you to continue being wonderful you while also knowing if someone is manipulating you or abusing you.

No, all your weaknesses that expose you as prey have not been identified here. Trust me when I tell you that the best human predators are superbly skilled at sizing up their prey before striking. Your idiosyncratic weaknesses are exposed to predators in a variety of ways, so when the ancient Greeks urged us to know ourselves as their prime directive, the best I can do here is to help motivate you to continuously look at yourself and build your defenses against being scammed.

Even if you choose not to read one more page of this book, these early warnings about your weaknesses will serve you well for the rest of your life. So let's look briefly at all the key messages I served up in this antipasto before we move on to the main course on how to see human predators coming a mile away.

KEY POINTS

1. Human predators look for weaknesses in the people they seek to use for their twisted agendas. Knowing what they look for is the first way human prey animals can protect themselves from predatory humans.

2. Our first shared weakness is the need human prey animals have for certainty. This need drives us to piece together a personal map of reality made up of our unique collection of core values, beliefs, biases, and expectations. As soon as we encounter events causing us to feel uncertain, we immediately look for ways to shore up our core beliefs and most cherished values. This tendency causes us to overlook clues that we are being stalked or are under attack by human predators. It also is a tendency that keeps us from using critical thinking about all information that bombards our lives daily. Hand in glove with our need for certainty is our projection of these individually created maps of reality, which we constantly display in our outward communication to others. Human predators look for the signals of our most cherished values, beliefs, biases, and expectations and then test them, confirm them, and use them against us for their nefarious purposes.

3. Our second shared weakness is the need human prey animals have for ego stroking. Ego stroking allows human predators to come close and gain trust as sensitive, caring individuals, but this is meant only to blind us to their hidden agenda(s) until it is too late for us to escape.

4. Our third great weakness to human predators is the follower impulse. Most human prey animals seek out what we believe are good people to lead us. We make our choices based on our need for leaders as determined by our personal beliefs and biases, as well

as the social-structural demand for a division of labor through-out society (since no one person can do everything for himself or herself). Over millions of years, evolution has created the follower impulse, which is still expressed by the tendency to trust completely those we select to lead, even without knowing much at all about the leaders we choose. Human predators take advantage of this weakness in extremely creative ways.

5. Our fourth biggest weakness to human predation is our hopes and dreams. By encouraging our hopes and dreams, human predators get close to us, use us, and scam us. Whenever we share our hopes and dreams with predatory humans, they will break our hearts and dash our dreams to dust through exploitation and abuse.

"

THE TEN COMMANDMENTS OF HUMAN PREDATORS

1. *No one is more important than I.*
2. *Nothing is more important than my needs.*
3. *I use others strictly to serve my needs.*
4. *My promises and commitments are empty.*
5. *Anyone who works against me is the enemy.*
6. *Anyone who threatens to expose me will be destroyed.*
7. *Children are pawns for manipulation, nothing more.*
8. *I am the final authority. Laws, rules, and social conventions mean nothing.*
9. *I am motivated strictly by domination, power, and control.*
10. *I take; you give.*

"

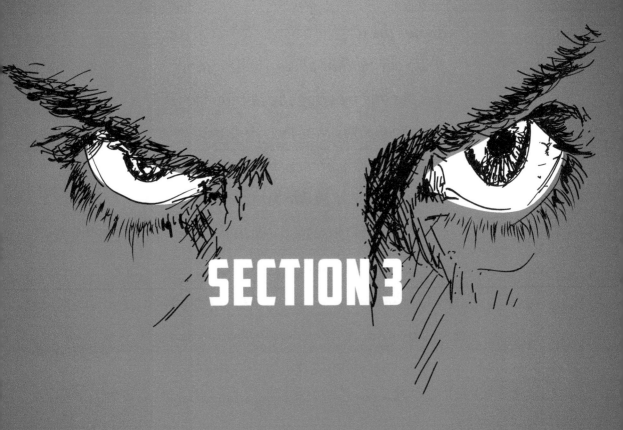

SECTION 3

"

It's not the outlandish lie that gets you.
It's the lie that poses as the truth.
It's the one wearing the familiar face.
It's the one that feels at home.
That pleases your sensibilities enough
to invite it inside for a while.
It's usually dressed a little finer,
wearing a bigger smile,
and speaking with a bit more confidence.
The one wearing Sunday clothes.
Looking like it's ready for church.
The knight in shining armor,
the princess, and the saint.
It's the lie that earns your trust.
That is where the devil hides.
– Kalen Dion

"

NINE BIG PERSONALITY TRAITS OF HUMAN PREDATORS

Meet the Mr. Hyde behind Every Dr. Jekyll

WOULD YOU BELIEVE THERE IS ONE MORE vulnerability we all share that human predators know about and seek to take advantage of? I'm talking about ignorance of what is at the core of all predatory behaviors. Your ignorance of what is going on inside them is their greatest advantage over you and your greatest blind spot. Fortunately, this particular vulnerability can be completely vanquished by learning the nine BIG personality traits of human predators—knowledge they don't want you to have.

At the end of this book is a presentation of red-flag warnings to help you spot human predators before they become a personal threat. Spotting human predators early when they are just starting to stalk you is extremely important if you want to avoid becoming their next meal. All these early red-flag warnings, however, are behaviors that emanate from a core collection of nine BIG personality characteristics of human predators.

Confoundingly, human predators will go to great lengths to make it hard for you to see these core personality characteristics. To make this even more challenging, none of these BIG human-predator personality traits may be fully developed in a human predator when you cross his or her path.

As human predators mature (chronologically or developmentally), they notice how they are different from people like you who have a conscience, empathy, and compassion. These observations cause them to hide their own way of relating to the world in various ways. Often, they go out of their way to create a supernormal persona, which becomes their presenting self. The red-flag warnings in this book are the breakthrough behaviors that should spook you, but often they don't have this effect because of your ignorance of what you are going to learn here. Even worse is that human prey animals with nurturing tendencies frequently willingly overlook such warnings as the person just having a bad day. People do have bad days, and on those days, humans are incapable of presenting their best selves. Yet when we are confronted with a collection of red-flag warnings and ignore repeatedly what we are seeing, we are self-blinded.

RED FLAG #2: Human predators will try to keep you away from anyone from their past who knows them intimately and may try to warn you about them. Their goal is never to reveal anything about their real lives, letting you fill in the blanks on your own.

The purposeful secreting of a human predator's real agenda is meant to blind you as well. Consider these well-constructed, normal-appearing strategies by human predators as a form of camouflage. As duck hunters build a duck blind, dress in clothing that allows them to blend in with the environment where ducks tend to congregate, use black pitch on their faces to mute the sun's reflection off their skin, and employ duck-calling devices that mimic the sound of female ducks in heat, so, too, do human predators do all they possibly can to blend in as they set their traps for hunting you.

WHEN SECONDS COUNT, THIS KNOWLEDGE MAY SAVE YOUR EMOTIONAL LIFE AND MUCH MORE

A few years back, my wife woke one morning with her entire right arm feeling like it had fallen numb from sleeping on it wrong during the night. She also felt that early-morning need we all tend to experience after a good night's sleep to relieve our bladder. Our master bathroom is equipped with a Toto toilet that automatically sees you coming, and the top of the toilet seat rapidly rises in anticipation, so there was no need for my wife to use her right arm to lift anything except her nightgown that day. Even this simple movement seemed oddly clumsy for her, so she shook her arm vigorously, hoping to get blood circulating to her fingers. This is a common response we all have when our arm or hand is "asleep." Strangely this didn't give her any relief. What was happening here?

Our little poochon puppy (a cross between a toy poodle and a bichon) is my wife's constant shadow. He leaves the bed if she leaves the bed, and he was at her feet curled up by the toilet as she went through her struggle that morning. How he knew what he knew will never be understood, but when the arm shaking started, Muffin began barking and ran into the bedroom to my side of the bed. I immediately knew something was wrong. He'd bark and then look at me, run back towards the bathroom, then jump up on my side of the bed, then jump down again, all while raising quite a ruckus so I would get his message: "Get the hell UP! Something is wrong with Mommy!"

I found Cay standing in front of the mirror over her sink trying to touch her nose with her right index finger. She couldn't do it. "What's wrong, Cay?" I asked.

Without any slurring of her words, she said calmly, "I think something is wrong with my arm."

Instantly, I said firmly, "Get dressed. We're going to the emergency room."

I'm guessing you already know what was happening to my wife, and you aren't a doctor. You know because the first signs of a stroke and the action to take have been drummed into us on television and in newspapers with a regular drumbeat (**FAST**—**F**acial drooping, **A**rm weakness, **S**peech difficulties, and **T**ime to call emergency services).

This is a good thing, by the way, because strokes can happen to people of any age. Now in our senior years, we see strokes among our peers that are frequently life-ending unless the early signs are spotted quickly and someone dials 911.

The next five hours were spent in the emergency room at the hospital just five minutes from our Sun Valley residence. Once I spoke the word *stroke* to the triage staff in the ER, the most beautifully choreographed sequence of events unfolded with precision and competence. The medical team knew exactly what to do, and they did it with the grace of a dance ensemble at the New York City Ballet. Working in tandem with a national Comprehensive Stroke Center in Florida via direct audio/video feed, the local team considered every possible diagnostic and treatment option and employed it before my wife was flown out of Sun Valley on a medevac to a Boise hospital, far better equipped to mitigate whatever damage the blood clot in her brain might possibly do to her.

Twenty-four hours after my wife's stroke, the blood clot in her brain had disappeared as suddenly as it had appeared. The rapid injection of blood thinners had given my wife and me the most favorable outcome we could have hoped for. Not only was the clot gone by the following afternoon, but the early signs of my wife's stroke had also disappeared.

Early recognition of what was happening to my wife was absolutely the most important event in the chain of events leading to Cay's miraculous recovery. And in this section, you will learn why it's equally essential for you to spot the early warning signs of another potentially life-threatening emergency—the presence of human predators on the hunt for prey. Your ability to identify someone who has a twisted predatory agenda may not be as clear as the early signs of a stroke at this moment, so we need to change that. Even spotting one of the early warning signs summarized at the end of this book can often allow you precious time to take defensive action that can save your emotional life, your financial life, your professional life, or any combination of the three. So let's get to it!

NINE PERSONALITY TRAITS OF HUMAN PREDATORS

From a purely scientific perspective, there are nine core traits of human-predator behaviors. All nine are accepted by psychiatrists and clinical psychologists as indicators they are treating (or attempting to treat) natural-born sociopaths or someone who presents as sociopathic due to addiction, emotional trauma, or brain damage caused by any number of contributing events.

None of these behavioral traits is considered criminal. A person can't be locked up or placed in a mental institution merely for displaying these traits. Furthermore, the intensity of each predatory trait will be dramatically muted by design. Predators do not want you to see them coming. For that reason, with each one of the nine, you will find in this section an example of someone with a full-on malignant display of the core behavioral trait

> **RED FLAG #35:** Human predators frequently come across as cold and punishing, overly punitive, and vengeful in both thoughts and actions.

and an example of a person who presents the personality characteristic in ways subtle enough that you fail to be alarmed. If red-flag warnings are missed, precious time and early exit opportunities can be lost.

Remember this presentation on the core personality traits of human predators is meant to give you conceptual handles for understanding these people from the inside out. While all human predators give early-warning signs, if uninformed about what those red-flag-warning behaviors are broadcasting, you will probably misinterpret them. Don't be one of the uninformed any longer. Both human predators who commit jailable offenses and those who do not are on the hunt and coming for you. If not involved in criminal activities that are jailable offenses, they are all thieves out to use your body or destroy your peace of mind, your emotional health, and your spiritual health. Many of these predators will also take away the physical health of their victims, and you will see how they do this through multiple examples provided in this section of the book.

Let's begin with a quick summary of the nine core personality traits. Please keep in mind that all human predators harbor these traits to some degree, and some of them (the most malignant and dangerous ones) are nakedly aggressive in their manifestation of all nine:

1. **Machiavellian Egocentricity** – a lack of empathy and a sense of detachment from others for the sake of achieving one's own goals.

2. **Social Influence** – the ability to charm and fool others while moving close for nefarious purposes. This quality is never sincere. It is the result of an observational astuteness and practice of what they see others do to successfully bring about desired responses from potential prey.

3. **Cold-Heartedness** – a distinct lack of emotion, guilt, or regard for others' feelings.

4. **Carefree Disorganization** – personal difficulty with planning ahead and considering the consequences of one's actions.

5. **Fearlessness and Fearless Dominance** – an eagerness for risk-seeking behaviors, as well as a lack of the fear that normally goes with them. These predators are also fearless in all social and work-related situations/relationships and dominate others without even thinking of or caring about what people around them are feeling (which often leads to their downfall).

6. **Blame Externalization** – inability to take responsibility for one's actions, instead blaming others or rationalizing one's own deviant behavior.

7. **Contemptuous Nonconformity** – a wanton disregard for social norms and socially acceptable behaviors.

8. Stress Immunity – a lack of typical reactions to traumatic or otherwise stress-inducing events.

9. Guiltless Lying – the ability to lie without micro-expression tells that typically give away lying behaviors. Anything from small lies to gigantic, world-class untruths can be offered up without any clue of guilt or shame.

DO ALL HUMAN PREDATORS MANIFEST THE SAME NINE TRAITS?

All human predators enjoy yanking your chain in twisted ways. Either they all have no conscience, or their conscience has been dulled or turned off completely through suffering traumatic events or by addictions (substance abuse addictions, drama addictions, or thought addictions). Yet not all of them want the same exact thing(s) from the prey animals they stalk and attack.

All human predators have no experience of shame or embarrassment resulting from their selfish, harmful, lazy, or immoral acts. None of them ever feels responsibility for negative outcomes caused by their behaviors, and all of them, when caught red-handed with their hands in the cookie jar, become angry to the point of being irate and then deny to your face what your eyes have seen and your ears have heard. Many of them will also threaten you under these very same circumstances, and then they will harass you until you back down. Even if you back down, they will often continue to harass you until they have extracted a huge pound of flesh from you. A large percentage of them will never stop harassing you, even when you catch them in their predatory acts.

All human predators act and think without consideration of consequences as they apply to others, and most of them, because they have no conscience, fail to grasp fully how negative consequences of their acts might come back to bite them hard somewhere down the road. Even the worst of all human predators, the psychopaths (including serial killers), believe at all times they will never be brought to justice because they are so much more intelligent and clever than the gullible fools who pursue them.

All human predators have ice in their veins, meaning they will take from you whatever they want while looking you straight in the eyes and smiling at you.

All human predators hold a distinct disgust for the idea of being caught and punished in any way. This disgust is not a feeling; it is a cold calculating disrespect for rules, laws, social acceptability, social norms, and anything like accountability. As a result, most human predators in the workplace seek a role where they are either top dog or a dog who answers to no one with people below them answering only to them. Many find a niche where they work completely by themselves without any oversight possibilities by anyone ever.

All human predators lie to get their way, their drug of choice, or their drama completed through the third act. The drama addicts are especially hard to spot because the drama is only fully viewed in their mind's eye. Only just before the curtain comes down will you see the bodies (the psyches) of their victims writhing in agony on the stage.

All human predators carry out their bullying and manipulation of victims without stress because their payoff is the thrill of dominating their victims or the even greater thrill they get every single day, anticipating the moment of domination over others, which they will very soon experience.

So the short and oversimplified answer is yes, all human predators manifest the same nine, core personality traits you will learn about in this section of the book.

What they don't have in common are their presenting personalities and ambitions. Every one of them has his or her own manufactured disguise, which is designed to make them blend in and look normal so they will be difficult to spot so you can't avoid their surprise attacks. Those surprise attacks can be aimed at grandiose, highly ambitious purposes (like world domination) or small gotchas meant to radically annoy their victims (like the neighbor next door who plays his stereo system at highest volume all night long, every single night).

DON'T NORMAL PEOPLE MANIFEST SOME OF THESE TRAITS?

Absolutely, yes! Each of us is capable of behaving as a predator to our fellow humans. A Latin proverb (*homo homini lupus*) expresses this truth simply: "A man is a wolf to another man." Every day and every hour of each day, we all battle the worst of our nature by making either wolf-like decisions about our actions or reaching up to be or become our highest and best selves, making choices in favor of goodness and decency that support the common good of society or, at the very least, the betterment of our affinity groups within society.

At times, under specific high-stress and high-fear conditions, humans can also experience what Carl Jung called a psychic epidemic that brings out wolf-like behaviors of man against man in large segments of society. Jung felt that such epidemics were far worse and capable of doing more damage than the worst of natural catastrophes.

The worst of these psychic epidemics is known as mass psychosis, which is an epidemic of madness that occurs when a large portion of a society loses touch with reality and descends into delusions. Mass psychosis manifests when a large cohort of people are suffering from threats or fears, real or imagined, that cause waves of terror in their minds. These threats become triggers that drive the fearful to act out in emotional, erratic, irrational, and unreliable ways. Eventually, if encouraged by leaders in a community who see a way to benefit from this mass terror, these groups reach a state of panic. In a panic state, large groups will commit crimes the individual would consider horrific and totally unacceptable under any other circumstances (think January 6, 2021). To make matters worse, those suffering from mass psychosis lose the ability to see what is happening to them.

Humans can't live for long in a panic state, and the need we all have for certainty (discussed in section 2 of this book) causes a psychic break. In truth, a psychic break is not a state of confusion and uncertainty but is a wild grasp at some new truth that offers to re-establish certainty. Sadly, however, when humans in a state of panic decide on a new truth to save them from their terrors, sound reasoning and logic never apply. Instead the group (and the individuals within the group) embraces a way of seeing reality that is a pathological insight. Some refer to this as a psychotic insight. It's called an insight because the group finally sees meaning and relationships that explain their confusing and alarming experiences, which led to a panic state. But this insight is referred to as psychotic because it isn't adaptive to the actual cause(s) of the group's fears.

A good example of the phenomenon of mass psychosis would be the witch-hunts that occurred in Europe and early colonial America between 1450 and 1750. During this time, it's estimated there were between thirty-five thousand and one hundred thousand executions of witches. The vast majority (70-80 percent) of those executed were women, not for any crimes they had committed but for their alleged subversive activities practiced in secret, which were supposedly causing unexplained events in the lives of normal people. We look back at these behaviors today and can hardly believe it happened. But isn't this what happened in Hitler's Germany with the Jews? And isn't this what is happening now with those who embrace QAnon?

Would you believe that witch-hunts still occur today in various places around the world? It's true. In Africa, Asia, and the Middle East, witch-hunts and executions continue, but you don't read about them or hear about them on nightly news broadcasts. Or do you? How about the horrible murder and dismembering of Jamal Khashoggi on October 18, 2018, a US-based journalist and critic of Saudi Arabia's government? Wasn't this a witch-hunt by the king of Saudi Arabia who rules his nation like a totalitarian dictator? A witch-hunt is also metaphorically applied to an investigation that is not conducted by legal authorities and results in a death sentence for anyone accused of subversive activity or disloyalty but with the real purpose of intimidating political opponents. Later in this section of the book, you will read about people who employ the phenomenon of mass psychosis to further their own political, power-hungry ambitions through liquidation of the life (or the reputation and, therefore, the ability to earn a living) of anyone who takes a stand against them or their authority.

So, yes, every human walking the planet can become a human predator. And on specific days, in the lives of nearly everyone, we do become predatory. It matters not if that day is forgotten or passes without harmful incident to others. When we are at our worst, feeling intensely angry or vindictive, ready to extract justice from anyone who has wronged us or who stands in the way of our ambitions, we do act as prosecutor, judge, and jury towards other people (and sometimes we execute them through character assassination). What is different in human predators from the rest of us is they consistently behave this way without conscience, day after day, until they are dead and buried and no longer a living threat to anyone.

THE NINE PREDATORY TRAITS IN DETAIL

Let's now break down these nine core traits and look at them under the microscope of literary focus so we can see the detailed reveal afforded by complete and exhaustive exposure.

1. MACHIAVELLIAN EGOCENTRICITY
*A lack of empathy and a sense of detachment from others
for the sake of achieving one's own goals*

If you are unfamiliar with Niccolò Machiavelli, you are easily forgiven. He lived in Florence, Italy, long before you were born, and died in 1527. But his name has certainly outlived him and for an extremely good reason. He was a cold-hearted politician, historian, and writer who championed unscrupulousness, deception, treachery, and crime in the world of politics. Some scholars claim Machiavelli's worldview was shaped by the tumultuous times in which he lived. His era was certainly turbulent. During his growing-up years and during his entire adult life, popes waged non-stop wars to acquire and rule over Italian city-states, little fiefdoms that looked like puzzle pieces all over Italy if you had a good map to look at back then. The entire Italian boot-like peninsula that we know as one united Italy today looked like a giant jigsaw puzzle during Machiavelli's life.

In fact, you could be a pope in those days only if you had a huge standing army ready to wage wars of acquisition all over Europe. This meant you had to be super-rich to be the head of the Holy Roman Church.

These wars were so unabating that the leaders of the many small city-states were in constant flux. Political-military alliances continually changed. To make things even more wild and disorderly, France and Spain were military competitors of the pope for control of the many city-states in Italy, and whenever one of these three would conquer and drive out the others, it would install its own mercenary leaders. These temporary, paid rulers were known as condottieri, and they were frequently bought off or changed sides without warning. As you might guess, this led to the rapid rise and fall of many governments.

I suspect good old Niccolò was a malignant human predator who was extremely intelligent and quite articulate, not just a product of his times. His skill at playing the political games of the tumultuous world he lived in required cold-hearted, calculating assessments about whose ass to kiss (or whose throat to cut) at all times.

RED FLAG #45: Human predators often present in sports activities as players who care only about the game, not about the other players. For them, winning is all-important, and they will employ any tactic to make sure they win (including cheating), no matter how irrational or inconsistent they may appear to others.

How different were Machiavelli's turbulent times from the world we live in? Can you name any current leaders around the world who are supremely treacherous, willing to employ any means to justify their personal or political goals? How about Kim Jong-un, the little fatty who rules over North Korea and is constantly rattling his nuclear arsenal in the faces of America's presidents?

1. Machiavellian Egocentricity
Example 1.1 – The Little Ruler from Hell

Above I mentioned that Machiavelli was an author. His most famous book is titled *The Prince*. I'm not joking when I write here that all political science majors attending college in the United States read this book as if it were the Bible. Kim Jong-un received his secondary education at the International School of Berne in Switzerland (an English-speaking school), and I'm willing to wager he read *The Prince* when there.

One of the most quoted teachings of *The Prince* is about being feared. Machiavelli wrote: "Is it better to be loved than feared or better to be feared than loved? Well, one would like to be both, but . . . when a choice has to be made it is safer to be feared." Machiavelli argues unashamedly that having too much clemency makes a prince vulnerable; therefore, when it comes to a choice, cruelty should be used because it is a way to instill fear in people so a prince can stand strong. Kim has been reported to have executed his perceived adversaries using such horrific means as death by piranhas and by firing anti-aircraft guns into his defense chief for falling asleep at an official event. Feared rather than loved? I'm thinking yes! In fact, it's a good bet that everyone in North Korea is fearful of Kim, even those who say they love him.

Does this make Kim Jung-un a human predator? It most certainly does. Human predators love using fear to frazzle prey, to freeze them in their tracks to make them compliant. Using fear like this requires ice in the veins and zero conscience. For human predators, the ends always justify the means. This is why you can point to so many world leaders as human predators. Yes, even in the United States, we have elected men as president who are without conscience and willing to employ all means to justify their own selfish goals.

By the way, life in North Korea is a living hell. The economy of North Korea is primarily based on the income generated by international criminal enterprises. The manufacturing of illegal drugs, counterfeit consumer goods, human trafficking, arms trafficking, wildlife trafficking, counterfeit currencies, and terrorism are all undertaken at the direction and under the control of the North Korean government. Without its international smuggling operations, North Korea would have no luxuries at all and certainly could never have developed its nuclear capabilities that keep the other national leaders around the world awake at night.

A question worth your consideration is: What happens to the masses of people who live in a nation led by a human predator? We know from social psychology experiments that have been repeated time and again that the extent to which authority dulls conscience is affected by the perceived legitimacy of that authority. In North Korea, Kim Jung-un's family—he, his father, and his grandfather—have ruled North Korea uninterrupted since 1948. All three generational leaders of North Korea have ruled with fear as their primary motivating force to keep both its own citizens and other nation's leaders off balance and in line. For the citizens of North Korea, their "Great Leader" has caused everyone's conscience to become dulled and in a trance-like state. Why do North Korea's citizens tolerate this sorrowful situation? Why don't they rise up and revolt? The answer can best be grasped by asking yourself why you don't rise up and revolt from the people you fear. Or, perhaps, you fear no one. Yet have you ever feared anyone? How about when you were little and just learning to make your way in the world?

I once thought I was fearless and able to manage anything life threw at me until my first safari in Africa (a sight-seeing safari). Then I came face-to-face with lions in the wild and had a mouthful of fear. You know I did not try to bluff these alpha predatory beasts, right?

To fully understand how fear keeps people in a trance-like state of obedience, you must know a bit about how the brains of humans are structured. Actually we humans have two brains, one much more primitive than the other (although these two structures are fully integrated with each other and neuroscientists see the brain as one unit of living tissue intelligence). The most primitive portion of the brain is often referred to as the reptilian brain (with all due apologies to reptiles), and it has been with us from the time we climbed down out of trees as ape-like creatures and started walking in order to locate new sources of food and water. The modern brain in its present evolved form is the Johnny-come-lately part of our brain structure, and for simplicity of understanding, it is identified by scientists as the cerebral cortex and appears to sit on top of the primitive brain like a giant scoop of ice cream. With all the superior benefits of the modern brain (rational thought, complex emotional capabilities, theoretical thinking, etc.), the reptilian (or primitive) brain is still more powerful and influential when triggered by the right external stimuli. Take the fear response to fear-inducing events, for example. The fear responses of human beings emanate from the reptilian brain structure. Once you poke someone's fear response, all kinds of higher brain activities temporarily shut down. History has proven that a leader who rules by fear can hypnotize the group conscience. Using fear-based propaganda to amplify a fear-based ideology can bring members of a frightened society to see everyone around them as mere things to be manipulated. This same approach to governing a nation can cause citizens to see anyone or any philosophy that opposes their own as an impediment that must be removed at all costs. Once this occurs, the belief systems of a society become one of "us against the evil ones," and that sets the stage for an epic endgame—a crusade to crush all opponents without pity or conscience.

While you look at this example of a human despotic predator and the comments above about how his leadership style allows for absolute control over his citizens, can you honestly relate to and understand someone like Kim Jong-un as a personal threat to you? On one level, you almost certainly can while you are reading stories about him. More likely than not, however, you will forget all about him fifteen minutes from now. That's because your brain sorts out potential threats according to their state of immediacy, and Kim Jong-un and his lovely cast of henchmen won't be following you around and posing their threat on a personal basis as you go through the rest of your day. What if, on the other hand, the United States elected someone who turned out to be a despotic ruler like Kim Jong-un? Would you stand up against such a ruler in this nation if that meant putting your life on the line? Or would your reptilian brain take over and cause you to do everything possible to preserve your life?

As I write this, the United States of America has pulled all its military assets out of the nation of Afghanistan, and that nation's capital city (Kabul) has just fallen. Thousands of citizens of Kabul are literally storming airplanes about to take off, grabbing onto the outsides of those planes to try to escape the feared Taliban who have taken over in just a matter of days. This is the reptilian brain in action. My hope, even my prayer, is that because of the right to vote, citizens of our nation will never have to face the horror of trying to escape mob justice as it is playing out right now in Afghanistan.

OK, I am sure you get the point being made here. Let's turn our attention to an example of this first personality trait of human predators in someone more likely to poke your fear response with immediacy.

1. Machiavellian Egocentricity
Example 1.2 – The Water Thief

Sun Valley is a wonderful place to visit, but having a home here is a mixed blessing. Idaho has long been a magnet for people who have low emotional intelligence and a high need for acting independently with little regard for the common good. The result is we have many citizens in this state who think laws apply only to the other guy and certainly not to them. Speed limits become speed suggestions for these folks. Pedestrian-rights zones are for target practice. Fireworks bans on July 4 are a reason to buy more fireworks than normal and set them off at all hours of the day and night. Talk about being egocentric!

We do have great turnouts for July 4 parades, though. And we see a lot of the United States flags on pickup trucks, if that sort of thing inspires patriotism in your heart. Generally speaking, in Idaho, everyone leaves everyone else alone, and we all just pretend we are a community of human beings that care about one another's welfare. But God forbid you find yourself in a conversation with someone about people on welfare. That could end in a fistfight.

During the pandemic, Sun Valley was the perfect place to ride out the lockdown. With gorgeous views of the mountains everywhere you turn, we have trails that allow us to hike for miles without seeing another person. The mandate for wearing masks didn't go over well, however, even after Sun Valley had the highest infection rate in the nation between December of 2019 and the end of February 2020. You see, folks around here don't cotton to being told to cover their faces by the government. Truth be told, they don't cotton to being told to do anything by the government. It's as though everyone in Idaho has read Machiavelli's *The Prince* and has decided to create a personal little city-state with its own laws and rules he or she expects everyone to tolerate.

During the pandemic, lockdown kept a lot of people at home that would otherwise have been out and about and seeing everything their neighbors were doing right or doing wrong. Low visibility leads to mischief, and I'm pretty sure that's why cattle are rustled in the darkness of night. Yes, it still happens. And so does stealing water.

Down at the neighborhood of East Fork, which is south of Sun Valley, there is a powerful snowmelt runoff stream from the Pioneer Mountains that feeds into the main river running through these parts known as Big Wood River. The families who have homes along the East Fork Creek are particularly independent minded. Some are so bent on having their own way about things they act like human predators on occasion, hellbent on getting their own way, no matter who gets hurt.

During shutdown, one of these people, one with a pretty good-sized piggy bank, became fed up with water restrictions to the point he built himself a huge, sophisticated reservoir while everyone was out of sight in the months during the government-ordered stay-at-home mandate. Then he stopped up the East Fork River and siphoned off a million gallons of snowmelt-provided river water into his nice new reservoir. Because they were all huddled inside their homes, the neighbors took a few days to realize that water along the East Fork River had slowed considerably. But then it stopped flowing altogether. That did get their attention.

Law enforcement was notified, and the search began for the reason why. This took three or four days because law enforcement officers around here, while good at searching for murderers and such, had zero experience at investigating the theft of water. Finally, the water thief was caught, and he had to unblock the river. No fool, however, the thief (let's call him a Machiavellian "Piggy" instead of a "Prince") knew the maximum penalty for the crime he committed was one hundred dollars. But because the one million gallons of water he diverted into his fancy new reservoir was now on his land, he couldn't be forced to give it up (that's what the law says, anyhow). Knowing the laws governing water in Idaho and waiting for the perfect moment to do it, Piggy (the human predator in this story) ripped off one million gallons of water for his personal use that legally should have been shared with all who live along the East Fork River.

I don't know about where you live, but up in these parts, that's a good reason for a hanging. Piggy didn't get hanged, however. He's just snubbed by all his independent-minded neighbors now, which is exactly how things were before the water theft occurred. You see, Piggy has no conscience and has no need to make friends with his neighbors. Piggy has only one master, and that is himself. The fact that he stabbed his water-poor neighbors in the back doesn't faze Piggy at all. He just didn't want to have to bend a knee to the water restrictions everyone else around these parts has to live with. Rules, guidelines, and laws be damned! Piggy is about as egocentric as a human can get.

What can you fairly conclude from the two examples above? Well, you might conclude the predatory expression of egocentricity is a trait that shows up a lot among the citizens of Idaho. Yet if there is one thing the COVID-19 pandemic has helped everyone see, it is how egocentric selfishness is widely seeded throughout human populations, not just in the highest, most powerful offices of governments around the world (or only in Idaho). It's so easy to see Machiavellian egocentricity play out in someone like Kim Jong-un, but what about the person who attacks and beats up a waitress in a restaurant because the waitress asked that patron to wear a mask to help protect everyone else in the restaurant? And what about the asshole who cuts you off in traffic or the person who occasionally shoplifts while grocery shopping? Are they displaying their own form of egocentricity? Perhaps these behaviors are just the tip of an iceberg of egocentricity in our society. Is it possible the universal (and totally selfish) desire for immediate gratification has been so pampered in America that all of us have become more egocentric, thus making the spotting of malignant practitioners of egocentricity much more difficult to see? If that's true, human predators may be counting on you to be easily fooled by your egocentric thoughts and using this against you to more easily hide their conscience-free egocentric behaviors when they bend or break rules, laws, and conventions that traditionally make a society work. All these questions and observations are offered to help you draw your own conclusions. But if allowed to offer you one conclusion as author of this book, I suggest all egocentric, self-centered behavior is predatory when it is carried out with no inner-moral dialogue or struggle with the question, "How will my decision affect others?"

2. SOCIAL INFLUENCE
The ability to charm and fool others
while moving close for nefarious purposes

Some say the truth of who they are is all about who they can persuade you to believe they are. This next personality trait validates how true this can be. What you see on the surface is not always what you get when it comes to some human beings. Human predators camouflage all they don't want you to see. Like mythical shapeshifters who become whatever they require to disguise their dark and demonic Mr. Hyde side, these Dr. Jekylls will serve up a presenting personality that is pleasant, well-mannered, and charming to suck you in before they pounce. Yet not all human predators have this ability to the same degree. The desire to blend in isn't always matched by a skill level that fully hides a predator's true nature, and this is true for many reasons. An example I like to use to illustrate this is my best friend's ex-father-in-law.

2. Social Influence
Example 2.1 – The Crime Boss and His Daughter

Fortunately, I can write about him now that the man you are about to learn of is no longer among the living, but he was (when alive) a crime boss in New York City and a malignant human predator of the first order.

My best friend during college hailed from New Jersey and was the most intelligent, kind, and caring soul I have ever known. Since I was from a midwestern family and grew up in South Bend, Indiana, Gary was able to share fascinating stories with me about how life in New Jersey was vastly different from the life I had known. His stories were riveting and included gang warfare, the fast and furious pace of life in the New York and New Jersey area, and an assortment of close calls he and his Italian family had with organized crime. Raised as a Roman Catholic, Gary was determined to become a missionary, but he had no interest at all in the priesthood. Family life was everything to him, and he wanted to have kids and raise a family like his parents. Besides, Gary was really good-looking, had a wonderful gift of gab, and the girls were all over him.

During summer months, Gary worked as a missionary in upstate New York around the Finger Lakes area to help migrant laborers, the families who traveled from various places to pick crops by hand. This is called *stoop-labor*, and it is hard, backbreaking work. The largest migrant laborer camp in the United States is in King Ferry, New York, which is located between Ithaca and Auburn along the shores of Lake Cayuga. Usually, the population of that camp exceeds two thousand laborers, who are made up of Puerto Ricans from New York City, Black farm workers from the Deep South, and Mexican American laborers from areas along the Texas and Mexico border.

When you read that these people travel with their families on huge school buses to make the sojourn to King Ferry, I want you to know this troop movement of many hundreds of miles includes infants as passengers. The state of New York provides and maintains a childcare center in this camp during working hours to keep the parents from taking those babies into the fields with them. One of the paid workers at the childcare center while Gary and his team of service providers helped adults at the labor camp was a college student who also wanted to be a missionary. She was ostensibly so devoted to this goal that until very recently she had been a novitiate among the Sisters of Mercy, a missionary order of the Roman Catholic Church.

The spark of love was almost instantly lit between my friend Gary and this like-minded young woman the day they met. Over two years of court-ing, they fell in love and decided to get married. Strangely, Gary's fiancé had kept him at arm's length from her family, which wasn't dif-ficult since Gary was attending college in Illinois while his new-found love attended college in New York City. I asked Gary about this more than once, but he brushed it off as just a logistics problem that would eventually have to sort itself out once they set a date to be married.

> **RED FLAG #3:** Human predators become extremely jealous if they see you enjoying yourself with other people.

That her father was a crime boss was never revealed to Gary until after they were married. But now I will turn to Gary to explain in a letter how this family merger was ultimately consummated:

> Looking back it's clear why my ex-wife kept me away from her family all those many years ago. Yes, it was intentional on her part. Yes, even after I met her parents, I ignored the creepy feeling I had about Mike [her father].
>
> On entering his home and shaking his hand, I could tell instantly something about him was off. He dressed impeccably, had a Rolex watch, and was wearing a pair of shoes that had to have been hand-made in Italy. Just the way he looked at me and talked reminded me of the phrase "lipstick on a pig." You know better than anyone I am super empathic and almost instantly aware of the energy peo-ple give off. Mike [his last name won't be revealed in this letter for obvious reasons] gave off the energy of a thug, and he was built like a tank. Oddly, his muscular build was not gym muscle. This man

had two Y chromosomes, meaning he had more testosterone than any man I had ever met. His wife was named "Tink" for Tinkerbell, and she suffered from agoraphobia. Both Mike and Tink smoked like nicotine was all they lived to breathe into their lungs. Mike wanted my respect. Giving it to him was easy since I wanted to marry his daughter, didn't know he was a crime boss, and had been brought up to respect all people until they proved by their behaviors they didn't deserve respect.

What Mike really did for a living wasn't revealed until after we were married and living two thousand miles away, working as missionaries on an Indian Reservation in Yuma, Arizona. He had said he sold equipment for retreading tires, and this, he explained, was what kept him on the road and away from home so much. But once I knew the truth, there was no way I would ever spend time with the man again. These particular people have no qualms about chopping up those they believe have betrayed them while the victim is still alive.

If all human predators can't fully disguise their true nature, why is it considered a core personality trait at all? It's because they all go to great effort to hide who they are, and you must know this truth and be able to easily retrieve it when you see any of the red-flag warnings in this book. Those red-flag warnings are your signal to dig deep and discover what's really going on. Mike the crime boss was certainly triggering a warning in my friend Gary. He was trying not to appear a dangerous man to my friend, but Gary's intuitive, empathic nature told him something was off. Still, Gary did not dig deep because he was in love and self-blinded by his hormones.

Those who are really good at shapeshifting frequently become chief executive officers of large enterprises, and we will look at one shortly who was outstanding at covering up his predatory nature. How do they become good at disguising the darkness of having no conscience? They have a unique kind of empathy. Called cold empathy, it is a tremendous ability to observe what personality types gain social influence, remember what they have seen, and fake the behaviors they observe. They can even fake tears if they are supergood at play-acting a role, but if you watch closely, they occasionally slip up and do something or say something that is out of character for the part they are playing.

While Mike the crime boss was lousy in his attempts to appear just an average, upper-middle-class resident of White Plains, New York, his daughter, it turns out, was brilliant at playing the girl next door with high standards and high intellect. Again, I'll let you read Gary's revealing letter to me:

Today, of course, we know so much more about genetics and how the gene pool influences personality, but I didn't know squat when I was twenty-two and courting her. I truly thought Janice was the real deal. She had grown up in the Catholic faith and the influence of the Sisters on her had been profound. I don't think Janice even knew what her father really did until she graduated high school. And Mike didn't want her to know. He and "Tink" had six daughters and no son. They lived in a middle-class neighborhood so as not to draw attention to themselves. And Janice never missed a day without going to church so she could celebrate communion.

This began to change after the kids were born. The deeply religious, self-sacrificing young woman I fell in love with had a short-temper with our two toddlers, and she dropped church entirely [after the children were born]. Then she began shoplifting and would even tell me about her scores. It was small stuff at first, but the more I pressed her to stop, the more she indulged. Then she started experimenting with street drugs. I knew none of this. She ran a halfway house for delinquent girls, and the girls hooked her. There were big behavioral changes at home, and she grew more distant from me and the children. But when she tried cocaine, she was a one-hit addict. I know you know this happens. The cocaine made her feel powerful, free, and happier than she had ever known. If you can believe it, she hid her cocaine habit brilliantly, never bringing the drugs into our home. But then she became sexually involved with a psychiatrist at the University of Arizona. She and her paramour were discovered having sex in the man's office by another doctor, for God's sake, who walked right in on them. At that point the jig was up.

How is it possible my friend Gary could meet one version of a woman who presented as so perfect to him and, a few years on, watch her grow into a human predator? Science has learned that epigenetics, or the influence of environment on a person's genetic leanings, can dramatically influence gene expression. In Catholic schools her entire life, Gary's wife became the center of attention by her extreme commitment to the Christian faith. She was the golden girl to the nuns who shaped her early life. The truth is she never actually felt drawn to the religious life, but she fed her narcissism by appearing to become the perfect disciple. This worked for her, even though she was a natural-born sociopath. The first sign of who she really was appeared when she refused to take her final vows as a Sister of Mercy. As a novitiate, she had felt not like a golden child but more like a slave with menial housekeeping assignments and hard manual labor. She secretly chafed and rebelled and plotted her revenge against the religious community. The best revenge was to refuse to take her vows as a bride of Christ, thus making the community who had sacrificed so much to train and educate her feel like failures. It wouldn't be the last time she would use this strategy on those she thought had made her suffer.

This story has an extremely tragic ending because Janice, Gary's wife, had a fatal heart attack two years after Gary divorced her. She was only thirty-three years old and had become by then exactly what you might expect of a cocaine addict, a homeless wretch living on the streets, doing whatever she could to feed her cocaine habit.

Shifting gears, what about the supernormal, white-collar predators? One study claimed that one in every five executives could be a sociopath (either natural born or an addict of some sort). Can you rely on that?

Highly doubtful! The study found that 21 percent of 261 senior professionals showed clinically significant levels of psychopathic traits, so it's an estimate at best. My own estimate would be a lot higher, but I'm not going to guess how many human predators are lurking in responsible business roles, either in the C suites or in middle-management roles. I'll just say this: if you think your manager is a human predator, you might be right.

The business world is loaded with famous names of human predators, so picking just one to use as an example is super hard. How about Martin Shkreli, the pharma CEO who raised the price of an AIDS drug by 5,000 percent? His actions were despicable, but he came off as friendly and charming. Yet why pick on Shkreli when there are tons of stories about horrible CEOs that have been turned into best-selling books. Let me tell you of one who was never written about. His name was Brian, and he was the CEO of a hospital I worked for in my career as a professional fundraising expert.

2. SOCIAL INFLUENCE
EXAMPLE 2.2 – THE HOSPITAL ADMINISTRATOR FROM HELL

Hospitals are where you find compassion heroes, right? So why did I find a human predator in the midst of these brilliant, kind, caring souls? What might possibly draw a human predator to this particular congregation of life-saving men and women?

The man I came to know as Brian the Terrible was initially my hero, and I referred to him admiringly as Brain the Wonderful. In the field of hospital administration, Brian was well-respected as a rising star. And the first time I heard him speak was on a telephone call he made to me when I was going through a contentious divorce. Auspiciously, Brian had called to offer me a job as vice president of his hospital's foundation, a position that did not yet exist. He offered to double my salary if I could relocate in thirty days. For me, at that time, it looked like divine intervention. Still, I offered up the truth of my marital status. "We know all about that," was Brian's deadpan response. His response made it clear I had been thoroughly scouted, investigated, and vetted. Even without a formal interview that might have revealed all kinds of problems with me, they wanted no one else to apply for the position.

As this all went down, I was flattered by the deep dive Brian had done into my life, both personally and professionally. But I should have been alarmed. It wasn't as if I had applied for a position and formally given permission for the hospital to contact my references. Later I discovered one of my senior mentors was serving as a consultant to Brian on fundraising and this dear friend of mine had been my behind-the-scenes, personal champion. Should that have mollified any concerns about their investigating me without my approval? No, it should have been a further red flag that Brian, the hospital's CEO, liked to push the boundaries of normal protocol. No other candidates were interviewed. No personality test had been administered to see if maybe I was a secret axe murderer. No one even knew what I looked like. Since there was no internet when this occurred, I could have had a rhino horn in the middle of my face.

When I actually met Brian for the first time, I was very impressed. He was tall, young, and handsome and had a superbly engaging personality. Every single one of his vice presidents (of operations, finance, nursing, strategic planning, and human resources) *and* Brian's personal assistant were movie-star handsome or beautiful. And they had sparkling personalities. Compared to them, I was as plain as oatmeal. Had they known this about me? And if they had known, how did I meet whatever standards they had in mind for me?

Soon enough, I found out. Not a single one of these highly educated, movie-star-appearing professionals knew a thing about hospital fundraising. On the other hand, I had recently received the highest award given in my profession. This was my superpower, and the hospital really needed someone like me. Still, I was only thirty-two years old and anywhere from five to ten years younger than all the other VPs. For me, the best news of all was the standing of this hospital among the elite, powerful, and wealthy. Serving as a volunteer board member/trustee was a sign you had truly arrived and were accepted among the old guard in this southwestern megacity. Better yet, the hospital had a women's fundraising cohort that had annually conducted a gigantic fundraising event for the last seventy-five years. These ladies represented the ultra-elite throughout the community. To say they were powerful women doesn't even approximate their material ability to sway public opinion.

Sensing something was off about the management team was unsettling, however, even if the off vibe was as opaque as a muddy river. I knew there was something fishy about all the members of top management, but what the hell was it? I began to look for clues, or red-flag behaviors, to tell me.

While there were a lot of red flags that got waved at me, the movie-star management-team bond did not easily break. It took five years before their secret seeped out, and when it did, I simply didn't know what to make of it. Actually, it's more accurate to say that, at first, I dismissed the entire news as rumor, or even a malicious lie. According to what surfaced from the loose lips of one man was that these people were all swingers and met up regularly after work at a gentlemen's club where a private room was always set aside for lap dances and drinks (and God knows what else). Frequently they would also meet up as a group for personal massages, the kind of massages that have happy endings. And Brian the Terrible was their leader—the head hedonist.

When sociopaths form a group like this, it's called a wolf pack. These wolves were hunting extreme sexual encounters, and they knew how to find them and keep what they were doing off the radar. What mistake did they make that caused the first leak?

While away at one of the many hospital administrator conferences they attended as a team, one of the most outstanding social workers at the hospital was a guest speaker at that conference. After this man's well-received address to the full body of attendees, our hospital's entire management team took him out to celebrate and congratulate him. Following a lovely dinner, gallons of alcohol, and a happy time had by all, everyone except the social worker excused himself or herself as if headed back to the hotel to get a good night's sleep. Instead, this team of swingers headed for a strip club. The social worker, who didn't like the idea of being left alone at the fancy restaurant, decided shortly once all had left to call it a night himself. And, wouldn't you know it, he caught the entire entourage on their way out the front door of the hotel, piling into a stretch limousine. Curious, he followed them in a taxi from a distance. When he witnessed their rented limousine drop them all at a high-end strip club twenty miles away from the hotel, their secret was no longer a secret. That social worker was a good and honest man who had played a prime-mover's role in starting an alcohol treatment center on the grounds of our hospital with millions donated to his project by our foundation supporters. He was a personal friend of mine, and he brought the information he'd detected to me first and immediately. What was revealed was the tip of the iceberg. And if even that had gotten out, the hospital and its foundation I had worked so hard to develop would have exploded like an atomic bomb was dropped on them. I had to move on, and I had to do so quickly and quietly. But before going, I was determined to dig up the whole story on the swingers in top management.

> **RED FLAG #25:** Human predators are superior at playing the victim when others confront them with behaving badly. A person with real confidence never needs to be in the victim position.

Since they had used the services of a PI on me without my permission, I thought the same for them would, indeed, be fair play. So while actively circulating my resume, I footed the bill for investigative services. When the dirt surfaced in toto, my head nearly exploded. Their little wolf pack regularly used cocaine, they had multiple affairs, and they employed hookers and strippers regularly for their sexual highs. Brian the Terrible and his VP for finance were in the process of a gigantic hospital bond issue that had kickbacks for them (off the books, of course). The bond issue required that 15 percent of the money needed had to come from private gifts, and that request was soon to be placed on the plates of my foundation trustees. I was sure this would not be a meal they would enjoy eating. I called in a well-known fundraising consulting firm to conduct a feasibility study while hoping the results would be so negative that my foundation board could take a pass on the project. As luck would have it, giving to our hospital was so prestigious that the campaign goal was determined to be easily achievable. Meanwhile, my search for new opportunities continued apace, and within six months, I was offered a position as a consultant organizing a thirty-million-dollar campaign for another local charity in the same metropolitan area.

To say I dodged a bullet, got out of Dodge City in the nick of time, and escaped a firing squad because of my discovery of Brian the Terrible's predatory sexual leadership (and the full participation of his hedonistic management team) would be a lie. That story will be told later in this section of the book when you read about Dr. Heartless. But I can say with certainty the hospital you just read about is closed now and in mothballs. All the players in the little sex club/wolf pack are deceased, and all the players in that club who had spouses back then got divorced within a year after I left.

What do I want you to take away from this sordid example? While it's easy to be shocked by the behavior of the hospital administrative team in this story, I prefer you focus on how it took me five years and a private investigator to connect all the dots about this wolf pack of human predators. That I sensed something was off about this group was not conclusive proof of anything. Also, I didn't have the collection of red-flag warnings that has been assembled in this book for you. Nor did I have the knowledge of how widespread human predatory behavior is in human populations. And maybe most important of all, these predators didn't want anyone to know about their extracurricular activities. Their presenting personas were supernormal, extremely intelligent, and highly attractive human beings. Brian the Terrible had handpicked each of the members of his management team. How he detected and choreographed their shared deviancy is still a mystery to me. How they all managed to keep their twisted, after-hours behavior hidden from almost everyone at the hospital is also still a mystery to me. The one slip-up that outed their secrets never would have come to my attention if my social worker friend hadn't wanted to follow their stretch limousine to see where they were going after seeming to ditch him at the restaurant in favor of getting a good night's sleep.

As you create your inner radar system of red-flag warnings about human predators, please remember that just one of these warning signs is never sufficient to allow you to conclude you are in the presence of a predator. If you see a cluster of warning signs, a big yellow light should come on in your head. More than five or six of these indicators and you should see a big red light. That's when to ask yourself if you are the potential prey. You must also ask why you might be the target of the predator stalking you.

Seeming to contradict the advice I just gave (but only to demonstrate how cleverly human predators can bury their worst intentions), let me share with you another example about a predator that gave zero early warning signs, yet when the first attack came, my jugular vein was the target.

2. Social Influence
Example 2.3 – The Dr. Jekyll and Mr. Hyde Alcoholic

Robert Thomas was an outrageous alcoholic whose behavior became completely unpredictable under the influence of a solid night of swimming face first in gin. The problem? No one in Tucson, Arizona, knew this. Bob (may God bless his departed soul) had just recently relocated to Tucson after several years employed by a famous author on the East Coast. While one of only a dozen world-class writers employed by James A. Michener to help develop his lengthy, fictional family sagas, Bob had a gift for writing unparalleled by anyone I had ever known. When he applied for a position on my staff with the assignment of developing a quarterly news magazine, there was more than a hint of serendipity in my interpretation of events. I needed a fabulous writer with the highest level of experience under his belt. Bob was seeking a retirement gig that would keep his mind occupied and his skills sharply honed (or so he said). It looked like a marriage made in heaven when his references all checked out.

The man who showed up for the interview was patrician looking, approximately sixty years of age, very well-dressed, and had a charming personality. I would have hired him on the spot but for the human resources protocols requiring a deep dive into his references. When I did hire Bob, he was happy, and I was thrilled. Together we came up with the name "Outreach" for the Saint Joseph's Hospital magazine, and Bob's writing was like the words of a Pulitzer Prize winner. No wonder his references were glowing.

Once the first issue of *Outreach* magazine was mailed to ten thousand of Tucson's wealthiest families, gifts to the hospital came flowing into my office. The magazine was meant only to cultivate interest in the hospital, but just in case, we had included a self-addressed, gift-return envelope. Tens of thousands of dollars resulted from the first mailing, and my stock in trade among the Sisters of Saint Joseph of Carondelet zoomed to heights never reached before. I was a hero. A fun fact is that I was only twenty-six years old.

When I first heard the quote that claims "what goes up must come down," I never thought this applied to me. When twenty-six years old and everything is going your way, it's easy to forget about all the Greek tragedies that were required reading in college. Like Icarus, however, the wings I had used to fly higher and higher at Saint Joseph's Hospital were about to quickly come loose from the hot hubris that held the feathers to my self-imagined angel's body.

On a Monday morning upon arriving at work, I was summoned immediately by the VP for human resources, and the door was closed behind me after entering his office. My new hire, it was reported, had come into the hospital over the weekend as drunk as a skunk. According to the nurses on several floors, Bob had terrorized all the nurses by shouting obscenities at the top of his voice, and when he was taken into custody by our security guards, Bob screamed that he was not to be touched because he was the publisher of "OUTRAGE MAGAZINE" and what they were doing to him was more outrageous than the magazine itself. The debriefing of Bob's embarrassing escapade over the weekend ended with a simple question. "What do you want to do about Mr. Robert Thomas, John?"

Once Robert Thomas was escorted off the property of Saint Joseph's Hospital that Monday morning, the VP for human resources and I decided we should recontact all his references. Why had not one of these people tipped us off about Bob's alcohol problem? Shockingly, we were stunned to learn they all did know, but they quickly faulted us for not asking them directly about drug or alcohol abuse when they had been contacted prior to our hiring Mr. Thomas.

What should you conclude from this shocking response to our follow-up calls after terminating Mr. Robert Thomas? I suggest you conclude you can never rely on others to tip you off about human predators, even if they know intimately about a predator's dangerous modus operandi. Two other take-aways are that the red-flag warnings in this book sometimes don't surface and you can get completely blind-sided by a human predator. Also, employers are wary of providing information that could cause them to be sued. Some companies and organizations take the simple (and cowardly) route of only answering questions asked of them and not volunteering info beyond those questions. In fact, this truth is one reason the book you are reading was written. It's almost as if there is a conspiracy of silence about human predators in our society, and often during the creation of this book, all involved with the project kept shaking their heads in disbelief that this book hadn't been written decades ago.

Are you ready to learn more? Brace yourself if you answered yes.

3. COLD-HEARTEDNESS
A distinct lack of emotion, guilt, or regard for others' feelings

Let's begin this unveiling with a question: Can you honestly say you understand what life is like for someone with absolutely no conscience? Whether an individual is born without a conscience or his or her conscience has been put to sleep with substance abuse, thought addictions, trauma, or brain damage, it doesn't matter. Can you comprehend what action without the filter of conscience feels like? I don't think you can.

We are talking about navigating through life, day after day, with no feelings of guilt or remorse, no matter what you do. And there are no limits on what you can do that will spark a sense of concern for the well-being of others, including those who are members of your immediate family. Here is a partial list of behaviors you can indulge in with absolutely no hesitation and no sense of immorality:

- You can have sex with anyone you wish, even if you have to drug them by using a date-rape pharmaceutical first.
- You can sell your child into prostitution to raise money for your drug habit.
- You are free to torture animals, even smash their heads open with a sledgehammer.
- You can shoplift just for the fun of it, not because you need to feed or clothe yourself.
- You can speed around town in your car with no regard for speed limits or for the safety of others.
- You can skip the funeral of your mother and father when they pass of natural causes because going to their funeral will just be boring for you.
- You can pretend to be friends with people, but if you are tired of them or if they offend you in the smallest way, you can dump them the way you would toss a facial tissue after blowing your nose.
- You never have to sign birthday cards to help co-workers celebrate their birthdays. Why bother?
- You can make fun of people who have lost their pets as being silly. Why would anyone grieve over the loss of a dumb animal?
- You can talk about yourself endlessly because why would you want to hear others talk about their lives? Literally, you can dominate every conversation you have with others your entire life by just talking about how great you are.

Let's look at some examples of human predator cold-heartedness. All these are ripped from headline stories that you may have recently read:

3. Cold-Heartedness
Example 3.1 – SoHo-Karen and Dog-Park-Karen

Unless you are reading with your eyes half shut, you have almost certainly noted the lack of moralizing in this book about human predators and the behaviors they display. There is a time and place for everything, and right now as you make your way through this Halloween Horror House, all you need to know is that around the next dark corner is a threat to you that you won't see coming without the knowledge imparted here.

If the monsters and goblins of real life were wearing the kinds of costumes found on Halloween night in Anytown, USA, that would be so much more convenient. But NO! These spooky snakes encroach from all directions, looking like harmless earthworms. Take the case of Lori Vallow Daybell, for instance. Here's a woman who, with little make-up and properly dressed, could easily be mistaken as a Hollywood screen star. In truth, she is a woman from Idaho who is the "doomsday cult" mom who is accused of murdering her children and ordering the murder of her husband so she could marry the cult's founder, Chad Daybell. How's that for cold-blooded? Wait! It gets worse. Currently on trial for these crimes, she has recently been declared by psychiatrists as unfit to stand trial. Really? Are these psychiatrists saying that a woman who murders her children, then immediately marries a cult leader, and runs off to Hawaii for an extended honeymoon with the man can't distinguish right from wrong and, therefore, should be locked up at a mental hospital until she is fully sane so we can then hold her accountable at some future date for her cold-blooded behavior? Imagine that!

Lori Vallow Daybell is too easy a target for this book, so let's rip a headline from a New York City incident that is as cold-blooded as an iceberg in Antarctica.

Have you heard of "SoHo Karen"? Just in case you don't know, Miya Ponsetto, age twenty-two, violently attacked a Black fourteen-year-old boy in a hotel lobby on December 16, 2020, and accused him of stealing her cell phone. This all went down at the Arlo Hotel in SoHo where Miya was caught on camera grabbing the boy, then tackling him to the ground when he refused to show his phone to Ponsetto. Forget about due process; Miya had performed her own investigation, tried the boy, found him guilty, and then began carrying out her sentence, which was to steal the boy's cell phone. Forget that justification for Miya's attack had happened only in her head. That's beside the point. Forget, too, that the boy was totally innocent. And while you are forgetting things, please also forget that soon after the incident occurred, an Uber driver returned Miya's phone to her in the lobby of the Arlo Hotel because she had absentmindedly left it in his car and he, being a totally honest man, tracked her down to return it.

For her behavior, Miya was labeled on the internet as a "Karen," which is an internet meme for a "white lady with a bone to pick." After her outrageous, cold-blooded behavior, Miya went blithely on her way back to California where she lives with her mother. Somehow, she had escaped arrest and imprisonment in New York City, but mainstream media hound dogs tracked her down in California and attempted repeatedly to interview SoHo-Karen on camera. They succeeded, too. And the film footage was on local news stations all over California before it made national

> **RED FLAG #12:** Human predators love to use self-esteem sabotage. Whatever you accomplish, they will always make it sound like it's nothing important. Downgrading your accomplishments and belittling you are all part of this same predatory behavior.

news. Would it surprise you that Miya's fifteen minutes of fame exposed her as someone who saw her behavior as fully justified? A grand jury in New York strongly disagreed and ordered her arrested for two counts of unlawful imprisonment as a hate crime, aggravated harassment, and endangering the welfare of a child. She's already appeared in court claiming innocence, but she could face a long imprisonment if found guilty.

No less famous, of course, is the original, most infamous Karen, Amy Cooper. Amy is a white woman who, when asked by a birdwatcher in New York City's Central Park to leash her dog, called 911 and accused the birdwatcher of threatening her life. She also accused the man of accidentally strangling her dog. All this outrageous, cold-blooded behavior was caught on cell-phone video and posted on the internet. To make matters worse, "Central Park Karen," as she became known, had unleashed her accusations at a Black man, and her racial profiling grenade was thrown at that man just two days after George Floyd was strangled to death in Minneapolis by a police officer. To say Amy Cooper suffered from bad timing in her cold-blooded, lying, racist rant is a monumental understatement. While she wasn't jailed for her attack (which was perfectly justified in her mind), after millions watched the video of her behavior on the internet, the investment firm where she worked fired Amy. The poor innocent dog Amy was protecting from the accused perpetrator was then temporarily taken from her by authorities, and she was charged with one count of falsely reporting a third-degree felony.

Does this kind of behavior happen a lot in our society? Yes, it does. COVID Karens have been a near epidemic of bad behaviors acted out by women who refused to wear masks in stores and restaurants across America. Everything from fist-fighting to pistol-presenting Karens have shown us how pervasively these ice-in-their-veins women (and men) will strike out with no conscience filters at anyone who crosses them.

More widespread and clearly more heinous are the men and women in authority who commit sexual assaults on children in our nation. Let's look at that behavior next.

3. Cold-Heartedness
Example 3.2 – Boy Scout Leader Sex Predators

If you had asked me when I was in my twenties if something like the next story could ever be true, you would have received a thunderclap "NO WAY!" answer. But only two days ago, the biggest headline feature story on national news was a report that the Boy Scouts of America had settled a sexual abuse, class-action lawsuit against the organization for $850,000,000. Forget the large amount of this settlement (which is rumored to be just the tip of an iceberg of billions the Boy Scouts of America will eventually pay to victims). Ask yourself how many lives were damaged or destroyed or both by the ice-in-their-veins, sexual predators those children had looked to for character-building leadership.

While the legal claims against the Boy Scouts have been percolating for years, the peak of those claims reached eighty-four thousand in February 2020. Does this figure help explain why scouting enrollment has dropped by 62 percent since 2019?

When growing up, I was a Boy Scout. Both of my brothers were also Boy Scouts. My mother was a den leader of the Cub Scouts that inspired in us the desire to join Boy Scouts. One of my most important mentors in the early part of my forty years in nonprofit fundraising was the man who established the Theodore Roosevelt Council of the Boy Scouts in Phoenix. This man was a true hero to me and to all the scouts and their parents for more than forty-five years. When he retired, the Phoenix community rented a high school football stadium so thirty-five thousand well-wishers could honor him and his wife, both of whom were the most dedicated builders of character that community has ever known. So what went wrong?

Sexual predators on the hunt to have sex with children are everywhere in societies around the world (and now they hunt your children on the internet). Yet, once again, there seems to be a conspiracy of silence about this horror. It doesn't matter if you wish to talk about the Boy Scouts or the Roman Catholic Church, the number of ice-in-the-veins predators going after children is legion. And if this isn't cold-blooded enough to chill your bones, nothing else written in this book will either.

Now that you probably want to go to your bathroom and throw up, there's no reason to dwell on this particular core-personality trait of human predators. Moving on to the next one may provide you some relief from your nausea.

4. CAREFREE DISORGANIZATION
Personal difficulty with planning ahead
and considering the consequences of one's actions

When much younger, I found it super-confusing that young women were attracted to men who were disorganized and sloppy in their personal habits. My parents taught us to organize everything, including our dresser drawers. We were even required to clean the bathroom every time we used it because we four children shared one bathroom (which never seemed problematic when I was a boy). Like everyone else who projects his or her values and personal worldviews onto others, I expected to find in the wider world these same family values and personal habits in others. I also expected women to find these personal habits and family values attractive. Big mistake on my part! It turns out huge numbers of women are attracted to the slobs, narcissists, abusers, spontaneously disorganized, high-risk-takers, and fearless non-conformists.

RED FLAG #29: Human predators can't take constructive criticism. If you try to correct them or confront them with their own issues, they become offended and even angry. Often, they will turn your most constructive suggestions into an attack on you.

My parents, like most parents, didn't teach us about human predators. That's basically why I entered early adulthood not aware of the red-flag warning signs you will find compiled at the end of this book. I thought sloppy and disorganized people were just sloppy and disorganized (and highly offensive to everyone).

A friend recently asked, "If humans predators often present as disorganized slobs, how can that be attractive to women?" I told him, "Many women are drawn to the challenge of remaking a man (especially the ones who present as carefree and disorganized). Their thinking is, "He will always be grateful, indebted, and faithfully loyal to me for my efforts, and I will have the man of my dreams."

Of course, no one explanation sufficiently applies because every person on Earth is attracted to different elements in people he or she chooses to approach or to love. Also, not everyone is attracted to predators (thank God!). But one of the most-often-cited reasons human prey animals are attracted to predators is a need they have to fix other people. My own sister married a man she thought she was going to fix, but after years of trying to get him organized and turn him into a good and decent husband and father, she discovered (sadly) that he could not be fixed. He eventually spent several years in federal prison for his white-collar, criminal activities, and he never changed his ways even after prison.

My sister admitted that even at the marriage altar she was thinking, "I can turn him into the man of my dreams." Is she the only one who has ever had this thought about the person he or she is about to marry? No way! But the women who are attracted to these men believe they have the power to shape the personalities of people, yet nothing could be further from the truth.

Now that I've taken you on a little detour (I'll get back to discussing carefree disorganization in a minute), I must explain about attractants that draw prey animals to these people. Let's look at three of the most common magnetic attractants of predatory humans their victims are willing to admit to. (We're leaving out the need-to-be-fixed attractant.) The three are:

1. **Mirroring.** While it's true you usually can't see them until it's too late, human predators know how to recognize human prey and to spot you through exposing your weaknesses. And one way they spot you as prey is your natural attraction to them. If you find yourself drawn to a predatory human and show it (no matter how subtle you think you are being), the predator will mirror a feigned return interest. Depending on the predator's agenda, the initial mirroring of your interest in him or her does not represent what you think it means. But how are you to know that? (Check the red-flag warnings at the end of the book.)

2. **Animal Magnetism.** Because they have no conscience, no shame, and no guilt, human predators give off an animal magnetism that we are not used to encountering in others. Something about this animal-on-the-hunt magnetism appeals to our reptilian brain, and this occurs far beneath our conscious awareness. Unfortunately, this leads potential prey to perceive a human predator's animal confidence as a cue to trust them and often to project competence onto them. Both of these can be a huge mistake, so how should you proceed when you encounter such magnetic people? (Check the red-flag warnings at the end of the book.)

3. **Spontaneity.** The carefree nature and spontaneousness of human predators tend to charm people who are often morality bound and living in a social convention straight-jacket, restricting them to act mostly by their personal rules for goodness and decency. The spontaneousness of human predators is often the magnetic force that makes them seductive to their potential prey. Human prey animals tend to let their hair down around those who are carefree and spontaneous, finding they like how they feel around such people. This same charming personality trait is what typically leads predatory humans to self-destruct, however, but this usually takes a long time, and as a prey animal victim who wakes up to how you've been trapped, you don't have enough time for your human predator to (maybe) self-destruct before he or she finishes messing up your life.

The third one of these powerful (usually subconscious) attractants is the one you need to focus on. Growing your understanding of how human predators' carefree disorganization can destroy their world (and yours) is my purpose now. So let's examine this powerful attractive quality of human predators a little more deeply.

As a reminder, section 2 of this book was dedicated entirely to shining a light on your weaknesses as potential prey. As it turns out, human predators also have weaknesses. One of their weaknesses is in how they read the emotional potential of human prey animals. Yes, they have trained themselves to ferret out the signals of your weaknesses, but this predatory skill is not emotionally based. It is a practiced skill based on cold observations, and it often leads to miscalculations of the signals you give off. This is one reason why human predators make mistakes—mistakes that get them into trouble.

Because they can't interpret your outgoing signals with anything close to 100 percent accuracy, they have to guess, based on what they have previously observed in other prey animals. As a result, they test out your responses for potential prey signals using mock charges and then watch to see how you respond. If they see the response they are looking for, they test you a little further to confirm the signal. Each test they put you through is higher risk for them because they may accidentally hit a super-hot-button issue that offends you in ways that cause you to outright reject them. They also will spontaneously abandon a carefully calculated plan of action if you do reject or surprise them, and this raises the potential for further miscalculation of their prey's responses and blinds the predatory human even more to unanticipated consequences. Still, the thrill of the hunt gives them a huge rush of the good brain chemicals you learned about in section 2. Let's look at an example.

Imagine you are a woman who plans a first date with someone on an internet dating site, someone you feel might be a good fit for you. A dinner is arranged at a lovely, upscale restaurant, but when your date arrives, he is inappropriately dressed. He is wearing spotlessly clean and pressed Bermuda shorts, tennis shoes with no socks, and a nicely fitting T-shirt, which shows off his amazing muscular physique. Yet he knew this was an upscale restaurant. You, on the other hand, are wearing a stunningly lovely, new dress for the occasion and heels. One part of your brain says, "What in God's name is he thinking?" Another part of your brain is fixated on the man's god-like good looks and wavy black hair. The concierge at the restaurant immediately recognizes your date and welcomes him warmly, and even though he's not wearing a collared shirt, you are seated at a table in a prime location.

What is going on here? Clearly, you are being tested to see how you react to this man's disrespect for the rules of the restaurant. Your date, as handsome as he is, has displayed his first act of disrespect for you, as well. Yet if you are still intrigued and go ahead with your planned dinner, you have given him a signal that he will now test further.

If during your dinner together you find yourself charmed by the man's attentiveness, great listening skills, handsome smile, and otherworldly good looks, you have given off another signal. You may be thinking, *OK, maybe I shouldn't jump to conclusions. Perhaps he's only eccentric, or maybe he came to our date having just finished a game of tennis with a friend. I'll stay through dinner and see who this man really is before giving him the brushoff.* But that's not what happens.

This man has your attention, and he knows it. In fact, you may actually be drawn to him in an animal way that is unlike other dates you've had, and you are super-curious about why you feel this way and perhaps a little giddy inside, too. Waking up in the morning with this Greek god by your side is a fantasy that quickly flashes through your mind. You think, *OH SHIT! What is H-A-P-P-E-N-I-N-G?*

In truth, you are responding to all three of the attractants of mirroring, animal magnetism, and spontaneity. Although this is all occurring at a subconscious level for you, the man with you knows exactly what he is doing. In fact, he is testing you to see how far he can push you, and you are discovering (and signaling) that you like it. That's what's H-A-P-P-E-N-I-N-G!

This testing by human predators of your weaknesses might be compared to an elephant's mock charges to see if you fear her, but a human predator's mock charge is designed to test your boundaries and see if you are still attracted to come closer. Remember the roof-replacement salesman in section 2 misreading me? Because I was quite pleasant and respectful to him, he read me as a potential prey who likes to be liked. This was, however, a guess on his part, and he was wrong, very wrong. He also saw I was a senior citizen and looked for a weakness often displayed by people my age—poor memory. That test failed when on his second visit

I greeted him by his first name and reminded him his roofing inspector hadn't yet called. There is no way that scam artist could have known I was then writing a book on human predators. While he was sizing me up, I was also sizing him up (he he).

What I didn't tell you earlier in the book is this same young man came by our home again. This third time he brought his fourteen-year-old son. This was another test for a weakness in me. He introduced his son to me by saying, "I just wanted my son to meet the nicest man I have ever met." Remember his roofing-inspector partner had already come by a few days earlier and I referred him to my builder and general contractor because we don't allow anyone to touch our home without our contractor's approval and supervision. So why did I receive a third visit from the young man who wanted me to meet his son? The test this time was to see if my niceness could be used to lure me into helping a man with a family to feed. It didn't work.

These trial runs at people are a human predator's tests to see what works and what doesn't work. They try all the angles that have worked previously to flush their prey out of hiding or to find a weakness they can exploit for their twisted agenda. If they don't see corroborating evidence that you can be lured into the trap they are setting (if they don't hook you with the bait they are using), they disappear.

Let's also revisit the ego-stroking example from section 2 to illustrate how both animal magnetism and mirroring work to ensnare prey animals.

You were asked to imagine an extremely attractive person of your favorite sex who approaches you and requests five minutes of your time for a private conversation. You broke away from others (or whatever you imagined yourself doing) to give the attractive lady (in this case) the five minutes she requested. And that five minutes you gave her turned into twenty minutes before you rushed out to make a meeting with your best friend across town. Those twenty minutes were magical for you. And once again, you learned how the brain responds to this approach by releasing five different feel-good brain chemicals. The unresolved question in that example is, "Was this a trap?" and more specifically, "Was this the honey-pot trap?"

A close, decades-long friend in the fundraising profession succumbed to this trap, which is all about animal magnetism in the beginning. The woman who trapped him was seeking employment on his hospital fundraising staff, and she had outstanding credentials (or so she said). When her references checked out, she was hired. Will it surprise you to learn that six months into her employment she and the hospital foundation vice president were embroiled in a hot and heavy affair? He was single, and so was she. On the surface, everything was peachy keen, right? Well, what about below the surface?

As the affair continued, the woman in this story slowly manipulated my friend into the subordinate role in the hospital's fundraising department. She was, in fact, far more intelligent than the fundraising VP, and she used her superior intelligence and her sexual powers over him to manipulate and dominate him. Yet her manipulations were no substitute for professional competence and wisdom about how to organize and manage a multi-faceted gift income development program, and my friend knew this. He alone on the five-person team understood that being charming was no substitute for knowledge of the principles and processes that lead to securing major gifts to the hospital foundation and renewing those gifts year after year.

Several times he tried to break things off with her, but she quietly let him know that was never going to happen. Eventually, my friend ran for his life, afraid for his life. His next position in the profession was fifteen hundred miles away, enough of a distance barrier to feel free of being stalked by this dragon lady who had emasculated him on every level. And what about her? How did she press on without her paramour?

She had always been able to rely on her magnetic and spontaneous personality to win people over. Planning beyond that was beyond her modus operandi, and she wasn't prepared to fill my friend's vacated job. So once she did take that fundraising VP position, she didn't have the knowledge of what to do and how to do it (just as my friend had suspected). Her winning persona couldn't make up for her lack of professional knowledge, and it often caused her to make disastrous missteps in managing her board of directors, the fundraising programs, and donor relationships she was now fully responsible for. An alcohol problem she had shown signs of for seven years then erupted into an out-of-control addiction. Her drinking added to her miscalculations and caused her to make even bigger errors in judgment. Within twenty-four months of becoming the fundraising VP, she was terminated.

Was this woman a human predator? Yes, in every way! She stalked and seduced my friend with great success, but always harboring a care-fully hidden agenda. She used her brilliant mind and manipulation skills to become the de facto VP of the fundraising department, but she lacked the professional knowledge and discipline required to perform at that level and succeed. And like most pred-

> **RED FLAG #28:** Human predators have an exaggerated view of their abilities. They consider themselves to be the best to handle or manage any situation, even if they have to rewrite history.

ators, she was playing a game of three-dimensional chess while my friend thought they were playing checkers.

The addiction to alcohol that brought this lady down is typical of how many human predators use substances to relieve their boredom with life and to increase their carefree disorganization. But those same addictions cause them to make spontaneous and even more disorganized decisions when under the influence. Her lack of a conscience and emotional depth, her superior intelligence, and her powers to manipulate everyone around her did not, by themselves, make her an effective professional in a position that required in-depth knowledge of the intricate, counter-intuitive fund-raising processes that lead to success. And her alcohol abuse caused her to sink deeper and deeper into a state of disorganization and confusion.

Much later in life, I learned that her entire adult career in fundraising had exposed the same pattern. Every single boss she had worked with fell victim to her seduction and superior intelligence, but when she was pro-moted to positions with greater responsibility and professional leadership, she bombed. And my good friend, with whom I stayed close until his death from cancer, was not the last victim of her charms and her weaknesses as a professional.

For human predators, sexual seduction is only one dimension of the three-dimensional game they are playing called domination. Though mirroring, animal magnetism, and carefree disorganization can be powerful attractants to human prey animals, these same traits inevitably are exposed as weaknesses. Yet I have watched many instances of these three initially attractive traits win predatory humans promotion after promotion only to reach a level of responsibility they don't have the competence for. This phenomenon is known as the Peter principle in the business world and was identified by Laurence J. Peter in his classic 1969 book *The Peter Principle*.

All who worked on the management team at this particular hospital were seduced by these three traits in this woman and misinterpreted her potential. But because she was always acting, everything she did was an illusion. Deception was easy for her. When she showed signs of emotion or intense interest in another person, righteous indignation, weepy sadness, or blushing modesty, she was acting. Not one interaction or relationship with others was spontaneous. Every move she made was designed to obtain a strategic or tactical outcome that would serve her purposes. And her purposes were all about domination by using other people's weaknesses. Section 4 is where you will learn how to build your defenses against these misreads and either avoid getting trapped or extract yourself from the grip of human predatory players of all types.

The human predators presented above don't hold a candle to the next one.

4. Carefree Disorganization
Example 4.1 – The Heart Surgeon Who Had No Heart

By day, he was almost certainly the most brilliant cardiovascular surgeon the world has ever known. By night, even though married with two amazing children, he hung with hookers where he entertained them at palatial hotel rooms and, after having sex with them, would beat them within an inch of their lives. Who does such things? A human predator who feels nothing emotionally for other people and whose narcissistic personality is boosted by being so incredibly handsome that women swooned from just being near him? Yes, that's who does these atrocious things to others. And through his operatic extremes at night with hookers, he was free to unleash his careless, cruel, and destructive spontaneity, which was the only time he felt anything at all. Of course, that side of his personality had to be suppressed in the surgical theater or when seeing patients at the clinic.

Our paths crossed in 1983 when he impulsively decided he wanted to establish a cardiac research center to complement his world-famous cardiovascular institute. To make this happen he needed money, lots of it. The estimated price tag was thirty million dollars. And at that time, I was the most famous fundraising consultant in the nation (which isn't saying much), and I had a one-man practice. When you hired me, you got *me*! You weren't sold a bill of goods by a slick salesman or con artist and then shuttled off under the campaign management of someone you had never met. Besides, my services came at half the price it would cost to contract with a large national firm. So one of the famous surgeon's major lieutenants approached me to explore my interest.

Once a contract had been negotiated and before the heartless doctor signed it, he and I met privately. He knew I had successfully raised money for a medical research facility once before, so I had street creds. He had lots of questions, but I had only one. My question was about the commitment of the foundation's board members. Were they 100 percent behind this project?

"They will do anything I ask them to do."

Quietly I said to myself, *Oh SHIT!*

Instantly Dr. Heartless had communicated that he was a narcissistic leader and his personal magnetism was all that held this project together. Because fundraising is all about heart-throbbing commitment of donors, the only thing that stood between me and unemployment was the iron-clad contract my attorney had drawn up. The heartless one hadn't signed it yet, and I had to obtain his signature before I left that meeting with him. With the flourish of a great and powerful man, his hand went to my contract, which sat on his desktop. I thought he was going to ask more questions, but with dependable swiftness and an arrogant grin, he dramatically went to the signature page, and with flare of authority, he signed. Talk about carefree disorganization. He hadn't even interviewed other consultants or consulting firms. He hadn't done a background check on me, and he had no idea what my contract said.

Immediately, I started interviewing board members in private, confidential meetings, one-on-one. Yes, everyone said he or she was on board with the entire project, and so we began discussing each one's personal gifts. That's when things went sideways. In fundraising, you must first win the hearts of people before they will commit large financial gifts. That hadn't happened before the project unanimously gained board approval. These trustees were robotically following their lord and master, who had no heart to win the hearts of others. Every response given to my questions about personal, sacrificial gifting was met with a word cloud designed to wiggle sideways on this topic. That meant the entire board would have to discover for themselves the real-life, measurable benefits of proceeding with developing the proposed cardiovascular research center.

There was one additional huge concern I had. Did Dr. Heartless understand he would be required to have the involved, detailed oversight and accountability to a major medical school willing to sign off on every research project undertaken at this new research center? In the field of medical research, without a medical school's involvement and oversight, no one in the scientific world will even pretend to take your research seriously. This meant having accountability from beginning to end of every research effort. Have you ever told a narcissist he or she must be accountable to senior oversight? Talk about an irresistible force meeting an immovable object!

To break this news to the fine organization paying me megabucks to lead them to the promised payoff, I brought in the best medical research-development consulting group on the planet. Having worked with them previously, I knew they were impressive, brilliant, connected, and ethical. Based in Houston, the lead consultant on the team instantly commanded respect when he met with the great heartless one. From his narcissistic perspective, Dr. Heartless only saw how the credentials of this planning firm would add prestige to his dream. He also thought such prestige would help bring in big philanthropic bucks. I didn't disabuse him of this notion, so he hired them on the spot. CA-CHING, CA-CHING! The cash register tally climbed by another $250,000.

While the planners planned, they were brilliantly doing my work for me. They insisted that half of the board of directors serve on a research center planning committee. Slowly, trustees began to see where the holes in cardiovascular research existed, and then they began connecting the dots to how they could help change the world of medicine. Weeks turned into six months, then nine months. Yet the process worked, and I began to hear talk of huge gift commitments by individual board members.

But the other shoe was about to be dropped, and when it did, I knew the heart institute's leader would go ballistic. He did!

Although I had ten million dollars committed from board members by the time the final planning report was submitted, I was in the boardroom when the planning team announced the entire research center would have to be under the oversight and supervision of a major medical school. If not, no scientific publications would even consider publishing the research results of the planned cardiovascular research center. Dr. Heartless turned red in the face when this news was shared. And that's when I knew the party was over.

The very next day, the ninety-day cancellation clause in my contract was exercised. The call came from the same major lieutenant who had first contacted me about taking the assignment. Not one volunteer called to express concern that I was leaving, but there was a wonderful consolation I had carried away from the board meeting the night before. While Dr. Heartless had said not one word, the chairman of the Research Center Planning Committee had reported each and every gift commitment from board members, which totaled ten million dollars. That the famous heart surgeon had had to call each donor after the board meeting and tell of his decision to cancel the project must have galled him to no end. I tried to imagine the line of crap he invented to explain his decision. Now, many years after his death, it still brings me enormous pleasure to know how painful this series of calls must have been for him.

This story illustrates how a brilliant man who never missed the smallest detail in the surgical suite was completely scattered in his approach to development of a thirty-million-dollar research center that would build his legacy. One has to question how a mind so detail-oriented in one setting could be so carefree and careless in another as to be clueless about how the medical research process works. Even without medical school oversight, any discoveries made in a research lab have to be repeated and validated by independent research laboratories. How could Dr. Heartless not know this? Or how could he not know how medical research publishing protocols work? The only explanation possible is that, like other narcissists, he lived in a world of his own, unaware on any level that others have importance or even significance. Everyone in the universe of Dr. Heartless was an objectified tool that existed to be used by him to get what he wanted, and this fact alone blocked his ability to see the consequences of ignoring the super-important roles others might play in the medical research process.

4. Carefree Disorganization
Example 4.2 – The Dating-Site, Romeo Rapist

Jason was so incredibly handsome you had to wonder what he was doing working as a Federal Express driver for three decades. But maybe this down-to-earth job validated him as the real deal. Everything else about him on the Christian dating site checked the boxes a woman about to turn fifty might rate as legitimate.

Jamie had recently divorced a man who, although the father of her three children, had gone completely off the rails since being diagnosed with type 2 diabetes. It took ten years for him to crash and burn, but when it happened, it was spectacular. The night he crashed his truck, he was drunk as a skunk and had a prostitute with him. Arrested and jailed, he got thirty days in lockup and two years of monitored driving. That meant his trucks had to be outfitted with breathalyzer equipment, forcing him to blow into a tube to check for alcohol on his breath before the vehicle could even be started. Jamie's truck also had to have breathalyzer equipment installed in case her husband (now ex-husband) tried to drive it. Try explaining all this to your friends or to your employer. How do you say "EMBARRASSING!"?

The love bombing by Jason began shortly after Jamie connected with him on the dating site. Measured at first, it quickly turned into an unstoppable carpet-bombing campaign. Should Jamie have seen and understood what was happening? Well, maybe. After all, Jamie was a therapist who had a specialty practice that included her cockapoo, named Pal. The focus of her work, however, was children who had suffered trauma due to abuse or illness. Pal was a natural at giving the children unconditional love, and often the kids would spend the entire therapy session hugging Pal as though she was a stuffed animal. Seldom had Jamie worked with anyone who was a human predator.

In fairness, Jason was not a natural-born human predator. Raised by a single mother who beat him with switches at the smallest provocation, Jason was a highly traumatized human being. The scars from those beatings were deep and had created a man who hated women with every fiber of his being. The adult drama he employed to act out his hate was serial monogamy. He was in his mid-fifties when he met Jamie, and he had mastered his seduction/destruction drama as performance art of the highest order. Find a beautiful woman who has just been divorced, love bomb her until she is high on brain chemicals and head-over-heels in love, marry her, and then within a few months deliver the coup de grace, which was his pornography addiction. Nothing kills a romantic relationship with a woman faster than knowing her new husband can't resist pornography. It's the ultimate way to destroy a woman's soul.

Jamie did know Jason had been married twice previously and he had children. They were grown children, but Jamie cared deeply about children and wanted to meet the ones Jason had brought into this world. Was this her way of measuring the soul of a parent? Perhaps. But even after she met them and grasped how damaged they were, her hormone-driven mind dismissed all this as being caused by their mothers' deviancies, not by their biological father.

The dating site did not reveal the other four marriages Jason had before meeting Jamie. And Jamie wouldn't know about those marriages until one week before the wedding. Wait! This gets worse.

The plans they made to be married happened after only six months of courtship. And the wedding itself was planned for late spring, just nine months after meeting for the first time. However, the word *wedding* isn't even close to describing the event these two had cooked up. Every person they knew had been invited. Money had been spent in large sums, gifts given and received, special clothing purchased, the wedding location reserved, a beautiful menu planned, and all the vows written by the bride and groom. A pig, dressed as a pig dresses for a wedding, was to be the ring bearer. Musicians were hired for the reception. Seating was planned so everyone's needs to be near or far away from others could be accommodated. It was at this point that Jason informed Jamie of his four additional marriages. Since the purpose of this drama was the killing of Jamie's soul, there should be a ceremonial wounding, thought Jason. If Jamie then proceeded to the altar, that meant the big reveal of his pornography addiction would surely kill this woman who was so deeply in love she would complete the last steps to the wedding altar egregiously wounded.

RED FLAG #26: A pervasive pattern of grandiosity in someone's storytelling, or the need for admiration demonstrated by exaggerating achievements and talents, is also a sign you are with a human predator.

The marriage itself lasted another nine months. What was it with the number nine? Nine months to get his prey to the wedding altar. Nine months to get himself unhitched from the dead or dying soul of his bride. And perhaps nine brides before all was said and done? Only two more to go after Jamie was dispatched. What a romantic!

In the example above, Jamie had been swept off her feet by the skillful love-bombing attack. Jason was so spontaneous, out-of-the-ordinary charming, and shamefully handsome Jamie dropped all her defenses as a woman. Once her brain was soaked in feel-good hormones, she became putty in the hands of her predator. Jason used her like a master sculptor. As with results from other predators who appeal to the reptilian (or primitive) brain with carefree spontaneity, Jamie was put in a trance. And while Jason thought he was in control, he didn't reckon with another player on the sidelines.

It turns out that Jamie's father was a man of considerable means and was adept at dealing with human predators. Shortly before the wedding, Jason retired from Federal Express on a pension. After the divorce, Jason wanted to continue working so he would appear employed and productive to his next potential victim. Using his considerable wealth, Jamie's father hired a dark web "consulting firm" to poison the well where Jason went to water his need to destroy women *and* the well where he went to seek employment. By the time the dirt about Jason was carefully placed by the "consulting firm," he was an untouchable. Sure, he tried his very best to get things straightened out, resurrect his reputation, and find employment again. He might have been better off by changing his identity or leaving the country. The stains on his name were indelible, and he still lives alone and unemployed. I guess it's true that karma never forgets where you live.

Nobody can keep track of all the variables that will ultimately come to bear on the outcome of any project he or she undertakes. The human condition is one of constant and often turbulent fluidity. Highly intelligent people may convince you on occasion that they alone have the power to guarantee a specific outcome, but this is a lie. For these reasons, anyone managing a project with a clearly stated goal must be highly organized and openly adaptive to changing conditions. If, on the other hand, such a project is managed by someone who is disorganized and carefree about the strategies and tactics he or she employs to achieve a project's objective, the person's chances of making a fatal mistake rise enormously. And this is exactly what happens to human predators in pursuit of their well-defined (at least in their minds) twisted objectives. They inevitably self-destruct due to miscalculations. On the other hand, they often succeed repeatedly before self-destructing and leave many bodies of human prey animals lying beside the road on their journey to eventual self-destruction. One way human predators make so much progress before their eventual downfall is due to the next BIG character trait—the one that works superbly to persuade people to follow them almost blindly at times. Let's examine that character trait next.

5. FEARLESSNESS AND FEARLESS DOMINANCE
*An eagerness for risk-seeking behaviors, as well as
a lack of the fear that normally goes with them*

"I just muscle my way into a controlling position."

I was interviewing a young man I know whose success at investing in commercial real estate is legendary, and I had just asked, "How did you manage to make so much progress this rapidly?" The above response was his answer. And it's an answer that isn't taught in classes on human motivation. Why not? Because if anyone except a human predator were to use this strategy, he or she couldn't do it with absolute fearlessness. And absolute fearlessness is the magic ingredient that stuns others into a state of fearful silence and acquiescence.

What does it feel like to be completely fearless? Does it equate with the idea of controlling your fears, setting them aside, and pushing on from there? Not even close! The kind of fearlessness this young human predator was talking about can happen only if you are born without the ability to feel anything at all unless you are participating in superhigh-adrenaline-releasing, ultra-high-risk activities. Even then, the feelings generated are minimal compared to what others feel in the same situations.

Can this same fearlessness be communicated by someone who has a malignant addiction? The answer is YES! Full-on addictions put to sleep that portion of the brain allowing humans to experience fear. So, too, do certain traumas and brain injuries.

The observations just made about addicts and certain trauma victims might lead you to wonder if the addiction itself would put off anyone who might be potential prey of fearless human predators. In explaining how deceptive addicts can be, let me tell you a story about a woman I dated and ultimately married who was a fearless human predator (just so you know I learned many of these lessons the hard way. UGH!).

Kathy was stunningly beautiful, and she stalked me. She had heard friends talk about me as a single male and decided she wanted them to arrange for me to meet her. None of this was known by me. One day when I took my thirteen-year-old daughter to her riding lesson, Kathy just happened to be at the stables where we kept my daughter's horse. It was easy to notice Kathy because she was unlike the strong women who hung out at the stables and masterfully dominated their powerful horses. Kathy was strong, but in a different way. I didn't know her strength was to get what she wanted through lying and acting.

Approximately a week after I met her, friends who owned the stables said she'd been asking about me. Was I dating someone? Was I a good man? Then they came out with a story about Kathy's recent divorce. None of this had been solicited by me, and later it would be revealed that Kathy herself had asked our mutual friends to play matchmaker roles in her twisted drama. That I didn't bite on the lure only pushed Kathy to be more aggressive. On my next visit to the stables with my daughter, the owners gave me Kathy's phone number. Weeks went by before I called Kathy and asked her out.

Boringly sweet and seemingly shy is how I read Kathy on our first date. Several more dates and I was close to certain this woman and I had no future. But on what I thought was to be our last date, the claws came out. I was forty-one, single, and sexually in my prime. (Or had I summited, started on the downhill slope, but wanted to prove there was no bottom?) What matters is that, when a woman is aggressively sexual, it's hard for a man to resist. And describing Kathy as sexually aggressive is an understatement. The woman was an animal in bed.

If any male reading this thinks he could never be hooked by someone like Kathy, I'll just say you are a better man than I am. After that first sexual performance, I was like a sex-addicted teenager. Blinded by lust, I was willing to overlook almost everything negative about Kathy that had previously surfaced in this mismatch. Within one year, we were married. But the wedding was private, took place in Lake Tahoe on the Nevada side of the lake, and there were no witnesses (like all good crimes). While all this may make for titillating copy to read (or not), you need to know that Kathy never drank alcohol during our entire courtship. While offered to her on all our dates, she always deferred, claiming she didn't drink. However, the night after we were married, Kathy became drunk out of her mind.

A one-off behavior? No chance. Kathy opened a new bottle of wine every day after I went to work, and she finished that bottle and another by the time I returned home. When confronted several times about her drinking, she shut me down so fast I didn't know what hit me. Within three months, we were divorced, and Kathy was in a world-famous alcohol treatment center that I paid for as part of our property settlement agreement. Still think it can't happen to you? Think again.

To get what they want from others, addicts of all types can perform amazing feats, including Oscar-winning performances of fearlessness. Let's examine a more famous incident where two human predators teamed up to take down thousands. One of the two was a natural-born, malignant sociopath. The other was his addicted partner.

5. Fearlessness and Fearless Dominance
Example 5.1 – The Sex Cult Masquerading as a Self-Help Group

Fearful and scarred people who say they escaped from NXIVM described personal experiences of brainwashing, manipulation, and even forced branding by the fearless and twisted Keith Raniere, founder of this cult/self-help organization.

Raniere had as his original founding partner a female hypnotherapist of great renown. What brought them together as partners can only be guessed at now because neither is willing to talk about it. The two of them began their search for clients in 1998, using all the catchy phrases proven to hook people to join their self-help sessions. Using hypnosis early with each new member, these two predators wanted to pry loose highly confidential and compromising personal information from each of their clients while they were in a trance state. Once captured, this information was then used against the victims as blackmail so they would perform in all kinds of compromising ways. These under-duress behaviors were then photographed, video-taped, and used to prey further on NXIVM's members.

As NXIVM expanded its membership, Raniere created a secret society for women named DOS, where members became Raniere's sex slaves and the initiates were even branded with his initials. Members of DOS were then required to recruit other young women to membership, behaviors they knew to be immoral and illegal. But they did it anyway because of the threats by NXIVM to release their compromised and defamatory behaviors, which, of course, were carefully stored secretly in places where the victims could never get them.

What if you had been Keith Raniere and wanted to make this scam explode with new members? If you answered that you'd recruit a big-name movie star to be your top lieutenant, you win! That's exactly what happened for NXIVM and DOS. Before we get to that part of the story, however, answer these questions: "What will you do about your sex slaves who break away from the cult and complain to authorities? How will you shut them up?" Short of murdering them, you would require deep pockets to tie them up with lawsuits accusing them of slander. This is an extremely effective way, used by all fearless predators, to beat such rebels into silence. Yet where will the money come from to hire the powerful law firms needed to bully these rebels into submission? Don't be shy! What do you believe a man like Keith Raniere did to get that kind of wealth? Of course, he spotted as prey two sisters whose father was a multi-billionaire.

Clare Bronfman, an heiress to the Seagram's liquor empire, was half of the sister duo that Raniere hunted and captured within the ranks of DOS to serve as financiers of his legal campaign to mute any rebels who broke away. Bronfman joined NXIVM in 2003 and rose to the top of its ranks as an executive board member over a period of fifteen years. She personally spent more than fifty million dollars on lawsuits on behalf of NXIVM. She also recruited women from outside the United States to membership in DOS, for which she was rewarded by her master, Keith Raniere, by giving her more highly trusted positions within the organization.

If a human predator is dangerous because fearlessness is a core personality trait, then that same person with money to burn is like a supervillain (think Darth Vader from *Star Wars*). But remember these people want to look legitimate. To do that, they must recruit men and women with credentials who are highly respected to either join their ranks or bless their organization publicly.

The first actress Raniere successfully recruited to NXIVM was Sarah Edmondson, a resident of Vancouver, British Columbia. She was, when recruited, going through a rough patch in her career and feeling lost. Looking for ways to improve her odds of success, she joined NXIVM. Raniere wanted to use her contacts in the film-making industry to bring in other stars and starlets. But because Edmondson and her husband both were members of NXIVM, he had to be careful. So he waited until one of Sarah's closest friends, a member of DOS, could be coaxed to approach Edmonson about becoming a member of the inner circle. When Sarah was branded in a secret ceremony with Keith Raniere's initials, she was so badly traumatized she and her husband left the cult and became outspoken critics of NXIVM. Essentially, this was a complete strikeout for Raniere. But fearless predators don't ever get discouraged by defeats.

The home run Raniere sought was scored in 2006 when Allison Mack, best known for her acting role in the series *Smallville*, joined NXIVM. Once successfully recruited into the inner circle of DOS, Mack become a star pupil and the perfect Hollywood connection Raniere felt he needed to give his twisted ambitions the wings to really fly.

Just in case you are curious, DOS stands for "*dominus obsequious sororium*," Latin for "dominant over submissive." The word *dominus* also has a masculine-specific translation of "master"; thus the true translation of DOS is male dominance over servile females. The idea that women could be persuaded to embrace such a concept in today's world is extremely difficult to comprehend, and indeed, many women within the cult never did know the meaning of DOS. But the ones who stayed in the organization all became submissive slaves to Raniere and were willing to do anything they were asked to do to please their master. This included committing criminal acts of all types. Yet not everyone stayed, and as mentioned, there were occasional rebellions.

> **RED FLAG #7:** Human predators will repeatedly test your boundaries. If you try to mark boundaries, they will label you reactive and narcissistic, and they will constantly attempt to push past them or get you to loosen your standards.

After multiple members left DOS, they organized and pressed charges. Subsequently, they spoke out for a *New York Times* exposé of the group. When that exposé hit the newsstands, Raniere fled to Mexico where he was eventually arrested by Mexican authorities in 2018.

You must be wondering how Raniere made money off NXIVM's members. In fact, there were multiple scams used to separate people from their money, but the primary strategy was to charge outrageous fees for seminars. Typically, it cost seven thousand dollars to attend a sixteen-day seminar. Nice money if you can get it, and Raniere and NXIVM got it over and over and over from many thousands of people who attended his Executive Success Programs.

This short summary of Keith Raniere and NXIVM is focused primarily on how a malignant human predator used his fearlessness to dupe people into behaving in ways they now regret enormously. Documentaries have been made, books have been written and published, and many NXIVM victims speak regularly about how they regrettably acquiesced to the demands of Keith Raniere. There have been trials and judgments, sentences, fines, and reparations demanded by the courts. Raniere himself is currently in jail, serving a 120-year sentence for sexual exploitation of a child, sex trafficking, identity theft, trafficking for labor and services, conspiracy to alter records for use in an official proceeding, sex trafficking conspiracy, forced labor conspiracy, racketeering conspiracy, and wire fraud conspiracy.

This man is a high-profile human predator who even managed to get the Dalai Lama essentially to publicly bless his organization. While hindsight is always 20/20, men and women of high standing around the world were duped by Keith Raniere because he was willing to do whatever it took to mask his true agendas. Reading his story, you may conclude that you could never be duped by such a predator. That conclusion is easy to make because the predator, in this case, was caught and punished. But the fearless ones don't always get caught because they don't always break laws and they operate in places where you would least expect to find them. Our next human predator is someone who did exactly that, and she will never face the consequences of her life-destroying predations.

5. Fearlessness and Fearless Dominance
Example 5.2 – The 9/11 Survivor

The attack on the Twin Towers of the World Trade Center may stand out in your mind as one of the most traumatic events of your life if you were living when it happened. Did you know there were approximately two thousand survivors of this heinous act by the Muslim terrorists who hijacked two passenger planes and crashed them into the twin 110-story buildings? What do you imagine life has been like for these people? What we know for certain is that each of these men and women was severely traumatized. They narrowly escaped death themselves, and some also were bereaved by the loss of loved ones who did die in the attack. One of the rare survivors on or above the point of impact went by the name of Tania Head.

Although these tragic events happened in 2001, Tania joined the World Trade Center Survivors' Network (WTCSN) in 2004. Prior to 2004, Tania had developed her own online support group for survivors of 9/11. When contacted by one of the founders of WTCSN, Tania agreed to merge her organization after many months of email exchanges. Initially, WTCSN's purpose was to provide support for survivors of the attacks, as well as the families of victims and first responders. However, they eventually wanted to expand their support, and that's one reason WTCSN reached out to Tania and others, including civilians present at the World Trade Center, as well as volunteers and personnel involved in the extensive rescue and recovery efforts afterward.

Tania claimed she had been inside the South Tower when United Flight 175 hit. Crawling through smoke and flames on the seventy-eighth floor with her right arm nearly torn off, she was one of only four people above the point of impact to survive. Her fiancé, David, was killed in the North Tower. Although the two of them had performed a private marriage ceremony on a beach in Maui only weeks previously, they planned a legal ceremony for early November when back in the States, according to Tania. Her actual rescue had been possible because of a man named Welles Crowther, a true hero whose courageous acts on that day had been widely reported in the media.

When her powerful story was finally picked up by the media, Tania received many invitations to speak, and in 2005, she was chosen to lead tours for the Tribute WTC Visitor Center. As a tour guide, she was photographed with dignitaries like New York City Mayor Michael Bloomberg, former Mayor Rudy Giuliani, and former New York Governor George Pataki.

On each of the tours she led or co-led with other survivors, Tania vividly recounted her Ground Zero experiences. She was even elected president of the World Trade Center Survivors' Network in 2006.

Then in 2007, the *New York Times* began investigating key details of Tania Head's story as part of an anniversary piece. Head had claimed a degree from Harvard and a graduate business degree from Stanford. But those institutions had no record of her. She claimed she had been working for Merrill Lynch in the South Tower, but Merrill Lynch had no record of her employment, nor did Merrill Lynch have offices in the South Tower at the time of the attacks. At this point, the investigation into Tania Head accelerated, and she began backing out of scheduled interviews, ultimately refusing to talk with any reporters.

You probably already know where this is going, so let's cut to the chase. First, Tania's real name is Alicia Esteve Head, and she wasn't even in New York City on 9/11. Nor was she a citizen of the United States. Alicia was born and raised in Spain by a very wealthy family of sociopathic narcissists. She was spoiled at home over the course of her entire childhood, and because she was homely and obese, her narcissistic needs had trouble being met on any level. So Alicia took to fearlessly creating monumental lies about all the boys who were after her, and she spread those stories liberally among her teenaged peer group, who tolerated her primarily because of her wealthy, influential family. In her late teens, Alicia was involved in a horrific auto accident that severed her right arm, but brilliant doctors in Barcelona were able to reattach it. This left enormous scars on her arm, which were immediately visible by anyone who met her. Everything she had told the World Trade Center Survivors' Network was a lie. After her fraud was exposed, she immediately left the United States and disappeared. Was she ever seen again by anyone? Yes, as a matter of fact, in 2011, Alicia was caught on film in New York City with her mother from Barcelona, Spain, by her side. To say the cameraman wasn't greeted with open arms would be a bit of an understatement. She ripped the camera out of his hands and assaulted the man. Talk about fearless!

Occasionally, fearlessness is expressed through combativeness. The kind of combativeness that is being identified here is not an oops moment where a person had a hiccup and ripped someone a new asshole in front of others. We're talking now about a lifestyle of combativeness where the human predator is self-centered, insensitive to the feelings of others, and always comes off to everyone within hearing distance with absolute certainty and authority. Good examples of these human predators would have to include Steve Jobs, Rush Limbaugh, Kanye West, and Sarah Palin. These people are (or were, in Jobs's case) masterful, seasoned, and accomplished at being combative, and anything you say will be challenged by them as if they want to stuff your words down your throat. The clinical name for this particular class B personality type is high-conflict personality (HCP).

The widespread expression of HCP among humans is almost universally denied as predatory. In fact, most people embrace high-conflict personalities as a leadership style. I'm guessing that's why there are no penalties (social or legal) for this kind of predatory behavior. In fact, the targets of these fearless, dominating predators nearly always end up blaming themselves for the predator's fearless rants against them. They wonder, "What did I do to deserve that?" No one deserves to be treated this way. And if you ever see someone viciously attacking others this way, be aware that sooner or later, he or she may attack you, too. Let's look at an example that is playing out with a nonprofit organization I advise in California.

5. Fearlessness and Fearless Dominance
Example 5.3 – The Conflict Addict

The following is a case study, using fictitious names, that actually happened to one of my nonprofit clients and demonstrates the four steps that high-conflict predators take to play out their conflict addictions—seduce, attack, divide, and dominate.

Shirley, with the high-conflict personality, and Leon, the normal human being, were board members of a nonprofit. This means they were volunteers who (supposedly) shared a motivation to serve others and make life better for all involved with the nonprofit's mission. Prior to joining the board, these two had known each other only casually, and neither had any animosity towards one another.

In the closed community setting of a nonprofit board of directors, Shirley was known as having very strong opinions about every topic. She would frequently exaggerate the negatives, make offensive comments about others who were in the room with her, and always act as if she were an authority on topics she had little real knowledge of or experience with.

She rarely smiled and never ever laughed. Other board members avoided teaming up in committee work with Shirley because of her negativity, posturing, and annoying behavior.

Having just served as chairman of the board for a year, Shirley decided the executive director, who had led the nonprofit faithfully and competently for nineteen years (and who had literally grown the organization from scratch into a juggernaut of high renown and outstanding achievement), needed to be retired. The first thing Shirley did to prepare for the war she wanted to fight was **seduce** the officers of the board's Executive Committee (including the chairman) to help her advocate against the executive director. In private one-on-one meetings (in person and over the phone), she persuaded each officer that at age seventy it was simply time to dump the current executive director. Her negative advocacy campaign was intensified when the COVID-19 pandemic changed the revenue streams that kept the nonprofit going during the national shutdown. Since it was clear a much-expanded charitable fundraising program would be required to keep the organization moving forward in future years, Shirley (along with her negative advocates on the Executive Committee) used this need to **attack** the long-serving and loyal executive director as not having the right stuff to take the organization down a new path in fundraising. "Besides," claimed Shirley, "the quadrupling of fundraising income going forward is a young person's game," implying the seventy-year-old executive director incumbent was on her last legs.

RED FLAG #48: A willingness for someone to use violence or threats of violence to achieve his or her ends, even when unnecessary, are warning signs you are with a human predator. This trait is often seen in abusive spouses.

The first formal attack occurred at a board meeting as an ad hoc discussion topic. Shirley's open announcement that interviews had already begun for the new executive director (a shock to all attending) declared the war was on.

In spite of the fact the current executive director was the trusted face of the organization to all its many stakeholders, Shirley wanted this woman released and given only thirty days to clean out her desk so a new executive director could be brought in immediately. Of course, the CEO almost dropped her jaw to the floor after hearing all this stated right in front of her.

Leon (the board chairman) chimed in by stating that the full board of directors hadn't yet approved a written transition plan for the current CEO but supported Shirley's statement. As shocked as anyone by these pronouncements, I pointed out that all the critical issues needing to be addressed in the process of changing executive leadership hadn't even been identified. So I asked (as an advisor) how could interviews with new executive director candidates be productive if they couldn't determine a candidate's potential fit into a plan to assure a smooth transition? It should be pointed out that all executive professional staff working for the executive director were also in attendance at this board meeting. And I could tell by the looks on their faces they, too, had never been told their beloved boss was being retired. They were in shock.

Then Leon asked that the full board take a few minutes to identify the critical issues facing the organization as it went forward with transition planning. All took this to mean Leon was trying to listen to my counsel. But was he really? Or was he simply attempting to placate me and others?

Board members wanted to know how the transition would be accepted by the many stakeholders of the nonprofit if the current executive director didn't participate in building relationship bridges to her replacement. What about all the operational knowledge accumulated by the current ED? How would that be captured for the new ED and used to assure a smooth transition? Other critical issues were identified that were also crucial to the nonprofit's success.

But as each question was raised, Shirley became more irritated and spoke up against the issues by saying they were insignificant and complaining that excellent candidates (available presently) would be snapped up by other nonprofits if this organization didn't grab one first. Basically,

Shirley's approach was "shoot now and aim later." Everyone not on the Executive Committee took Leon's side, calling for a rational, respectful, well-thought-out plan of action first.

Shirley was intent on **dividing** the formerly unified group. As the discussion on Zoom continued between the four Executive Committee officers and the full board of eighteen members, the ground was perfectly laid for combat, which is exactly what Shirley wanted. Then Leon pulled a switcheroo by reversing his position and suddenly spoke up for Shirley's point of view. "Shirley, you are right. We *have to* strike while the iron is hot. If there are candidates right now available, we should be interviewing them." BAM! The shock around the table was palpable. So was the anger.

Shirley immediately fired another volley of ammunition meant to intensify the divide in the room. "I am conducting interviews now because the Executive Committee authorized me to do so, and only the Executive Committee has the authority to decide when it's time to retire the executive director. The authority to hire a new executive is also fully in our hands."

This attempt to **dominate** was met with a volley of shots from other board members, but many simply signed out of the Zoom meeting to show their disgust with Shirley. Those who remained on the Zoom screen were about to go to war, all-out-thermonuclear war! But then came the surprise! After each board member shot back in protest of Shirley's power grab, he or she also signed off the Zoom call, deciding not to wait to be shouted down by Shirley's rather shrill retorts.

Finally, the board chairman spoke up and was fully supported by the board treasurer in stating that the Executive Committee would suspend the interview process and immediately appoint a special committee to work with staff on development of an appropriate transition plan. Another switcheroo? At this point Shirley had been abandoned by her best negative advocates and stood alone on the battlefield. As the board chairman finally realized he was losing his entire board, he had also connected the dots to how he had been set up by Shirley. Determined to have the last word, Shirley stated she could not just drop the people she had been interviewing without extreme embarrassment, and on-the-spot she stated her plans to continue her interviews.

While Shirley is a true high-conflict personality, she's not very good at it. She didn't count on the power people have to simply sign out of a Zoom conference call. Still, that didn't matter because Shirley gets her high from the anticipation of the conflicts she stirs up and from the combative experiences. For her, it's not about winning the war. Her brain chemicals (the good ones) release just by stirring the pot of relationships she has. You may already have met someone like Shirley who creates upset, chaos, and damage wherever possible. My guess is you didn't enjoy the experience.

Pay special attention to the four steps these combat specialists go through to create their chaos. First, they **seduce** a team of negative advocates. These are typically people in power who have authority to represent them and their case for or against someone they see as their opponent. Second, they **attack**. This could take place in a court of law, on a political stage, or in a board meeting. The goal is to achieve the third step, which is to seriously **divide** the stakeholders against one another, unleashing a civil war within the organization. The final act in this four-act drama is to **dominate** everyone involved, which can occur either by staying involved and fighting or by withdrawing and watching from the sidelines as the now-divided and angry stakeholders fight one another (the upset and conflict the high-conflict predator is always seeking to provoke). This drama plays out daily on internet social media platforms that create chatrooms and discussion groups that are really stages for this type of predator to manufacture upset, which leads to fighting.

As long as you know HCP predators exist, you can keep them from seducing you to serve their pot-stirring purposes.

Please remember fearlessness helps make human predators much harder to see, but occasionally fearlessness has the opposite effect. In rare instances when fearlessness is combined with extreme narcissism and blame externalization, human predators are easy to see. These overt predators take high-profile positions in public and business life, and they demand being the center of attention at all times. But when their loudly voiced plans or ideas go haywire and blow up, they never assume responsibility. Instead, they blame others liberally and demand the heads of those others served to them on a silver platter. This book isn't only about the overt predators. This book is also about how to see covert human predators, too, like Tania Head and Keith Raniere, who hide behind a cause or behind their victims who have been coerced to do their dirty work.

Since externalizing blame is also one of the core personality traits of human predators, let's examine that topic next.

6. BLAME EXTERNALIZATION
Inability to take responsibility for one's actions,
instead blaming others or rationalizing one's own deviant behavior

Even in death, some human predators deny their responsibility for any wrongdoing or responsibility for their misdeeds. I'll always remember reading a headstone inscribed as follows:

> Let Me OUT!
> I'm Innocent!

The man who was laid to rest in the grave at the foot of this headstone had shot three men in the back in 1848, and he'd done it in front of witnesses. According to the historical accounts, the deceased claimed his victims committed suicide by showing up in Tombstone after a gambling altercation in which they had accused their attacker of cheating. I was visiting the OK Corral as a tourist at the time I read this. The lawless frontier of the Old West was crawling with human predators, and Tombstone had more than its share.

Denying responsibility for acts of cruelty, lying, cheating, and outright theft have been a mark of human predators since Cain killed his brother Abel. Of course, the engraving on that headstone was humorous when I read it, and that it had been carved at the deceased's request reveals to me that the citizens of the Old West either had a highly developed sense of humor or were recording for posterity the trait in human predators you will learn about now.

Imagine this situation: a four-year-old has chocolate cake all over her face and hands, there is a mangled chocolate cake on the floor, and the child's eyes are wide with surprise because you just walked into the kitchen and discovered her in the act.

You say, "Tell me what happened." Your voice is soft and yet suspicious.

"The puppy got into the cake."

"The puppy got into the cake?"

"Yup."

"Why is there cake and frosting all over your hands and face?"

"I'm cleaning up."

"But the puppy doesn't have any cake on his paws or his face."

"I cleaned it off."

"That was very nice of you. Shall I clean the cake off you like you did for the puppy?"

"OK."

This imaginary conversation is not outrageous because it is with a four-year-old child. As a good parent, you aren't giving the child permission to lie, but you are entering into the child's world gently so a bond will be created for the next step. While cleaning the child, you will explain why getting into the cake was a bad thing for the puppy to do. Then you will ask the child how the puppy should be punished. The child will most likely say the puppy should not get any cake for dinner. Your next step will probably be to agree, and then you will explain that no one will be able to have any cake for dinner, not even you or the child's siblings. If normal, the four-year-old will ask, "Why not?" And you will explain the cake must now be thrown out because the puppy's germs on its paws and mouth are also in the cake and those germs would be bad for the family and make them all sick.

The above is a normal exchange if you are dealing with a toddler who is still learning right and wrong. It also assumes the child has a normal brain with a conscience. Learning about natural consequences is the least traumatic way to help little ones grow their consciences, although some of you reading this may prefer creating strong impressions with little ones using a more direct, authoritarian approach.

Now let's change the situation. Imagine you come home from work and discover your wife in bed with another man. Assume your wife and the man she's with have no conscience and deny what you witness with your own eyes. She and the man scold you as they calmly go about getting dressed, "Would you, please, have the decency to wait downstairs until we both finish dressing, and then we will explain the therapy session we were having before you rudely interrupted." Sound insane? Of course, but human predators are extremely adept at accusing their victims of wrongdoing when they are caught in the act. This is called *gaslighting*, and just because the situation you were asked to imagine is grotesquely exaggerated doesn't mean it couldn't or wouldn't happen. In fact, gaslighting happens all the time on a much larger stage in today's world. We just don't recognize this crazy-making for what it is. The use of expressions like "fake news" and "controlling the narrative" and "spinning a story" are really meant to attack fact finders who dig up inconvenient truths that either politicians or business leaders (the guilty parties) want suppressed. If you find a fact about me that I don't want the world to know about and I accuse you of spreading fake news, I'm essentially saying you are incompetent, lying, and insane and shifting the focus from me (the guilty one) to you (the innocent).

Today, everyone is accusing journalists and on-air reporters of spreading fake news to make it look like the profession of journalism is conducting witch-hunts when they uncover a human predator's dirty deeds. So it's probably fair to say that gaslighting has become the most on-display form of blame externalization in our society.

This shows, I think, we are all under enormous stress and stress is making most of us a bit more predatory than we have been in past decades. When life becomes nearly unmanageable (like now) and social and economic turbulence reaches a tipping point, our need for certainty about what to expect from life can't be met. That's when we panic and start blaming others for the mess we are in. While it's sad to witness this happening, it's shocking when you are the one being blamed.

Of course, the worst form of gaslighting is racial gaslighting—the untruth that claims dark-skinned people are lesser beings than Caucasians. Let's look at that narrative next.

6. Blame Externalization
Example 6.1 – The World's Deadliest Conspiracy Theory

Blaming others for the challenges of life you might be having is, in truth, a form of denying responsibility for your own life. And anyone who does this is acting the part of a human predator. How can this be true? It's true because we are claiming our life's burdens exist primarily because we are victims and because blaming others always, at the very least, demeans the ones who are being blamed. Frequently, blaming others leads to supposed righteous attacks on, or even murder of, those we blame for our perceived challenges or, if you must, our problems.

The idea of white supremacy is the conspiracy theory that has probably created the most damage to other people, especially to anyone born Black. While there are many variations on the theme of white supremacy, basically it is a body of beliefs stating darker-skinned people are inferior to white people and that's the natural order of things. This core tenet of white supremacy implies that people with dark-colored skin do not have the same rights as white-skinned people. But the truth is white-skinned people are using this way of thinking to steal the rights of Black people for selfish purposes (like enslaving them, denying them jobs they are fully qualified to do, and denying them access to opportunities of all types that white supremacists claim are only for whites). From this single tenet springs every evil White people have ever perpetrated against Black people, including slavery. When immoral actors (Black people or White people with liberal ideas) try to overthrow this natural order, white supremacists claim this is the putative cause of all Caucasians' problems.

Therefore, these immoral actors must be put down or put back in their place to make the problems of White people go away. As twisted as this logic may be, try to explain to a white supremacist that the original tenet of white superiority is morally, factually, intellectually flawed.

The atrocities committed against Black people during the era of slavery in America show how completely inhuman humans can become when they start minimizing the importance of others by saying those others (Blacks in this case) are lesser beings and, therefore, Whites are higher, more valued beings. In fact, white supremacists also blame dark-skinned people as the cause of all problems in white society, and by doing this, they set themselves up to be victims in a great drama between right and wrong that never ends for White people. Reflexively, white supremacists believe their problems can be solved only by keeping Black people (and White liberal thinkers) in their place. Playing the victim card is a huge red flag that you are dealing with a human predator, by the way, but not everyone claims the victim role due to this particular reason.

RED FLAG #50: Online dating sites are a favorite hunting ground of human predators looking for human prey animals. Because their potential targets on dating sites are people who openly declare they have lonely hearts, those who use these platforms make easy pickings.

Others claim victimhood due to a difficult childhood of trauma, neglect, rape, sexual molestation, homelessness, and so on. All are legitimate causes of suffering, but claiming victimhood can also lead to adopting the role of professional victim and exploiting it as an excuse for all manner of predatory behavior. Buying into an individual's claim to victimhood and encouraging the role of the professional victim is like giving a person with a broken leg permission to never walk again. And when a society buys into assigning victimhood status to anyone and everyone who claims this role, a culture of victimhood can be created. That's when you see people whose worst trauma ever was a paper cut claiming the right to play the victim card.

What's most interesting is how blaming others and playing the victim card tends to shut down the conscience of those on the sidelines or those who see themselves as not involved. For some reason, still unexplained by modern psychology and psychiatry, those on the sidelines tend to grant a pass to anyone claiming he or she is a victim with a righteous cause to go after his or her victimizer(s). Let's look at that phenomenon next.

6. Blame Externalization
Example 6.2 – Beware Those Playing the Victim Card

"I was robbed!"

"They cheated me!"

"Who could have seen that coming?"

"They made me do it!"

"I was just following orders!"

"You must hate me!"

"If you hadn't _____, I wouldn't have done that!"

The above are each a claim of innocence or mistreatment by those wishing to play the victim card. And what's the point of playing the victim card? The point is to get others to feel sorry for the victim. No act or verbal expression by a human predator is a bigger tell than claiming victim status and seeking the pity of other people.

What ever happened to owning your own shit? My favorite expression about those playing the victim card is "putting a turd in someone else's pocket." And when you witness someone putting his or her turd in your pocket, trying to get your pity so the person can play the role of victim, your antenna should go up immediately. Why? Because such people are highly likely to be trying to shut down your justifiable outrage for acts they have committed or lies they have told. In fact, they are probably setting you up for an even bigger lie if you show signs that you feel sorry for them.

Is this always true? Of course not. If someone is the victim of a hit-and-run auto accident, there is a clear perpetrator and a clear victim.

You can offer up a host of scenarios where the role of victim is absolutely justified. How about the battered wife or someone who is robbed by muggers? Clearly there are situations with sharp edges defining criminal and victim. We have both criminal and civil courts for dealing with those situations.

On the other hand, those who tell a sad story that you can't verify with well-documented facts are creating a word cloud to hide their less-than-honorable intentions or guilty behavior. The unanswered question is, "Will you fall for this ploy when someone tries it on you?"

Another question you might wish to consider thinking about is, "Who should you expect to try playing the victim card?" Would you answer, "Only toddlers and the usual adult suspects"? If so, allow me to enlighten you with another story.

In 2007, the economy of the United States experienced a financial meltdown. My personal investment portfolio was being managed by a major Wall Street investment banking firm. In a matter of a few days, the value of my investments dropped nearly 40 percent. My wife, who had ten times as much money invested with this firm, also lost nearly 40 percent of her net worth. The bankers with whom we met personally every three months flew from New York to meet with us in Seattle. Their song and dance consisted of "No one on Wall Street saw this coming." Really?

Those bankers were wanting us to feel sorry for them, *and* they wanted us to believe the lie they were telling us. Through in-depth research, however, I learned the real estate crisis that caused the markets to crash had been amply signaled to this banking firm. Actually, I had well-documented proof this same investment bank was deeply participating in the mortgage-backed security disaster that led to the financial crash of 2007 and 2008. Its international representatives had sold the crap they had created through sub-prime mortgage-backed securities to retirement funds around the world. They knew well in advance the market would crash, and they were playing with fire when they sold this tainted paper to clients. That meant our personal investment bankers were trying to put a turd in our pockets when they claimed, "No one on Wall Street saw this coming!"

This story is shared not because everyone in the financial services world is uniquely predatory. It's because my experience has been that nearly all who screw up tend to cover their ass by playing the victim card. This is why you must always watch for this red-flag pattern of blaming others because human predators *always* wave this flag when trying to squirm out of accepting responsibility for their failures. Sadly, the character trait of stepping up and owning responsibility for screwing up is no longer taught to most children growing up in America. And this fact of life makes it almost acceptable to play the victim card by anyone and everyone.

Does this mean the red-flag warning sign of blaming others doesn't apply any longer? No! It still is an early-warning sign that is extraordinarily trustworthy for signaling you may be involved with a human predator. When this red flag is waved in your face, pay attention. Go on high alert. Dig out the facts. And get your defenses up.

Finally, no matter how tempting you may find the narrative for blaming others, don't give into that temptation as it leads to a very slippery slope of denying you are 100 percent responsible for your life, your choices, and the consequences of your choices. And most importantly, don't ever bend the rules or the laws that govern civilized behavior, unless you are prepared to accept the consequences. Otherwise, you will be just like the people you will learn about next.

7. CONTEMPTUOUS NONCONFORMITY
A wanton disregard for social norms and socially acceptable behaviors

Have you ever been tempted to bend or break a rule? How about a law?

These are not trick questions. Of course, you've been tempted in both, and you've bent or broken rules and laws. Even if all you've ever done is exceed the speed limit one time, that would be an infraction of a law.

Why ask? The only purpose of this question is to help establish how different it is to experience the temptation to bend or break rules and laws from having a wanton, reckless disregard for all rules and laws. And right from the get-go, you must grasp this difference is so great that trying to claim they are even similar is like comparing a football to an atom.

Yet now that this metaphor of the difference between a football and an atom has been used, does it sufficiently explain how your posture towards rules and laws is so vastly different from someone acting in a predatory way? I don't think so. Let me try again.

When you feel tempted to bend or break a rule or a law, you likely ask, "Should I do this?" A human predator, on the other hand asks, "How can I use rules or laws against others to get my way?" The question, "Should I do this?" is weighed against your conscience and a personal commitment to always consider the rightness or wrongness of your choices. By contrast, the question, "How can I use rules and laws against others to get my way?" is asked from a completely different contextual posture where there is no conscience at all, no respect for any rules or laws, and the belief you and your overall respect for rules and laws are weaknesses that can (righteously) be used against you. Perhaps a good example will help you grasp the full implications of this contrast.

7. Contemptuous Nonconformity
Example 7.1 – The Lawmaker as Human Predator

Shouldn't those who protect or make our laws be the ones who most respect them? While I'm suggesting the answer is yes, voters continue to elect to office men and women who are super-predators. Why is that?

Additionally, it should be noted that while passing the bar examination is a highly challenging intellectual test, no one admitted to the bar in these United States of America is required to take a test to determine mental or emotional fitness to practice law. Should lawyers *and* politicians be required to submit to in-depth psychological examinations to participate in lawmaking and legal protection?

Richard Nixon has been posthumously diagnosed as demonstrating all the characteristics of a sociopathic narcissist (a human predator by any stretch of the imagination), but he did resign when his connection to the Watergate Hotel break-in was undeniable. Was resigning a mea culpa, an apology, and a confession? Not really! Nixon's last words in his resignation speech were, "I am not a crook!" Yes, he said that, but had he been prosecuted for authorizing crooks to break into the National Democratic Headquarters, steal the opposition's documents, and plant microphones, wouldn't he have been convicted as a crook? Wasn't his resignation a way to avoid prosecution and conviction?

What's mind-blowing is that an Emory University project in 2013 that analyzed a trait called *grandiose narcissism* in America's first forty-two presidents rated former President Richard Nixon as sixth. Since narcissism is all about "me first" and "me forever," doesn't having this trait guarantee that a person is unfit to serve (or even run) for the highest elected office in the land? If you answer yes, you will receive a lot of pushback from people who disagree with you. Some folks are of the opinion that only those with narcissistic personality disorder can survive in Washington, DC.

I'm of the opinion that the best way to stop electing human predators to public office is to have term limits. But that will never happen. In 1976, I gave everything I had to help a man I knew well to become a United States senator. This man had impeccable character. He was both a former trustee of a hospital foundation I directed and a friend of many years. When he became a candidate for US senator, I got involved because he campaigned for election on a platform of term limits. While running for the office, this man declared time and again the maximum he would serve (the maximum that anyone should serve in the US senate) was two terms. He stayed in DC for four terms. And I'm convinced, once he got a taste of real power as a senator, he became addicted to that power and broke his word because of that addiction.

Certainly, you've noticed how stingy I'm being when it comes to naming names and telling my personal stories about lawyers and politicians who are known human predators. The reason, of course, is fear of getting sued by these people. I won't ever share my lawyer stories.

If you really want to read a good lawyer-as-human-predator story, pick up a copy of *Confessions of a Sociopath* by M. E. Thomas. Written under a pseudonym, this lawyer explains how having no conscience, no feelings, and no emotions to muddy her thinking about right and wrong and possessing absolute self-confidence about any action she takes made her a far better court advocate for her clients. This book also outs many of her professional peers as human predators who exceled in the legal profession, and when she did that, the legal profession across America was infuriated. Problem is they couldn't sue M. E. Thomas because no one (at that time) knew who she was. She has since been outed, and if you are curious enough, you can learn on your own who she is.

Politicians, on the other hand, are fair game for stories about what they do as predators when they get caught. That information is on the public record. However, the predatory behaviors of politicians who don't get caught are deeper than the ocean. Let's look at only five of the crimes committed (proven in courts across our land) by some of our nation's notorious politicians.

BOSS TWEED – US REPRESENTATIVE, 1852

His first name is a strong hint that this American symbol of inner-city corruption was a human predator. Actually, his first name was William, and Boss was only a nickname. His nickname refers to his skilled trading of votes, money, and power for favors he granted to his constituents and business partners during the Civil War. If these acts didn't make him Boss, what would it take? Tweed was convicted in 1873 for his role in a corruption ring that stole at least one billion dollars in today's dollars and was sentenced to twelve years in prison. He wasn't very pleased about this, so he escaped from prison and fled to Spain where he was arrested and sent back to New York City, where he eventually died in prison of pneumonia. While political law breaking (and rule breaking) can be traced back to the founding of our nation, Boss Tweed holds a special place in history books as someone who symbolized political greed over respect for the law.

RANDY "DUKE" CUNNINGHAM

What is it with the nicknames? Are these people wanting to get caught? Anyway, Cunningham had been a decorated navy fighter pilot in the Vietnam War before election to the US House of Representatives from 1991 to 2005. He resigned from Congress in disgrace in 2005 for taking bribes of more than $2.4 million from at least three defense contractors in exchange for government business. Even worse than his nickname, this dodo used the bribes to make extravagant purchases such as a yacht, a Rolls-Royce, and a palatial mansion. I guess people noticed.

THE KEATING FIVE

In the 1980s, the savings and loan banks in America (which don't exist today) had become cesspools of risky investments and corruption. Nothing was worse than Charles Keating's Lincoln Savings and Loan in California. This particular bank collapsed completely in 1989, leaving thousands of investors penniless. How did Keating get away with his high-risk investment schemes for so long? Keating had five US senators in his pocket, all of whom had helped keep Department of Justice investigations of Lincoln Savings and Loan from moving forward. Those five Senators were Dennis DeConcini, Arizona; Alan Cranston, California; Donald Riegle, Michigan; John McCain, Arizona; and John Glenn, Ohio. Keating had lavishly entertained all five men and made huge contributions to their re-election funds over many years. While all except Cranston were subsequently exonerated of any wrongdoing, they were roundly criticized for having exercised "poor judgment" by interfering with the formal investigation of Lincoln Savings and Loan. Yet isn't interfering with a formal investigation a criminal act? Oh, well! Who says American political influence isn't for sale?

ROD BLAGOJEVICH

As governor of Illinois, Rod Blagojevich was charged with corruption in 2008, impeached, and then tried and found guilty of seventeen charges, including trying to sell then President Barack Obama's former Senate seat. Unfortunately for him, Blagojevich was recorded in a wiretap operation by the FBI as saying about that Senate seat, "I've got this thing and it's f------ golden. I'm just not giving it up for f------ nothing." Other criminal offenses included wire fraud, attempted extortion, and conspiracy to solicit bribes. On December 11, 2011, Blagojevich was sentenced to fourteen years in prison. After serving eight of those years, Blagojevich was pardoned by then President Donald Trump. Blagojevich is prohibited from ever again running for public office. Can you imagine why?

KWAME M. KILPATRICK

In 2002, Detroit's sixty-eighth mayor was a rising Democratic star when he took office. Back then, they called Kwame M. Kilpatrick the *hip-hop mayor*. Once in office, however, he reportedly set about building a criminal enterprise at city hall. Leading Detroit as mayor until 2008, he had had been dogged for years by rumors of hundreds of thousands of dollars deposited to his personal bank account that supposedly originated from a pay-for-play system of fleecing contractors and taxpayers for personal gain. Yet these rumors weren't pursued by law enforcement as no one dared take him on in a court of law. Then in 2013, the city of Detroit declared bankruptcy, and the ensuing federal investigation proved Kilpatrick's rumored antics were all true. A federal jury sent him off to jail for twenty-eight years. In January 2021, then President Donald Trump commuted Kilpatrick's sentence. He was released, having served only seven years. Now fifty-one years old, he claims he is done with politics and headed for the pulpit. God help us all!

One of the breaking headlines on the news just one hour ago as I write today (July 16, 2021) announced the recent discovery that former President Bill Clinton took two (previously undisclosed) international trips with Ghislaine Maxwell, Jeffrey Epstein's madam. Maxwell was convicted for sex trafficking of minors with the now deceased Epstein in late December 2021, a case that ensnared billionaire moguls and multiple political leaders around the world. Of course, you would have to have lived under a rock for the last five decades to be uninformed of the twisted sexual appetites of former President Bill Clinton. Talk about a disregard for conventional mores and the rules of married life!

> **RED FLAG #19:** Human predators frequently engage in truth bullying. They will beat you up with their version of the truth until you acquiesce. If you attempt to argue or defend your version of the truth, they will belittle your argument or dismiss it.

Is it fair to say these half-dozen examples of politicians who were proven to have a wanton disregard for rules and laws represent how all politicians should be seen? No! No way! What these examples prove is that human predators show up everywhere, including in the highest political environments in this nation. How could it be otherwise when nearly a third of all those walking among us are human predators?

But wait! Are these duly elected rule-breaker/law-breaker politicians worse than those who elect them? Well, those of you reading this can answer yes! And you're learning about the group of people that should answer no.

7. CONTEMPTUOUS NONCONFORMITY
EXAMPLE 7.2 – THE COVID PANDEMIC PREDATORS

Can economic and social circumstances create human predators? This question would be difficult to answer in more placid times, but since the start of the COVID-19 pandemic, turbulence has pretty much penetrated every level of society. This particular pandemic is only one contributing cause of the turbulence now being experienced around the globe. Global warming and human overpopulation are the two big contributors to worldwide, socioeconomic turbulence, and the influence of both in our lives has been rapidly expanding for the last fifty years. Yet we humans are like the frog slowly boiling in a pot of water on the stove during that fifty-year period. Because the changes in the numbers of humans on the planet and the warming trends in climate didn't dramatically disrupt our lives, we didn't hit the panic button and jump out of the pot as it was moving towards the boiling point. Sadly, the vast majority of human beings have to be in a gun-at-your-head confrontation with reality before they contemplate hitting the panic button. And believe it or not, even such a desperate encounter with impending death will never move a large percentage of humanity. The COVID-19 pandemic has proven this in spades.

The years of 2020 and 2021 demonstrated also that humans tend to be or become their worst selves when worldwide, life-threatening diseases threaten the economic and social order. Look at these numbers for example:

- Gun violence increased significantly during the COVID-19 pandemic and continued to rise in 2021.
- In early 2021, the FAA reported a dramatic rise in violent conduct at airports and on planes, most of it due to passengers who objected to rules about wearing masks to protect against spreading COVID-19.
- In 2020 through 2022, gang violence increased dramatically in Central America and Mexico, thus driving immigrants to flee to America's southern borders.
- The CDC has reported that deaths from drug overdosing increased by 29.4 percent in 2020. That's up from a mere 5 percent increase in the previous year.
- Scams hit their highest number on record in 2020 and 2021. According to the Federal Trade Commission, Americans have filed over half a million COVID-19 fraud reports and lost over $480,000,000.

Of course, if more pandemics follow on the heels of COVID-19, government leaders around the globe will attempt heroic acts. Throwing money at desperately suffering populations will be (and has been) one strategy you can count on, and that will be its own temptation for scams like this one:

7. Contemptuous Nonconformity
Example 7.3 – How Economic Stress
Creates Human Predators

Prior to the COVID-19 pandemic and the PPP loans, Bob's construction business had a superb launch, and new business for the firm was developing far faster than projected. Then came the lockdown. Bob saw all this coming before the lockdown was announced, including the PPP loans. Bob was no dummy. He read the papers. He watched the news on TV. And he thought creatively. So he staffed up . . . fast!

One of his new hires was David. Bob promised David the world to get him to leave his current employer. One promise was that David would be groomed as his business partner, and another was that in four years David would own the business outright, when Bob planned to enter retirement. This was enticing stuff for a forty-something like David who had worked his way up in the construction business, learning everything he now knew as an apprentice. David gave notice to his current employer, and his last shift happened to be the day before the COVID-19 lockdown was announced.

When PPP loans became available, Bob applied swiftly. Before his application was submitted, Bob moved even faster. He purchased a house adjacent to his own home, claiming on his PPP loan application his ownership of that property was part of a long-term plan to turn it into a bed and breakfast. David was told he'd be the one working on remodeling the planned B&B property and other properties owned and currently managed by Bob's contracting business. "Forget the slowdown," he told David. "I've got lots of work for you right now."

Instantly, David was making more than ever before in his life, and he was thrilled Bob started him at ten dollars an hour higher than what had been promised. It seemed like every other day Bob added to his promises of greater gains and growing opportunities for property management and company advancement. It all seemed too good to be true when compared with what was happening in the rest of the building trades industry. Each night was doom and gloom on television. However, David noticed after a few weeks on the job that Bob's management style was growing scattered and disorganized and occasionally Bob became explosive. Should David be worried?

When some of Bob's promises about greater gains and real estate management opportunities didn't pan out, the occasional temper tantrum became a steady diatribe, and most times they were directed at David. Then, without a word, Bob cut David's hourly pay in half. Fear gripped his heart. Hey, this was all happening in the middle of a pandemic lockdown. David had bills to pay. Did David dare confront Bob?

It took a year before David figured out that Bob had hired him only to get help from the federal government to buy the house next door and pay David out of the PPP money.

The straw that broke David's back happened while Bob was out of town and called one day to notify David that a newly hired employee functioning in a limited office role had to be paid immediately. Bob practically demanded Dave pay the employee out of his personal funds, but only as a loan until Bob could return and sort everything out. Always considerate and loyal, David asked the hourly pay rate of this new employee. That the new guy with a limited job description was being paid more than David delivered the final indication that Bob was now more than struggling to make ends meet to the extent he was willing to sacrifice a loyal, hard-working employee without reservation.

At this point, your reading must be interrupted. Please stop and ask one question, "What would you have done if you had been David?" Because you have read this far, you know Bob has turned into a human predator. But, based on what you have learned so far from this book, what advice would you give David about how he should proceed? Remember, Bob has become a volatile person with huge mood swings.

He takes giant steps without ever sharing his thinking with David, and he blames David frequently for consequences of decisions gone bad.

Was Bob a human predator before the crunch caused by the pandemic lockdown? It's hard to know. His early moves to purchase the house next door and hire David might simply have reflected a man who was good at reading the direction of current events, or those same behaviors and instincts might have been predatory. Giving Bob the benefit of the doubt, wasn't he like everyone else who felt panic in those early days after COVID-19 came to our nation's shores? Didn't a great many suffer from the cascading collapse of the economic shutdown of businesses everywhere? And how many adopted predatory behaviors to try to survive?

Whether you believe humans have only a thin veneer of civility covering their much more powerful reptilian brain impulses, there is ample evidence from historical economic meltdowns that economically displaced people become their worst selves under the stress. Because I'm in my late seventies, the path of my life has taken me through several large social and economic shake-ups. There is nothing on the horizon that allows any of us to conclude there are fewer shocks and economic displacements ahead.

If you are to survive the coming economic earthquakes in the next ten years, your chances will be dramatically improved because you read this book and know how to spot human predatory behavior and how to take evasive action when human predators are on the prowl.

To wrap this up, please keep in mind that every rule you see bent or broken isn't proof you are witnessing a human predator in action. On the other hand, don't close your eyes and forget what you have witnessed when rules are bent or broken. The guy who runs a red light you stopped for may be rushing his wife to the hospital in the middle of labor. But if he flips you the bird when he runs that red light, stay away from this asshole, and don't become an asshole yourself by trying to chase him down and confronting him.

8. STRESS IMMUNITY

A lack of typical reactions to traumatic or otherwise stress-inducing events

Which of the following options fairly describes your emotional life?

- **Option A** – I am generally free of entangling and irrational emotions. I am strategic and cunning, intelligent and confident. In situations where others feel stress, I am the poster child of calm, even cold and calculating, though I notice that others around me are confused and emotionally agitated under the same stressful conditions.

- Option B – My emotions are the paintbrush I use to color the events of my life. Feelings of love, joy, and general happiness are my go-to emotions, and I seek a life that brings out such feelings in me. Yet I am also capable of feeling loss, grief, anger, and disgust appropriately when events and situations call for it. Stressful situations are easily managed when they arise, unless of course the stress is life-threatening for me or others I care about. Seldom do my emotions run my life, but I can't imagine how anyone might exist without feelings.

- Option C – I am hypersensitive emotionally. Small events can, and do, trigger major emotional responses within. I am also extremely detail oriented. I see elements others generally miss, and I am never happy until all the *i*'s are dotted and the *t*'s crossed. I am slow and methodical in making decisions, but I love music and both write music and produce music other artists create. Often, I have a knee-jerk emotional reaction to behaviors or events that displease me, and for this reason, I can easily get hijacked by my emotions. Criticism from others is especially hard to take, and often I overreact to being judged by others about anything. I love a calm, quiet working environment and am easily stressed out by loud, unexpected noises. Even the presence of other people when I'm trying to concentrate or focus on my work is highly stressful for me.

Can you imagine how hard it might be for three people, each with a different emotional profile as presented above, to relate with the others or to even comprehend what the life of the other two would be like? Forget about the adage that cautions, "Do not judge another until you have walked a mile in their shoes." In my early life (my twenties through my early thirties), I was the father in a young family where the mother fit the profile of Option A, our child fit the profile of Option C, and I fit the emotional profile of Option B. Need I explain how that turned out?

While there are many themes and variations on the three emotional profiles you were given above as forced choices, it's probably more useful to think of these three as a continuum where Option A is at one far end, Option B is somewhere close to the middle, and Option C is close to the opposite end. Believe it or not, under a multitude of circumstances, each of these emotional profiles has benefits, and each has severe weaknesses.

As an example, while the expression *human predator* tends to have pejorative implications most of the time, in wartime, being a human predator can serve the war fighter in extremely positive ways. Battle situations require the war fighter to control stress reactions and maintain situational awareness at all times. If, however, the war fighter is highly trained and fully prepared to do battle with enemy forces *and* has the benefit of never feeling the stress of battle (in fact, never feeling stress at all), then he or she can function at the highest level of efficiency for longer than other soldiers. That is the very definition of a Navy Seal, isn't it? The more emotional sensitivity one has built into one's natural biological make-up, the more likely he or she operates inefficiently during combat and will suffer PTSD from the experience of battle.

During World War II, Adolph Hitler knew well that the greatest enemies his soldiers would meet on the battlefield were stress and exhaustion, not the Russian soldiers or British, French, or Americans. To give his war fighters an edge, Hitler ordered his military leaders to provide all German soldiers ample amounts of amphetamine in tablet form (which most celebrity addicts, including Elvis and Johnny Cash, have been hooked on). This worked extremely well in the beginning. The drug would keep the

German army up and fully energized for days. It was also the reason Nazi soldiers were seen as ferocious fighters. Little did Hitler know the Allied Forces were taking these same drugs and even more powerful stimulants. However, the use of all drugs like this carries risks. In addition to the high possibility of addiction and abuse, your body has no chance to recover from the fatigue it is suffering. So there comes a point where a soldier comes off the drug and just collapses and he can't function at all in battle. This is not a desirable outcome.

Now that we are addressing addiction related to substance abuse and its implications on human predation, it's worthwhile to note the problem of escalation for drug abusers and how escalation leads to more predation on the part of addicts. Just to be clear, escalation is the expanding desire for drugs that drives drug addicts to want more frequent and larger doses of their drug of choice (including trying new and more powerful drugs like fentanyl, which frequently leads to overdosing and death). Escalation also leads to a more thorough shutdown of their conscience and causes addicts to be more manipulative, violent, and dangerous. In this state, these addicts are as capable of committing predatory acts with the same ferocity and focus as any of Hitler's soldiers.

> **RED FLAG #56:** Human predators can't tolerate hearing any perspective that threatens their self-perception, and if you or any audience is nearby when this occurs, they will tell their version of the story loudly and with great vigor to erase the cognitive dissonance of your differing account. This is called identity-protective cognition.

What about the non-drug-addicted human predators? What does it mean to be stress immune for them? First, it means they don't ever experience stress the way you feel it. There are never any panic or mental breakdowns with these people when they commit their ugly acts or even criminal acts. What they do experience is an intense focus, mixed with adrenaline, which is caused by the anticipation of getting what they want in terms of control or hurting others in mean and nasty ways. Even thought addictions take away the neurotypical way of experiencing stress. For example, those who are addicted to becoming more and more wealthy actually feel nothing a normal person feels, but they are adrenalized and experience a rush of feel-good brain chemicals over making the big score that elevates their net worth. This is the closest they come to feeling anything, let alone feeling anything like stress.

In selecting a story that illustrates what the human predator experiences in living without stress, the choices have been abundant. The options considered ranged from the Sackler family that owns Purdue Pharma, which many point to as the most influential power behind creation of the opioid crisis in this nation, to William Neil "Doc" Gallagher, a radio host on Christian radio networks in Texas who formed and advertised his Gallagher Financial Group liberally to mom-and-pop followers of his broadcasts that turned out to be a Ponzi scheme, which ruthlessly stole from his clients who trusted him for almost a decade.

Gallagher took thirty-two million dollars from senior citizens in the name of Christianity, and he loved every minute of it (but he doesn't really love serving three life sentences in jail because he's eighty years old now and he will never see the light of another day of freedom again). The Sackler family's FDA-approved drug, OxyContin, has been linked conclusively to the beginning of the opioid crisis and overdose deaths of more than five hundred thousand people (due to OxyContin and many other opioids) while OxyContin was making the Sacklers billionaires. Yet never in twenty-five years did they pause or stop denying they were liable, even though Purdue Pharma aggressively and purposely lied about the addiction potential of OxyContin from day one. The Sackler family will be allowed to keep their vast fortune (all ill-gotten gains), and none of the members of the family will spend one day in jail under terms of a settlement in 2020. Although the Sacklers agreed to pay $4.5 billion to claimants and place Purdue Pharma into bankruptcy while being shielded from further opioid-related lawsuits, recently that settlement agreement was disallowed by a higher court. This means the

Sacklers may yet serve jail time or be forced to give up most of their ill-gotten gains.

These individuals have stayed away from the press and won't reveal their deeply disturbing inner selves to anyone. This is true of nearly all human predators. There is no benefit to them in disclosing what their inner life is like. But a few have talked anonymously about what their inner world is like as they live their lives. In a nutshell, they admit to feeling nothing. They are also totally absorbed with their own agendas. For them, this life is their party, and it's all about them. Depending on who else is attending the party, human predators will express emotion (happiness, joy, excitement, incredulity, shock, disappointment, sadness, and grief) if it helps them get what they want. These false feelings are purely superficial. They never feel their heart race in anticipation or pound in fear. But they do experience the primitive emotions of intense anger, frustration, and rage. Typically, these emotions last only an instant and then morph into a feeling of intense calm and focused rage. They always remember who caused the rage they felt, and that person now and forever has a target on his or her back.

The most forthright and revealing expression of a human predator's stress immunity is described in the previously mentioned *Confessions of a Sociopath* by M. E. Thomas. Here are a few examples from the book:

8. STRESS IMMUNITY
EXAMPLE 8.1 – VULTURES IN VIRTUE'S CLOTHING

M. E. Thomas is an accomplished lawyer somewhere in the United States and the following excerpts are her own words. Because she is a lawyer, she is supposed to be one of the good guys helping bring justice to a complex world. Remember as you read these excerpts that M. E. Thomas is a pseudonym.

Once while visiting Washington, DC, for a law conference, a metro worker tried to shame me about using an escalator that was closed. He asked in thickly accented English, "Didn't you see the yellow gate?"

Me: Yellow gate?

Him: The gate! I just put the gate up and you had to walk around it!

Silence. My face is blank.

Him: That's trespassing! Don't you know it's wrong to trespass! The escalator was closed, you broke the law!

I stare at him silently.

Him: [*visibly rattled by my lack of reaction*] Well, next time, you don't trespass, okay?

It was not okay. People often say, in explaining their horrible actions, that they "just snapped." I know that feeling well. I stood there for a moment, letting my rage reach that decision-making part of my brain, and I suddenly became filled with a sense of calm purpose. I blinked my eyes and set my jaw. I started following him. Adrenaline started flowing. I felt so sure of myself, so focused on this one thing I felt I had to do. An image sprang to mind of my hands wrapped around his neck, my thumbs digging deeply into his throat, his life slipping away from him under my unrelenting grasp. How right that would feel.

. . . I had been caught in a fit of megalomaniacal fantasy, but in the end it didn't matter anyway. I lost him in the crowd.

· · ·

I am a sociopath. . . . Key among the characteristics of the diagnosis are a lack of remorse, a penchant for deceit. . . . I am generally free of entangling and irrational emotions. I am strategic and canny. I am intelligent and confident and charming, but I also struggle to react appropriately to other people's confusing and emotion-driven social cues.

· · ·

Perhaps the most noticeable aspect of my confidence is the way I sustain eye contact. Some people have called it the "predator stare," and it appears most sociopaths have it. . . . We are unfazed by uninterrupted eye contact. Our failure to look away politely is often perceived as being aggressive, seductive, or predatory. It can throw people off balance, but often in an exciting way that imitates the unsettling feeling of infatuation.

Ever find yourself using that charm and confidence to get people to do things for you that they otherwise wouldn't? Some might call it manipulation, but I like to consider it simply using what God gave me.

. . .

I was actually a great lawyer when I was trying. At one point, I worked as a prosecutor in the misdemeanor department of the district attorney's office. My sociopathic traits make me a particularly excellent trial lawyer. I'm cool under pressure. I feel no guilt or compunction, which is handy in such a dirty business. Misdemeanor prosecutors almost always have to walk into a trial with cases they've never worked on before. All you can do is bluff and hope that you'll be able to scramble through it. **The thing with sociopaths is that we are largely unaffected by fear. Besides, the nature of the crime is of no moral concern to me; I am interested only in winning the legal game** [emphasis added].

8. Stress Immunity
Example 8.2 – Predators Don't Get Butterflies

You know that feeling when you're nervous, like butterflies are fluttering in your stomach? Human predators have no idea what that's like. Basically, natural-born human predators have two gears. Either they are in a state of super-calm resolve to get what they want, or they are super-angry. When pushed too far, cornered, caught in a lie, or caught with their hand in the proverbial cookie jar, they fly into a rage. In a rage state, they are a threat to your physical safety, and they will bring harm to others nearby. Many (if not most) emotionally abusive spouses are human predators, and when they don't get their way or don't hear their spouse saying exactly what they want to hear (and in the way they want to hear it), they become batterers and commit physical violence against their spouse, as well as daily dish out emotional abuse.

Natural-born human predators also experience intense focus mixed with adrenaline that is very different from nervousness or anxiety. When human predators set in motion a drama that involves conflict leading to a response they want from others, the anticipation of getting what they want triggers this mix of intense focus and adrenaline they enjoy.

Let's look at an example that shows the explosive anger predators can unleash and the enjoyment they receive from trying to yank the chain of their intended prey.

Janice had been cornered. Her lover called to inform her that her about-to-be ex-husband had filed an alienation of affection lawsuit against him. If this lawsuit went forward, his reputation as a psychiatrist would be in tatters. He was married and the father of five children. "Somehow, you have to get him to drop this," pleaded her lover.

Her first thoughts were murderous. That was followed by a moment of nothingness. Then she was good, calm, focused. She thought, "He's coming over to pick up the children this evening for the weekend. I'll have the time of my life going hammer and tongs with him. After he takes the children to the car and straps them into their car seats, I'll ask for a private word with him in the house. With the children out of sight and unable to witness, I'll let him have it."

For the next few hours, Janice calmly gathered all the knives, hand tools, and other implements she might use to murder her husband. She hid them. Certain she was now capable of cold-blooded murder, she didn't want to go there just yet.

When Gary arrived, exactly on time, Janice was excited by the adrenaline she felt released within her. She could barely keep the grin off her face. Ready to rip this man a new asshole, and no matter what it took, she would get him to back down.

The plan was implemented easily because Gary was a polite and considerate person (and in her opinion boring) who did not want to see his children upset. Once Janice had him alone inside the house, she didn't care if the children sat out in the car strapped to their safety seats for hours, even though the outside temperature was in the nineties.

Screw them! At first, she kept her voice calm and confronted Gary with the facts.

Oddly, he remained perfectly calm. "Yes," he said, "my attorney has been instructed to unleash legal hell on your lover unless, of course, you and I can reach an agreement about custody and child support first."

That's when Janice began raising her voice. She hadn't anticipated Gary's calm. The emotional temperature was going up, and she didn't care if this went on for hours. She was going to find a way to make him take a swing at her. Then she would call the police and have him arrested and prosecuted for assault and battery.

Surprisingly, Gary just listened quietly, not engaging Janice in any way. Then, after a particularly threatening tirade by Janice, Gary turned his back and walked away. She couldn't allow that. Janice picked up a lamp, a large lamp, and went to bludgeon Gary. She didn't care. He was going to back down, right here, right now.

Fortunately, out of the corner of his left eye, Gary saw the swift movement of the huge lamp coming at him like an asteroid. It wasn't thrown. The driving force behind the lamp was her hand, and the target was the back of his head. He ducked, raising his left arm, and the lamp missed. No harm to him. The lamp, however, shattered against the door he was about to exit. Gary understood instantly that this was meant to be a homicidal blow. He swiftly opened the door with his right hand and left the house.

Meanwhile, the children had not stayed belted in their seats. Both had escaped when they had heard their mother shouting. They witnessed the entire event through the huge picture window into the living room and saw their mother swing the lamp viciously at their father's head. Gary swept them both up, threw them into the backseat like ragdolls, jumped in the driver's seat, and sped away.

The above event is a real one. The human predator in this marriage was the wife who was having an affair. Need I tell you the husband never went to the house again on advice of counsel? The children were always delivered in a public setting after the lamp attack—a setting with many witnesses.

Notice that the mother of the two young children had very little attachment to them, as expressed by her non-concern they might overheat in the car. Creating deep and lasting attachments to anyone is a typical problem for human predators. Additionally, although the marriage had lasted eight years, Janice found her partner boring and had taken a lover to spice up her life. Why she hadn't requested a divorce instead of taking a lover goes to the personal objective of yanking the chain of her boring husband. Why divorce when you can have all the benefits of a live-in father for your children while you take lovers on the side?

Also notice how the alarm of learning about a legal move against Janice's lover quickly resolved into a calm that came over her. This came only after she had a plan—to verbally attack (out of sight of the children) and provoke Gary to strike her, then to call the police, press charges, and make Gary out to be a battering husband. Just as Gary arrived to take the children for their weekend together, Janice could barely keep from smiling as adrenaline rushed through her body, knowing she had the upper hand.

If you lean toward thinking of the adrenalized state Janice experienced as emotion, I assure you it is not. The brains of human predators overvalue the pleasure associated with getting what they want. Joshua Buckholtz, a neuroscientist at Vanderbilt University in Nashville, Tennessee, discovered the brains of people with sociopathic tendencies are rich in dopamine, which you now know is a reward chemical that makes us seek out pleasure. Buckholtz concluded from his experiments on highly antisocial subjects that they do have a need for pleasure that is extreme, but the only way to get the release of dopamine is to pursue activities that reward them at the expense of others without considering the costs of their actions—such as hurting others. Even Ted Bundy described his first killing as falling short of his expectations. This, he explained, was why he had to keep killing. He was trying to perfect reality to match the intensity of his anticipation. But only the anticipation of killing ever released the dopamine reward he sought, never the actual killing ritual itself.

Another finding of the Vanderbilt University studies was that sociopaths are far more likely than other criminals to abuse drugs and alcohol.

In the story shared with you about Janice and Gary, it was later discovered that Janice was addicted to cocaine. Her psychiatrist lover had encouraged her use of this street drug (supplying her with ample amounts of it) because he wanted to get her into a relationship. Since Janice was not a client, he knew he wasn't violating professional practice standards. What he did on his own time was nobody's business, or at least that was his take on things. What he didn't know is that Janice turned out to be a one-hit wonder, someone who becomes irreversibly addicted by taking cocaine just one time. She didn't need his encouragement, but she did need a steady supply, and her psychiatrist lover was the source of that supply.

Naturally you noticed Gary's calm, cool, and collected response to the rage leveled at him in this story. What you may have guessed is that Gary had been trained by a professional coach to be prepared for Janice's tirade. Did this training pay off? He certainly avoided doing harm to anyone, and he didn't get arrested and charged with wife battering. That is often a win for someone trying to disentangle from a human predator. And you are wise to take note of this now as disentangling from human predators will be thoroughly covered in section 4 of this book.

Of course, every word written in section 3, plus the red-flag warnings at the end of the book, is meant to give you multiple ways to see human predators coming and avoid engagements with them. Yet this isn't always possible. Their abilities at stealth by employing deceits of all kinds allow human predators to weasel their way into your life in impressively creative ways. Let's look closely at the lying ways of human predators next.

9. GUILTLESS LYING

The ability to lie without micro-expression
tells that typically give away lying behaviors

How many sad songs have been written about lovers who lied and got caught? I always liked Linda Ronstadt's song, "You're No Good." Here's a quick reminder of the lyrics:

Feelin' better, now that we're through
Feelin' better cause I'm over you
I've learned my lesson, it left a scar
Now I see how you really are

You're no good, you're no good, you're no good
Baby, you're no good

The reason I adore this song is because that's how prey animals feel about all human predators once they catch them in their lies and deceptions. After being lied to, you find yourself feeling betrayed and ready to go on stage and sing at the top of your voice, "You're no good, you're no good, you are NO DAMN GOOD!"

Another part of the song that catches my attention is, "it left a scar/Now I know who you really are." Let's talk about those scars on the hearts of people who have been lied to. I have a dear friend who married a man she loved with all her heart. She's a straight arrow in every way. But this man lied to her in so many ways it's

> **RED FLAG #4:** Human predators have little to no empathy for anyone or any living creature. Occasionally they can appear to have empathy for family members (especially their own children), but this is actually an expression of their ego as they see their offspring as mere extensions of themselves.

mind-blowing. Being a Roman Catholic, however, she kept forgiving him because marriage for her was a sacred commitment. Finally divorced, she is deeply scarred and states clearly and consistently when asked about marrying in the future, "I'll never get married again. Why would I? Why would anyone?" How deep is that scar?

Human predators are liars, and I want to write that all liars are human predators, but that flies in the face of a hard reality about humans. All humans lie. If you claim you never lie, well, you're a liar. One study found that Americans, on average tell about eleven lies per week. If this is true (and, yes, little white lies were being counted in this study), how can a finger be pointed at human predators for the lies they tell?

The answer to this question is that conscience draws the line. And human predators have no conscience. This means no line is ever drawn by human predators when they lie. Even when their lying might lead to loss of life, emotional damage, or devastating financial losses for their victims, human predators will lie with none of the tried and proven tells of micro-expressions, body-language giveaways, or eye movements (including changes in the aperture of the retina).

The difference between pathological lies and those little white lies we tell all the time is thin, but we can delineate the difference in a few words. You, as a normal liar, may tell your wife you forgot your wedding anniversary because you are struggling with the challenges and stresses of breaking in a new team of salespeople at work (the truth is you simply forgot). You would also explain to her how awful you feel (that part is true) to let work ever become more important than your relationship with her (that is also true but not truly relevant here). Then you would ask her forgiveness and plan with her a special weekend getaway. This is normal lying. There is a morally acceptable purpose behind this lie. Blaming work is a little lame, but it may keep your wife's feelings from being so hurt she can't forgive you. Playing the pity card can be justified only if you are intent on making up for your forgetfulness with deep sincerity.

But what if you tell lies about your past life that have no clear purpose? For example, instead of telling people you grew up in Muncie, Indiana, you tell people you grew up in New York City. Or what if you explain to your co-workers that your apparent cold symptoms are actually caused by the chemo treatments you are receiving for cancer? These lies are doing nothing but meeting some twisted internal need and have no empathic purpose whatsoever. On the other hand, these kinds of lies aren't specifically intended to harm others, either. They are awful lies, but those who voice them aren't full-on human predators. They are compulsive liars who often get caught in the web of lies they create.

Pathological liars, however, tell lies to harm others with no regard at all for the damage their lying will exact on their victims. This can happen only when the liar has no conscience and no ability to empathize. Furthermore, pathological liars lie with such conviction they actually believe the lies they tell. This is the case even if the lie contradicts another lie the person told just five minutes earlier.

Micro expressions, certain body-language tells, and eye-movement giveaways of normal liars are all caused by conflict within a normal person and his or her conscience. If you have no conscience or your conscience has been put to sleep by an addiction or severe trauma, these physical tells don't manifest. In one way, you could express all this by pointing out that *no conscience* equals *con science*. Conning science—and you—is the specialty of human predators. While believing you are dealing with an honest broker, you are being conned.

Making the problem of pathological lying much worse is the internet. Cyber-bullying, dating-site lying, broadcasting lies (or even half-truths) about the dangers of a pandemic vaccine, spreading conspiracy theories, posting false testimonials (either negative or positive in nature), and selling counterfeit products or services online are just a few examples of how the internet allows pathological liars to harm others and even do it using a false identity or anonymously.

9. Guiltless Lying
Example 9.1 – Owner of Free Tours by Foot Sees Something Afoot

Ethics and morals, at the very least, are principles that allow humans to regulate cooperative behaviors. Here in the United States, we have always attempted to mix individual freedoms with cooperative efforts. Now that we have online communities through the internet where there is less accountability, the anonymity of our online neighbors allows those with predatory agendas to mix freely with prey animals. And this is a gigantic problem because the potential for predatory humans to do immense harm to others on the internet is limitless.

In the offline world, almost all the predatory behaviors that take place on the internet would be crimes, and the perpetrators of those crimes would be swiftly dragged before a judge. Further complicating online misdeeds is the protection given to online platforms under Section 230 of the Communications Decency Act. In essence, if an online user of a sponsoring platform posts anything that is illegal (or controversial), the platform sponsor can't be sued in a court of law. What Section 230 actually does is give online sponsors the legal status of a distributor rather than a publisher. Was this an error in judgment by our lawmakers? Time will tell. The better question is, "What did Section 230 do to benefit human predators who use their lies (including half-truths) to take advantage of others for personal gain?"

Stephen Pickhardt founded Free Tours by Foot in 2007. His business model was simple and elegant. His guests were asked to pay only "what you like." The business was available in nine cities around the world, including Berlin, London, New York, and New Orleans. Everything went swimmingly until 2019 when Pickhardt noticed a disturbing trend on his business review page. With no change in the way he operated his tours, reviews by customers turned negative, but only those reviews posted on an influential travel website. According to Pickhardt, "They were so, so bad." His tour guides in New Orleans were the prime target of these bad reviews. They were accused of taking people down dark alleys and strong-arming the tour guests.

Pickhardt decided to get to the bottom of this. He personally researched the writers of the reviews online and soon discovered they were all coming from the same Facebook profile. The profile was a staff member of a rival firm. Once the problem was discovered, the well-known travel website removed all the negative reviews and shut out the reviewer by making it impossible for him to log in to Free Tours by Foot's website.

Did Free Tours by Foot lose business because of these unethical acts by Pickhardt's competitor? That's a harder question to answer because you never know who saw those reviews and decided not to use Pickhardt's services. What's shocking is the lowlife behavior a competitor chose to smear a decent business operation. Has the saying "all's fair in love and war" now changed to "all's fair in love and war and business"?

And what consequences did the rival business suffer? Probably none. Like it or not, our system for operating the internet allows human predators to do enormous damage before they are even called out. How is it we have created such exposure to a system that allows these people to do so much damage? How is it none of the rules applied to every other part of life do not apply to internet communities? And just in case this kind of predatory behavior is news to you, going on any internet platform without this knowledge is akin to being a fawn in a wide-open meadow surrounded by forests filled with lions. The endgame won't be like a Disney Studios, happily-ever-after movie.

The story just related is a violation of business ethics as we have known them in the United States. The perpetrator of this business ethics breach wasn't even using sophisticated online strategies to hide. Much more egregious and sophisticated online predators are those who use the internet to hunt for children to lure into the worldwide sex trafficking trade.

9. Guiltless Lying
Example 9.2 – Internet Lying to Abuse Minors Is No Minor Problem

Hopefully you agree that one of the worst of the online lying practices by human predators is luring children into the world of sex trafficking. Things have gotten so bad even online multiplayer video games and chat apps are being used to connect with children and lure them to sex traffickers. Did you know more than 150,000 new escort ads are posted on the internet every day? A 2012 Thorn survey of child sex-trafficking survivors found that 75 percent had been sold online, most of them through escort websites.

Of course, buyers drive the market making child sexual exploitation lucrative for traffickers. Few of these buyers ever face serious consequences. However, more than one thousand children are arrested for prostitution each year. Legally speaking there is no such thing as a child prostitute. Children cannot consent to sex. They are victims, not criminals. Yet when children are arrested for prostitution, they have a criminal record that prevents them from access to critical resources to rehabilitate their lives like jobs and housing. And this sets them up for further exploitation by sex traffickers.

Let's look at just one story that demonstrates how minors become prey for these human predators.

Nicole was only seventeen, living in London, when she met a man on Facebook who offered to take care of her. Nicole was, at that moment, parentless and had posted on her Facebook site that her mother had just been sent to prison for white-collar crimes.

Surely you are thinking, "OMG, girl, don't go there!" Of course, Nicole did go there. Once she met up with the man, instead of looking after her, he sold Nicole to men across the United States. It was only when she was in her early twenties that she was finally able to escape sex work.

The goal here is not to pick on Facebook, although in 2020, 59 percent of online victim recruitment in active sex trafficking cases occurred on Facebook. It's also not the goal here to gross you out with stories showing how widespread the problem of sex trafficking is around the world. Specifically, the purpose here is to draw your attention to how pathological lying can now happen more easily than ever in the anonymous universe of online communities. Prey animals, BEWARE!

9. Guiltless Lying
Example 9.3 – The Lyingest Liars in Liar Land

Now we have a dilemma, and we have to make a choice to resolve it. Who is the biggest liar in modern times in the world of business? Is it Trevor Milton of Nikola or Elizabeth Holmes of Theranos? These two people are perfect examples of human predators who lie without demonstrating any clues that they are lying.

Trevor Milton is currently being prosecuted by the SEC and the United States Department of Justice for deceiving investors about his semi-truck that, supposedly, is capable of running on a hydrogen-powered battery. The problem is Nikola never had the technology it claimed for this truck, but Milton sure wasn't shy about taking money from people who trusted his lies. He also claimed he had dropped the cost of producing the hydrogen (a source of clean energy) by 81 percent. How interesting! The Nikola enterprise wasn't even producing hydrogen. Yet the company claimed it had the largest hydrogen production station in the Western Hemisphere at its headquarters in Phoenix. In fact, Milton stated on video that this hydrogen production station could produce one thousand grams of hydrogen per day. You can watch him making this statement on YouTube, and I dare you to identify any signs the man is lying. Later, in a recorded interview, Milton had to admit Nikola didn't even have a permit to build a hydrogen producing station. Did it bother him to get caught in this bold-faced lie? Not a bit! Are there other lies? Oh yes! Milton also claimed Nikola's headquarters was completely off the grid by using 3.5 megawatts of solar energy from solar panels installed on its roof. Strangely, aerial photographs taken of that building after this claim show no solar panels on the roof at all. It gets much worse, believe me. Claiming Nikola had hired one of the best teams in the world to develop its patented technology, Trevor had actually hired his brother, Travis (a general contractor with no experience at all with hydrogen), and placed several additional family members (and other "select early employees") on Nikola's payroll, paying them $110 million from round one's investor funds. This isn't the end of Trevor Milton's lying, but let's look at his competitor in this imaginary world-class lie-off competition.

Elizabeth Holmes of Theranos infamy has already been convicted by the SEC of deceiving investors who plowed billions into her start-up between 2003 and 2018. What Theranos promised was a revolutionary blood analyzer that could run hundreds of tests just from your finger-prick blood in the comfort of your home. At one point, Theranos was worth nine billion dollars. That's one for the record books in Silicon Valley, the incubator of revolutionary start-ups. Her patent idea was meant, in her mind at least, to change the world and to make the Stanford dropout a billionaire. But can you begin with both goals without the drive for wealth corrupting the higher-minded goal?

In the beginning, Holmes relied heavily on the reputation of her investors to bring on more investors. But elite medical endorsements were not forthcoming. Maybe Holmes didn't impress scientists because she had little education in medicine and chemistry.

Consider carefully that the in-home machine she was developing was to relay the data gleaned from your finger-prick blood to a specialized lab that would interpret the results and send a report back to the consumer. How hard could this be? Right? Well, it turns out this is impossible. So far, medical science can assure physicians of reliable results only if you go into a blood-draw center and send the vial of blood to a lab that uses a very large machine to analyze for specific requests, and the lab then requires several days to deliver the results to the ordering physician. Theranos was promising to scale down the massive machines now in use to the size of a large computer printer that could fit into a box and bypass physicians completely. Do you think eliminating doctors from the process had something to do with why her idea was poorly received by medical scientists? DUH!

The big lie here was the machine Elizabeth Holmes dreamed of didn't exist, and anyone with a lick of medical training knew her requests for high-ranking medical endorsements were filled with multiple promises that relied on scientific impossibilities. When the hard questions came, Elizabeth (the only employee of Theranos at that time) couldn't provide answers about how to overcome these scientific impossibilities.

Wouldn't you stop right here if you had been her? But NO! Elizabeth, her deep pockets now filled with investor funds, hired engineers to design and build her machine. Then she started running tests that didn't work yet on cancer patients. The well-known pharmaceutical firm Pfizer worked with her on this, in spite of knowing the Theranos tests couldn't be relied on to adjust the medications of test patients. In the interim, while testing proceeded, Holmes had been outright lying to investors about how well the tests worked. A man who shall remain unnamed, working as CFO for Theranos by then, caught her lies and confronted Holmes. She fired him on the spot and never hired another CFO.

By 2007, still with no working product, Holmes was labeled the next Steve Jobs by a Silicon Valley news rag. Talk about investigative reporting standards hitting a new low!

Yes, her board of directors was made up of A-list men and women from the business world, but she lied to them too. And most important of all, she made them believe her without any demands for accountability. How did she do that? She lied with no shame, no conscience, and she practically hypnotized people with her fake, baritone-range voice. You really should go on YouTube and listen to some clips of her using that voice to tell her lies. She was supremely accomplished at conning everyone who met her.

By 2009, a Pakistani named Ramesh "Sunny" Balwani (also Elizabeth's boyfriend) became Elizabeth's new mouthpiece at Theranos. Sunny was also a malignant human predator, who lied without shame or any indication of inner conflict. As few as two such people working together is known as a wolf pack. And through team hunting for investor prey, these two were unrelenting. Together they talked Walmart and Walgreens into signing a contract with Theranos for more than one hundred tests it could provide their in-store customers. The only problem was that less than half of the tests were even theoretically possible. And worse? None of the tests could be performed on the prototype machine Theranos had now created, named Edison. That, dear reader, is world-class lying!

All this came crashing down around Holmes in 2018 when she ran out of money and liar's luck. Multiple lawsuits, investigation by the SEC, and ultimately criminal fraud charges by the Department of Justice brought her face-to-face with the harsh consequences of her fifteen-year lying spree. Holmes and Balwani were scheduled for criminal trial in August of 2020, but the trial was delayed due to the COVID-19 pandemic. Her trial is now over, and she was found guilty on four of eleven counts, which means she faces up to twenty years behind bars.

You may think I'm being arbitrary in making this decision, but I give the trophy for the Lyingest Liar in Liar Land to Elizabeth Holmes. Sure, Trevor Milton is a terrific predatory liar, and he gets second place only because he hasn't crossed the finish line in this race to harsh consequences. Maybe he will escape judgment by the SEC and never be held liable to pay back his investors (although General Motors, one of Nikola's biggest investors, sued him and won). Maybe he will win his criminal case. But Elizabeth Holmes has already lost to the SEC, and her criminal trial will probably see her separated from her child and new husband for many years. At least that's my take on the contest. But hey, if this were the Olympics (which are going on in Tokyo as I write this) and you were a judge, whom would you pick as the winner of this imaginary contest?

HUMAN PREDATORS HUNTING AS WOLF PACKS

The word *poison* perfectly describes what human predators of all stripes represent to anyone who becomes caught in their elaborate traps. Forget about the word *toxic* as a descriptor for human predators. Your chances of having a brief encounter with just one of these people should be enough to motivate you to learn how to defend against them. Where are you likely to encounter them? Consider this list:

- Family members
- Your marriage partner
- People you date
- Anyone you work with
- Friends
- Professionals—lawyers, doctors, psychologists, contractors, gardeners, insurance sales professionals, real estate sales representatives, pastors and priests, police officers, judges, teachers, elected officials of all types, money managers, and investment advisors
- Those you connect with on the internet

OMG! Is there anywhere these people don't show up in normal society? NO! For my part, working in the nonprofit field as a professional fundraising consultant protected me from encountering as many as most. Still, as you've read, I did run across a few, and two of them hired me as a consultant during my fifty-year career. Fortunately, with those two, I had suspected they were human predators, so the contracts I had with them were bulletproof. But had I not been alert to the signs of a human predator and had I not taken steps to protect myself on the front end of those professional relationships, they would have destroyed me.

At this point, you are owed a discussion about human predator wolf packs.

It's an absolute fact that human predators of all kinds form predator groups to con, rip off, and steal money from their marks. They are called *wolf packs* because they hunt like wolves with each member of the pack playing a special role in bringing down their prey. Some wolf packs operate with as few as two human predators working in tandem (as was the case with Elizabeth Holmes and Sunny Balwani).

Another great example of predators in wolf packs is the beautiful couple (apparently husband and wife, but no one ever did ask) that joins your church. They drive a beautiful, high-end automobile, dress in superbly tailored clothing when they attend church, are charming and charismatic, and always say the right things to everyone they meet at church on Sundays. They carry beautiful Bibles and know the Bible forwards and backwards. Citing biblical passages at just the right time and in prescient ways demonstrates they are disciplined students of the Good Book. Certainly, these people are the real deal, and God has blessed them in spectacular ways (or so it seems). When asked what they do professionally, they hesitate, but with lots of encouragement reluctantly admit they are personal financial advisors. And then they add, "This is all we can tell you because our clients are very high-net-worth individuals and we're bound by confidentiality agreements to be very discreet." Thus ends the digging into their background.

> **RED FLAG #13:** Human predators manipulate human prey animals by attacking a person's character. For example, a dear friend was once told she would make a horrible mother because her pet cat whined constantly. She was dating a man who wanted the cat out of her life, perhaps because the cat was receiving more attention than he was. Human predators will stoop to anything to get what they want.

But then the church Finance Committee finds itself struggling to successfully navigate the economic downturn caused by the 2007 housing finance debacle that has wracked the stock market. Wringing of hands and late-night discussions won't bring back the 30 percent losses to the church's stock and bond portfolio. Suddenly someone remembers the couple who joined the church several months back and who, by admission and appearance, are successful financial advisors to high-net-worth individuals. Could God have sent them to this very church at this particular point in time to guide the congregation's leadership through one of the worst financial downturns the nation has ever known?

At last, someone suggests, "Let's go talk with them. What harm is there in talking?" But, dear reader, you already know what harm there is in following that suggestion. You know how this will end, don't you? You know the new member couple represent two foxes in the henhouse and once the church decides to place its financial assets in the hands of this demonic duo, they will simply disappear.

And that's exactly how this story ended. Exactly one week after all the papers were signed, giving them full trustee control over those precious church assets, the beautiful, new church-member couple didn't show up at worship services the following Sunday. The most insightful members of the congregation made an afternoon hospitality visit to their home that Sunday to see if they were ill or if, perhaps, they had suffered a tragedy in their family. Of course, the discovery was made that they never even lived at the address given for church records when they joined the church and took their vows of membership. And the fancy car they drove to church every Sunday? Its plates turned out to be stolen from another part of town entirely. Once this information surfaced, members of the church Finance Committee held an emergency meeting in the sanctuary and opened the meeting with prayer.

Is a greater and deeper explanation of wolf pack behavior required? Hopefully not! This short discussion is totally unfair to wolves that at least are open and honest about what they do and why they exist. Only a fool would approach a wild wolf or a pack of wild wolves and expect anything less than predatory responses. Now, after learning about predatory human wolves, working alone or as a pack, can you (or will you) ever approach anyone without your antenna up for the one (or two or four or more) of the early red-flag warnings at the end of this book? And what should your antenna be searching for if not the nine core character traits of human predators discussed here? Trust me when I warn you these people will nearly always be wearing sheep's clothing.

WHEN A NEIGHBOR IS A HUMAN PREDATOR

Unless you live in the country on a farm or on a palatial estate, chances are you have to live with a neighbor or two. Mostly, your interactions with neighbors are, well, neighborly. When they aren't, when you find you live next to the neighbor from hell, things can go south so, so fast!

My wife and I had such a neighbor living next door in a very high-end neighborhood. The fact that he had money and could afford a lovely home didn't tell us a thing about his living habits, however. Right after he moved in, he began leaving his garbage at the curb in plastic bags at night, instead of in the large garbage bins we were all provided by the county garbage service. We had racoons, skunks, and coyotes in the neighborhood, and they had no problem tearing through those plastic bags.

As you might expect, the next morning there was garbage strewn all over the neighborhood. What the racoons, skunks, and coyotes hadn't scattered around, the wind spread like autumn leaves. Seeing the new homeowner later that day on the street, I kindly and politely approached him and suggested next time he might want to use one of the garbage bins in his driveway. In response, he told me to go fuck myself. Then he continued using the bags every week thereafter. Every morning on garbage day, some of us would collect all the half-eaten and rotten trash from our lawns and toss it into the maniac's front lawn. Then he re-collected it in his plastic bags and strolled the neighborhood, throwing everything back onto the lawns of every single house up and down the street. He even crammed the stuff into our bushes. Sometimes we would find garbage in our mailboxes.

Eventually the police were called, the health inspectors were notified, and lawyers entered the picture. It really got ugly. He also called the police and the health inspectors and his lawyers, complaining about his disorderly, disrespectful neighbors. After receiving a letter from a very powerful attorney representing my wife and me, he filed a nuisance lawsuit against us. His case was dismissed with prejudice when our attorney showed the court photos of this man's outrageous behaviors. This went on for a full year before he moved out. Was this man a human predator? Absolutely, he was. He lived for conflict, and if no one threw the first stone, he was going to throw it. What kind of human predator does that? Let me answer your question with a question. What difference does it make? When you live next to a neighbor who is seeking conflict with others as his only reason for getting up each day, you can say adios to your peace of mind.

ECCENTRIC FAMILY MEMBERS AS HUMAN PREDATORS

Some human predators are easy to spot, but not all of them are. Those most easily identified (the worst of them) are rated 10 on a scale from 1 to 10. Others are less obvious and are down in the range of a 1 or 2, often are considered eccentric or weird, and are rated by most in society as harmless. They are definitely not harmless, however. They are just harder to spot early to avoid or defend against. And they can even be living in the same household with you. Who hasn't heard of the wonderful parent who is a model citizen, a member of the four-square church, and an upstanding member of the business community who sexually molests his or her children or of an uncle or a cousin that commits child rape? If you want to read about a real example of child abuse by a mother who was a respected church member, see the book *A Child Called It*.

My wife's stepmother was considered an eccentric woman, and she tried to seduce me when I was in my mid-fifties and she was seventy-five. (Don't even think about asking for details.) It doesn't matter that I was able to counter her behavior with disarming humor that defused the hand grenade she was about to throw at me. That woman was seriously trying to harm me and my wife. Why? Who in the name of sanity knows? My wife had always referred to her as the "wicked stepmother" in her life, and my wife was right. The woman's internal logic was so out of step with the worldview of other people that seeing her as bonkers was easy. At least for me it was easy to see what she was. Yet to everyone in my wife's family, she was still only an eccentric older woman. And that's a good example of the problem we often have in seeing these dangerous family members. Those who aren't obviously malignant in their behavior towards others twenty-four hours a day are given a pass way too quickly. Furthermore, seeing those who are lesser predators requires readjusting the lenses through which we look at the world, and that's hard to do if the reality of sociopathic predators isn't taught to us when we are in our teen years.

In fact, teenagers can often behave like human predators because of their raging hormones. Puberty is frequently expressed with all the outward symptoms of total narcissism and zero empathy and compassion described of adult human predators. But we wouldn't seriously consider placing teens in jail for these traits! Or would we?

Speaking as someone who lived a single-parent life raising two children from ages six and eight, I will admit that during their teen years, they both behaved very badly. Their lack of empathy and compassion, their tendency to stomp on rules, social conventions, and even laws, and their nasty little psychological games were enough to inspire murderous thoughts in me. Am I the only one who has ever felt this way about their teenagers? Jail time for each of them would have been my second choice when they pulled some of their teenage stunts. Yet today, they are my best friends, and both are healers. Go figure!

CAVES, CLUBS, AND BATTLE AXES

This morning while hiking in the beautiful mountains surrounding our home in Sun Valley, listening to the Grateful Dead singing "Casey Jones," I thought one verse of that song summed up perfectly the problem this book is trying to help you solve. The words of that verse are:

> *Trouble with you is*
> *The trouble with me*
> *Got two good eyes*
> *But we still don't see*

While technology has evolved exponentially in the last one hundred years, humans have not. Sure, we can rattle off a list of new products and services that have been developed in the last one hundred years because the changes in technology and science, digital communications, and social media have come fast and furious. But basic human behavior has not changed. Yes, we are going through subtle changes all the time by suddenly being glued to computer screens and cell phone screens for hours on end. But the basic underlying structure of the human brain has not changed. Still today, hard-wired at the base of our skulls is the reptilian (or primitive) brain we share with almost every living creature on Earth. So while technology has changed, we as biological beings are often still using technology the way our caveman ancestors did—as clubs and battle axes.

RED FLAG #34: Many human predators see themselves as superior to everyone, and if they don't receive treatment reflecting their superiority, they often become rude or even abusive.

Oh sure, we also use technology to heal, to teach, to learn, to inform, and to help create new technologies. Still, we as a species haven't connected the dots to the fact that we are reproducing like rabbits (albeit industrialized nations have lowered their birthrates to below replacement numbers), burning fossil fuels that pollute our atmosphere, dumping our garbage and waste into oceans and rivers, and burying toxic waste in soil everywhere we can get away with it. And every time a national leader anywhere in the world gets his or her feelings hurt, the war drums start beating, and in today's world, we have nuclear weapons instead of clubs and battle axes.

In every conceivable way, humans are still subject to the same follies of mania, greed, and a race to win over our fellow humans at almost any cost. The idea of winning, however, is also an illusion. And this is especially true if the so-called winner employs predatory strategies to destroy other humans emotionally, financially, spiritually, and environmentally.

There has been an explosion of human predatory behavior in recent years, and in my humble opinion, this is all driven by a new consciousness that, due to climate change, we are, every one of us, under threat. What's worse, even damning, is that once these behaviors are modeled by people in positions of power, an impressionable populace will see this as a green light to use predatory behaviors towards everyone as a morally accepted norm. Fear, mass fear, and our selfish instincts always bring out the worst in us. If that happens to the vast majority of humans around the globe, mass adoption of human predatory behaviors will lead to overall societal breakdown. In that environment, the human predator thrives.

Only awareness of our vulnerabilities as prey animals and broadly dispersed education about how easily the masses can become manipulated to follow the most dominant predators stand between social order and chaos.

If you know what to look for (which is the very purpose of this book), you need not proceed into the future with fear. Read, reread, and memorize the early warning signs of human predators so you spot them when predators still think they are invisible. Up to now, you have been walking among these people, oblivious to their existence. But you know now how to use your two good eyes and spot them early. In section 4, you will learn how to avoid, disarm, disengage, and defeat them.

The greatest battle you will have to fight in this world is the one within yourself, the fight to never give up your own moral compass and never become a human predator yourself simply because all others are caving in and abandoning their moral compass. The authors of this book believe in the human capacity for good. Therefore, we are determined to educate so you and everyone who reads this book can make moral and ethical choices to stop being just prey animals who follow the strong, immoral, or amoral who hold positions of power.

Please, do not stop your education here. Press on and learn how to use a form of mental martial arts to counter those who are determined to dominate you and lead us all back to the cave of ignorance, war, and slaughter. Do this now before you see any more degradation of social and moral order.

RECENT EXAMPLES OF PREDATORY BEHAVIORS IN AMERICA

1. How the world's largest bank turned all its employees into human predators—the cross-selling scandal at Wells Fargo Bank that stole billions from its seventy million customers between 1993 and 2017—only to end up paying three billion dollars in criminal charges from its widespread mistreatment of customers: envzone. com/how-greed-led-the-giant-wells-fargo-to-the-fraud-scandals/.

2. How one sociopathic narcissist scammed hundreds of rich kids and social influencers out of tens of millions of dollars and made their lives a living hell while stranded on a Bahamian island in 2017: "Fyre Festival: Inside the World's Biggest Festival Flop," https://www.bbc.com/news/newsbeat-46904445.

3. The true story of a sociopath who made her way in New York's high society and fleeced them for hundreds of thousands of dollars with nothing but lies about her sixty-five-million-dollar trust fund and royal lineage: "The True Story behind Netflix's *Inventing Anna*," https://time.com/6147088/inventing-anna-true-story.

4. A dating-site predator who scammed ten million dollars from lonely women looking for love—watch *The Tinder Swindler* on Netflix: https://www.netflix.com/title/81254340.

5. The payday loan shark who lived off the poor and near poor, charging them illegal fees and interest on five-hundred-dollar payday loans: "Scott Tucker Sentenced to More Than 16 Years in Prison for Running a $3.5 Billion Unlawful Internet Payday Lending Enterprise," https://www.justice.gov/usao-sdny/pr/scott-tucker-sentenced-more-16-years-prison-running-35-billion-un-lawful-internet-payday.

KEY POINTS

1. Our ignorance of the nine core personality traits of human predators keeps us blind to how very dangerous these people are.

2. Predatory humans don't want us to know about these nine core personality traits and go to great lengths to cover them up by presenting themselves as normal (even super normal). Through studying human prey animals with cold, calculating empathy, human predators learn how to mimic our behaviors so they can camouflage their predatory nature and get close to us. The best of them are tremendous actors and can even cry a river of tears on demand if that's what it takes to keep us off balance, emotionally confused, and feeling sympathetic towards them.

3. It doesn't matter if a human predator is genetically predisposed to predatory behavior or is created by addictions (either substance abuse addictions or thought addictions), emotional trauma, physical trauma, or cultural dogmas. The nine core personality traits presented in this section are the foundational elements of who

they truly are when on the hunt and determined to carry out their twisted agendas and nefarious goals.

4. The only important predatory behavior is the ambition that drives each human predator to use others. Some are megalomaniacs like Vladimir Putin who is currently invading Ukraine with his vastly superior military, and others just want to hook up with someone with money (or only a steady job and, therefore, a steady income) so they can live off their target like a blood-sucking leech.

5. Even those who get snared as prey can become predatory humans (think about wartime behaviors, cult behaviors, gang violence, and conspiracy theory addictions and the resulting behaviors from those who act out towards anyone who disagrees with their conspiracy theory beliefs). Additionally, highly stressful socio-economic circumstances can drive the best of humans to become predatory, and this truth has been born out repeatedly in recorded history.

6. In order to grasp the reality of the depth and breadth of human predatory actors living among us, we have to open our eyes. Only by facing our vulnerabilities as prey animals and the constant threat from human predators will we enthusiastically invest the energy to learn how to avoid and defend against these dangerous people.

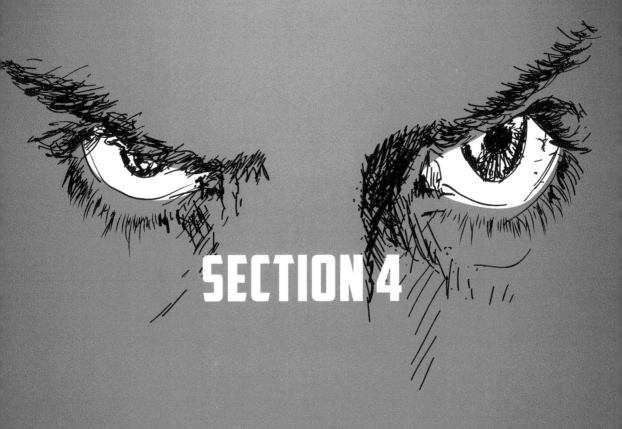

SECTION 4

"

Sometimes you just have
to accept that some
people are shitty humans
and stop trying to see
the good
that isn't there.
— The Minds Journal

"

THE ART OF WAR AGAINST HUMAN PREDATORS

How to Stay off the Menu of Human Predators Seeking Fresh Meat for Their Twisted Agendas

TRAIN YOUR MIND TO BE CALM IN ALL SITUATIONS

HUMAN PREDATORS SEEK THOSE who appear to them as weak and vulnerable. Unfortunately, in most instances these are compassionate, trusting, good-hearted human beings like you. As is true of parasites, human predators are strongest when they can get their claws into a healthy host. Slowly, predators suck their victims' healthy love and respect until the victim is destroyed. But unlike parasites, these human predators don't do this for survival. They do it for fun and entertainment in order to alleviate their twisted state of living in contempt, envy, and boredom.

You can't change human predators! This is an unconditional declaration of truth. You can't charm them, persuade them with brilliant rhetoric, shame them, guilt them, or threaten them with consequences to stop them from carrying through with their twisted, destructive agendas. Once human predators are on the hunt, no matter what the cause of their predatory behavior, you must treat them the way you would treat a lion on the hunt in Africa.

As a thought experiment, how would you proceed were you to find yourself alone on foot in the African savannah where lions are on the hunt all the time? This alpha predator is, of course, not the only danger you will face out on the savannah, but you certainly don't want to meet a lion face-to-face. What would be the early warning signs you should look for? Of course, you wouldn't know! You have never been taught these lessons. Yet in the pages of this book, you *are* being taught about behaviors that indicate a *human* predator is close by and on the hunt. With this knowledge, will you be fully prepared to deal with these carefully disguised predators? Not really!

You know and I know you also need weapons to fight human predators. Just as with lions on the hunt in the savannah, you need (1) ways to blind predators to your presence, (2) to take evasive action to make sure your paths don't cross, and (3) a high-powered strategy to bring down something as ferocious as a lion once you become the prey animal they decide to attack. Giving you the strategies and tactics to succeed with each of these objectives is exactly what this book must now provide you.

AVOID, AVOID, AVOID!

Let's begin by reminding you that the subtitle of this book is *How to Recognize, Avoid, and Defend Yourself against Liars, Cheaters, Manipulators, and Abusers*, referring, of course, to human predators. Using the red-flag warnings at the end of this book in combination with the in-depth explanations of the nine core personality characteristics of human predators provides you only with the high-powered lenses to see what you could not see before. But avoiding and defending against predatory humans is an art form requiring specific strategies and tactics you don't yet know about. Most important, you must not blind yourself to red-flag warnings when they are right in front of you.

Sometimes, you may not always be able to avoid engaging with human predators. There will be times when you suddenly realize they have you cornered. If you should find yourself facing combat with one, how do you defend yourself? Addressing these issues is the primary purpose of section 4. And the preparatory work to stay off the radar of human predators or to do battle with them begins with making yourself strong.

THIS IS WAR! HOW WILL YOU PREPARE?
Ten Strengths for Combatting Human Predators

Living in the jungle populated with human predators, you must be a special forces–conditioned fighting machine. Why? Because sooner or later you will encounter human predators on the hunt and, eventually, you will see battle. How can you prepare? What conditioning is required to make your body, mind, and spirit a force unafraid and certain of victory against predatory humans?

How you prepare yourself depends on your definition of victory. Most often, victory against human predators must be defined as early identification of and avoiding engagement with them. And the first lesson to learn is how to make yourself as strong as possible on every level. Human predators are put off by prey that is preparing to be strong, coming across as strong, and having real strength. Here's a list of the obvious and not so obvious strengths you must develop.

1. Physical strength
2. Emotional strength
3. Spiritual strength
4. Mental strength
5. Observational strength
6. Relationship network strength
7. Financial strength

8. Skills in your chosen field of endeavor
9. Strength in spotting predators
10. Counterattack strength

Let's look at these personal strengths selectively, focusing on the defensive power each skill set can provide.

1. PHYSICAL STRENGTH

All preparation for either battle or inner peace begins with developing your physical strength through diet, exercise, and proper amounts of sleep. You can read or grow your knowledge about building up your strength through access to many authors, online training instructors, or even membership in a local gym where you can receive training in a broad array of physical fitness programs (including yoga and martial arts training). You must make your own choices about strength building, but every predatory human thinks twice about approaching those who give off signals that they are strong, physically disciplined creatures. Those in such condition have a vibe that says, "I am not to be messed with."

Experts tell us that criminals decide in seven seconds if you will be their next victim. Human predators are just like criminals whose greatest concern is getting hurt or getting caught by choosing the wrong prey animal to pick on. Yes, human predators, for all the reasons identified in section 3 of this book, often miscalculate, but they do calculate.

If your physical appearance makes a statement that you are easy to overpower and control, that's inviting trouble. In fact, simply by modifying your walking behavior will show strength to the world and make you less vulnerable. By taking forceful, dynamic steps you can convey assertiveness and confidence. Holding yourself, especially your spine, erect when talking to people or walking from point A to point B is a repelling signal to most human predators. Chin up, spine straight, and shoulders back are the three most important ways to signal you are strong on every level of your being. If you build your physical strength through an hour of intense physical fitness routines every day, then the mantra of chin up, spine straight, and shoulders back becomes the real you, not an act or a role you are playing.

Your eyes are also a powerful way to communicate strength, and they are definitely part of your physical self. Whether or not this comes naturally to you, make strong eye contact with people all day long. Let them know you see them, feel them, and have registered their existence as part of your surroundings. Yes, you can do this with a smile on your face. Your smile will open doors that otherwise might not open for you, but behind that smile, your eyes have to send a more powerful message to the subconscious mind of human predators—that you are fully alive, strong of character, and a force in this world that sees everything.

Above all, you must develop through physical strength the message that says, "I am calm, cool, and collected." All human predators, from the nasty behaving neighbor next door to the bully at work to the alpha predator seeking to crush your spirit, want to get you in panic mode so all your weaknesses are exposed and on display for them to take advantage of. They are more likely to hesitate just a bit if they see their potential victim presenting calm in the face of their first mock attack. Staying physically fit through constant aerobic and anaerobic exercise causes your brain to give off high levels of endorphins, which keep you in a natural state of calm. If you have low confidence around a predator, do some exercise and notice how your brain chemistry has changed. You'll feel confident and calm from the inside out. Physical fitness may have bigger benefits to your state of mind than your stature. When facing a bully, your calm and relaxed brain will be a buffer against attack. Remember that predators love to trigger your adrenaline to throw you off. A calm body and mind prevent this. Both calm and self-assurance are the ultimate states of readiness for all life's challenges. Working to keep yourself physically fit is step one of basic training for your own inner calm and self-confidence. The second step is emotional focus and developing your sense of self-belonging.

2. EMOTIONAL STRENGTH

Let's not make light of the importance of emotional strength and the often-not-taken road to mastering our emotions. Who you are emotionally is made up of a complex mix of your genetics, your parental influences, your exposure to emotional challenges and overcoming them, and your exposure to emotional trauma.

Earlier in this book, you were informed about the emotional burdens that weigh on those who are hypersensitive. Human predators know some prey animals are easier to pick on emotionally than others, and they quickly assess the hypersensitive among us to isolate for their nefarious purposes. What do they look for? Fear!

RED FLAG #22: Human predators often use guilt trips on their intimate partners to dominate them. The point of laying guilt trips on intimate others is to flood their minds with feelings of taking responsibility for everything that happens in the relationship, which is a form of imprisoning them.

Fear is the one specific emotion all human prey animals work on to prepare themselves to deal with human predators. In all its many guises, fear is the one emotion predatory humans seem able to surface quickly in emotionally weak people. How do you work on eliminating your natural fear response as you make your way through the human jungle? While there are multiple ways to answer this question, the best way to learn constant calm when fear triggers are being pulled (or pushed) is to participate whenever you can in an Outward Bound type of experience.

There is nothing to compare to learning survival skills out in nature under the watchful eye of a highly qualified coach. When you face challenging environments in the wild—ranging from desert climates to high mountains, catching your own food with bare hands, finding water, building shelters, and making your own fire—you will be transformed in many ways. Each time I have done this, I have felt less fear and greater personal worth just knowing I can survive for several weeks in the wilderness with nothing but a knife and a bottle of water.

The day you meet up with a human predator and you feel that first unexpected yank on your survival chain, you have to respond appropriately or suffer the consequences. Reacting with fear sends the wrong signal to predators and will shut off your ability to think clearly.

As this section of the book unfolds with counsel about how to handle various attacks from predatory humans, you will be able to survive only if you can hold in check your natural fear responses. When you do survive the modern peril of an in-your-face encounter with another human's attack on your psyche, you emerge with new confidence. You learn you can maneuver on your own without anyone else intervening on your behalf.

By the way, this guidance is not male or female directed. Unless you are a natural-born alpha female, all women should be wary of the paradigm taught (mostly subliminally) that it's more feminine to depend on male might and manpower to keep you safe from life-threatening situations. By going through an Outward Bound experience, women, just like men, will discover higher levels of functioning in the prefrontal cortex, which mitigates fear-based thinking.

If you've never had the opportunity to develop basic survival skills, it's not too late to pick them up and jump-start your brain's combat neurons later in life. Just remember, when you know on some level that you're capable of surviving under the most fundamental conditions, then your sense of self-worth and confidence are supercharged. By demanding fundamental survival skills in yourself, you are positioned to expand into learning the warrior skills that will be presented later in this section.

A crucial skill you learn in wilderness survival is that in situations where nature throws you a surprise or a shock, first you must pause, breathe deeply, and keep your emotions in check. This is also true of your social interactions with all humans with whom you relate, and it's especially true with human predators.

All your interactions with others hold potential surprises and even potentially shocking responses from them. While you can be as spontaneous as you wish when good news is shared, letting yourself enjoy effusive responses to the joy of others, any negative or shockingly negative responses from others should trigger a perfectly calm *pause*, allowing you to process what you have heard and seen. Allow there to be a satellite delay in your response. There are no rules that say how fast you have to respond to anyone. They go fast, you slow down. Now you are playing by your rules, not theirs. If you practice this *pause* response in all your reactions to surprises, ask thoughtful questions to surface more information, and listen carefully and actively to those serving up negative, shocking news or even threatening news, you can become adept at this supremely important skill.

Many years ago, I was on a wilderness hike before sunup with my sister in Yellowstone National Park when we spotted a grizzly bear walking directly towards us. My sister and I have done many wilderness treks together, and we both immediately paused at the sighting of the bear. She asked calmly, "What do we do now?" Since we were on a designated trail (as was the bear), I invited her to stand with me five yards off the trail, hold hands and raise our arms high above our heads. In my right hand (my free hand), I held a can of powerful bear spray that I knew how to use on bears. Plus, I had used it on a charging grizzly and knew it stopped them in their tracks, completely disabling them. Then I instructed my sister to not make eye contact with the bear and to breathe normally to keep our fear levels low. Grizzlies can sense fear. When the bear came within fifty yards, he stopped and stood on his hind legs showing his full height of at least seven feet (the bear in that moment seemed ten feet tall). He sniffed while turning his head back and forth, then dropped to his left, and did a hard turn, galloping at full speed into a stand of trees a few yards away. We immediately turned to our left and bushwhacked our way down to the Yellowstone River, making our scent a little harder for the bear to track and our exit to the river and back across swift in case the bear decided to stalk us.

On returning to our campground and safely back where others in our group were just waking up, we laughed until we cried. By pausing, staying calm, and not confronting the bear or showing any fear, we escaped a disastrous early-morning trek and confrontation with an alpha, four-legged predator. You will soon discover this same protocol is what you have to follow when face-to-face with human predators, too.

3. SPIRITUAL STRENGTH

This is not a self-help book; it is a self-defense book. So here I will severely limit my comments, as building your spiritual strength is a deeply personal process. As I assume you are a person with empathy and compassion, you must also be capable of creating warm, loving attachments to others. Good for you, but bad for you if you encounter a human predator. Human predators do not have this capacity at all. They feel nothing, or nearly nothing, most of the time. Remember, they were either born without this capacity, or this capacity has been shut down due to their addictions or the traumas they have suffered.

If you have a spiritual belief system, then dive into your spiritual space as deeply as you can and grow your spiritual living space as you may need to retreat there for perspective when under attack by a human predator. One of my favorite lines from William Shakespeare is, "Hell is empty, and all the devils are here." A few encounters with human predators will make you believe the truth in this prose. If you do not have a spiritual belief system, you can grow your spiritual strength by surrounding yourself with three types of people—the inspired, the excited, and the grateful. Then when you encounter the dark and threatening specter of a human predator in your life, your relief from dealing with this devil will come from spending time with the people you love being with.

My favorite way to look at human predators is as black holes, very much like those in the cosmos. These people suck all the light within their event horizon into themselves, never to be seen again. People like you are the light, and you are what makes our little corner of the cosmos beautiful and meaningful. These metaphors of light and darkness are as close to spiritual expressions that I can give you without stepping on toes. And that is as close to a discussion of spirituality as I honestly need to have with you. Please continue being the light to your corner of the universe and make your light as bright as you can during your time on planet Earth. Stay away from the black holes of this life with all your might because you know without exception exactly what those black holes will do to you.

4. MENTAL STRENGTH

In the world-renowned book, *The Art of War* by Sun Tzu, written sometime around 500 BCE, the reader is counseled to "never be where your enemy expects you to be." This is also my prime directive for avoiding human predators. Sun Tzu's teachings have been carefully followed by some of the greatest military generals who ever lived. When it comes to your life, you are the military general, and you are also the highest-ranking soldier in your own army. Yet this advice prompts the question, "What does it mean to never be where your enemy expects you to be?" One answer, of course, is you do not have to fight with every human predator who crosses your path. Combat should always be a last resort.

What you must do when facing down an enemy playing war on a level you may never have imagined before reading this book is allow every attack and every intended blow from human predators to hit nothing but thin air when they strike out at you. Here you will discover how to move artfully out of the way of those strikes.

Problematically, however, you will not do this skillfully unless you grow your mind's powers to see the blows coming long in advance. And you can only grow your knowledge and skills for dodging these blows by embracing the reality that human predators are out there, always seeking combat and domination on some level.

Unlike your mind, which releases the five good brain chemicals when stimulated by love, kindness, service to others, joy, awe, and astonishment, **human predators release feel-good brain chemicals only when anticipating the approaching battles they wish to fight and win and by landing their blows intended to bring you down**. Once you fully grasp this truth, you are ready to start practicing the art of war against those who are determined to crush you like a cockroach under their powerful, well-shod shoes.

When you see the blows coming from a human predator, you can never be successful by reacting with rash, knee-jerk emotional responses or poorly thought-out counterattacks. Instead, you must mentally step aside to make the blows miss. Or better yet, you must simply vanish from the sight of predators just as they commit to their attack. All this must be accomplished using your intellect, not your emotions. Doing this can be especially challenging when the predatory human you are up against is extremely charming or persuasive, strokes your ego, or has power over you in some way. So how do you practice and prepare for this?

The short answer is you must use your mind and intellect to avoid the predators when you see them, you must never panic and give them a hot reaction when they are attacking, and you must disentangle yourself from them with cunning and deception of your own if they get their claws into you.

Imagine how insane it would have been for my sister and me to have attempted angering the bear we met on our early-morning hike in Yellowstone National Park. Humans in their right mind don't do things like that.

The greatest exercise for your mind is to engage in critical thinking about every thought and experience coming your way. How do you do that?

Socrates once said, "The only true wisdom is in knowing you know nothing." Think for a moment about any firm idea or belief you held fast to as a small child. Then consider how your thinking has changed from those early days in your life because you have learned so much since then. Now imagine how much you will learn over the next ten or twenty years. We humans are naturally curious beings, and our curiosity prompts us daily to learn something new in order, at the very least, to keep surviving in a rapidly changing world. Yet so many of us turn off our curiosity in adulthood and cling everlastingly to ideas that we believe give us certainty. As pointed out in section 2, the need for certainty is universal, but the grasps we make for absolute certainty are nearly always delusional.

Another way to say this is that every person has a map of the world in his or her head. We imagine it's an accurate map, but it is always wrong because we only have tiny pieces of the truth out there. We feel better if we convince ourselves we have an accurate map of the world, but in truth our personal map is based on partial information, wrong information, and broad (sometimes false) assumptions. Critical thinking is all about accepting that your map of the world always needs updating because it's always incomplete. Staying open to new information that may change your map is the first lesson of survival in a complex world. Old maps get you lost or injured. Always be revising your map!

By humbly embracing what knowledge you presently have as only what you have learned so far on life's journey, the call to remain curious and constantly learning is easier to embrace. I believe this is what Socrates was imploring us all to do. Always remain openly curious. Openly curious people are the only ones who go looking for new ideas and new ways of managing life's challenges, which also happens to be step one in the critical thinking process.

Step two in the critical thinking process is to question everything. Please, don't ever accept anything at face value or just because some so-called authority claims something as true. If you are intellectually curious, dig deep into any topic that may have an impact on your ability to navigate this life. Become your own expert on these topics. Even when you read voraciously and become extremely well-informed on a topic, any conclusions you draw from your personal investigations serve you best by seeing those conclusions as temporary. Remain curious to new information and new data at all times because so much of what humans used to know with absolute certainty is simply no longer so.

The third pillar of critical thinking is adaptability. To make your way in this world successfully, you must adjust and change with your environments. Our bodies evolve and adjust, and our perspectives and the way we do things have to, as well. If you don't shift and adjust as needed, life can become super difficult and extremely hard to manage. Take global warming, for example.

Scientists have been urging us to think globally for decades about how the byproducts of fossil fuels and toxic chemicals used in various ways by humans are harming the environment. With few exceptions, however, humanity has ignored these warnings and pleas. Now the Earth's atmosphere is heating rapidly from carbon dioxide emissions from burning fossil fuels, and methane gas is being released by tundra thawing in the far northern latitudes. This is a prescription for disaster. And it's all the result of human failure to adapt and adjust to changing conditions. Now (because we didn't adapt and adjust when we had time to do so) we face an existential threat from rapidly growing forest fires in the summer months and warming oceans making hurricanes and tornados more frequent and more powerful. Potable water and tillable soil for growing crops are becoming scarce, and food shortages around the world have the potential to cause great suffering.

RED FLAG #30: Human predators always say no to invitations you extend to them that are important to you but from their point of view not useful to them and their highly focused agenda.

Critical thinkers also have self-control. The critical thinker practices the *pause* before every response and action taken to current events and emotional triggers. Here's a fun test to see how good you are at self-control. Imagine I offered to write you a check for one hundred thousand dollars today or to give you one penny today and double it every day for thirty days. Which would you choose? Critical thinkers always choose the second option. But why? Because they are the ones who practice the *pause* and do the math before answering.

The final element critical thinkers display is keeping everything in perspective. This means you must know your own long-term goals and objectives and measure every move you make against those goals and objectives. When my sister and I confronted that grizzly bear, our overarching long-term goal was simply to survive. Yet in that moment, the conditions for our long-term survival had dramatically changed. Face-to-face with a new (and surprising) threat to our long-term goal, we needed to keep cool heads and follow every caution we had ever been taught about what to do to defend ourselves. Reacting emotionally would have gotten us killed by that bear. If we had turned and run, the bear would have seen our running as a prey signal and chased and killed us. The same is true with human predators. In the pages ahead, you will be given ample guidance on what to do when you encounter human predators. The unanswered question is, "Will you remain calm and follow that guidance?" Only time will tell.

5. OBSERVATIONAL STRENGTH

The counsel to become a better observer must be the one strength-building recommendation you embrace with your whole heart and mind. There are more than five dozen red-flag warnings at the end of this book about how to spot a human predator early. Be familiar with them and dedicate a part of your mind to serving as your lookout for behaviors that make you extremely uncomfortable as you navigate the human jungle. If it helps, think of this as your GPS system for avoiding assholes! Like Siri, you will hear instructions, "On your left up ahead is a gas station and a Starbucks. On your right is a malignant asshole! Turn left to avoid the asshole!"

In the military, this lookout ability is taught as situational awareness, and it simply means knowing at all times what is going on around us. It is the ability to draw a kind of mental map to help us understand where we are, what surrounds us, and the challenges that lie ahead. Those who develop their situational awareness are better able to see what is really happening and then develop better, more effective coping plans. It does not mean walking through life as if the ground beneath you is covered with freshly laid eggs. It does mean, however, that in addition to being yourself, your very best, most fun-loving, kind, and generous self, you know that some people you meet may be looking at you in a predatory way.

Yesterday afternoon, while working on this book, a knock came at our back door. The knocking proved to be from a man who is right now building a home on a 7.5-acre development our family owns and has subdivided over the last six years. We own the house and pool adjacent to his construction site and use it as our guest house. His foundations are now poured, but his new home has a long way to go, and it is already late August. Builders up here in the mountains try to time their work so new homes are framed in and can at least be covered in plastic during the winter months, thus allowing subcontractors to work inside all winter long on plumbing, pulling electrical wire, and so on. This particular new owner probably won't get his home framed in before winter snow begins falling. But right now, he has another problem. He needs water the city planners won't give him for another lot he owns in the development. The man came by yesterday to request permission to tap into our well water (we own and use the only well on that 7.5 acres) until the city grants him permission to use city water.

While listening and interacting with the man, I became aware that he is a human predator. He was extremely vague about how long he needed our well water. He talked only about himself and all the money he has made in real estate over the years. He complained about being a victim of rapid turnover at the city planning department. And not once did he mention he was willing to pay for using our well water. Even though we stood outside and talked, he invited himself into our house when he clearly saw I wasn't going to invite him in. In doing this, he was pushing boundaries, testing me to see what he could get away with. His entire appeal was wrapped in charm, self-assuredness, and boasting about his many real estate conquests. I played along, observing every move he made, and promised him I would share his request with family members that very evening.

We have only one family member who is a real estate expert, and I warned him immediately about the predatory signs I saw in this man. "Watch out for this one," I counseled. "He is a seasoned human predator who is only out for himself. Don't give the man an inch, or he will take a mile."

The need to be on the lookout for signs someone may be a human predator is second-nature to me now, and the energy required never interferes with my living with joy, humor, kindness, and goodwill towards others. For me, the challenge is no different from walking along a beautiful ocean beach and enjoying fully the wonders, mystery, and beauty of the experience while keeping an eye open for ocean life washed ashore or seashells in the sand, both of which might be a danger to my bare feet.

6. RELATIONSHIP NETWORK STRENGTH

In *The Art of War*, Sun Tzu offers his students seven questions to ask (and answer) before ever adventuring into battle. Two of those questions are "Which army is stronger?" and "In which army is there the greater constancy both in reward and punishment?" You must never take on a human predator in conflict without answering these two questions. The question to entertain first, however, is this one—"Do you have an army, and if not, why not?"

In all life, there are battles to be fought, and no one is exempt from this truth. Our society says it embraces rugged individualism as a highly valued quality, and indeed, there are times when this trait will serve you well. One of those times is when you are on the run from an enemy that is bigger and stronger than you. But rugged individualism is a terrible liability when you are in direct conflict with a human predator. Such times demand you stand against the predator with vastly superior forces of men and women who are highly motivated by a common bond and shared values. Otherwise, you will go down in defeat.

Growing up, I was enthralled by the television series created by Walt Disney regarding the life of Davy Crockett. While it aired way back in 1954 and 1955, today I can still recall the melody and the words of that show's theme song. The opening lines were:

Born on a mountaintop in Tennessee,
Greenest state in the land of the free,
Raised in the woods so he knew ev'ry tree,
Kilt him a b'ar when he was only three,
Davy, Davy Crockett, king of the wild frontier!

Of course, the series ended when Davy Crockett and all the other rugged individualists at the Alamo were slaughtered by the Mexican Army while they were fighting for Texas to become a territory of the United States (at that time it was known as Tejas because the entire territory was ruled by Mexico). Outnumbered by an estimated fifteen Mexican soldiers to every single fighter defending the Alamo, Santa Anna's men brutally destroyed the Alamo's ragtag, very brave, little army.

Until that episode of Disney's series on Crockett, I was enthralled by everything about "the king of the wild frontier," and I wanted to be just like him. But when these one hundred great frontiersmen went to war with an army outnumbering them fifteen to one, I lost all respect for them. Even at age twelve, I knew they were simply a bunch of dumb asses.

War is never fought with the intent of losing. Instead, war is fought to win, to be victorious, never to become a martyr. And even when you go to war, deception, as Sun Tzu teaches, is your greatest advantage. Yet at the Alamo, not a single man who died fighting Santa Anna and his vastly superior army seemed to understand this. Yes, as martyrs they inspired huge numbers of Americans to join together and defeat Santa Anna, but the men and women who made that happen understood fully that wars are fought to be won.

So answer this question: "Who stands with you and is ready, able, and willing to fight by your side when you have to do battle with human predators?" In case you are thinking you are going to be the first human to traverse the journey from birth to death without ever facing battle, it's time to disabuse yourself of this fantasy. The most peace-loving human to pass along this mortal highway couldn't escape making enemies intent on killing him, and neither will you. Remember, you may never do a thing to anyone that should result in an attack on your life or on your psyche, but with human predators always on the hunt and seeking to dominate human prey, you can be sure you will become their target sooner or later. Then you will know exactly who and how many are truly committed to you as members of your tribe, willing to stand by you and fight.

This is definitely not the place to teach you the basics of bringing good and strong people close, how to bond with them, and how to cultivate such people into symbiotic, mutually rewarding, enriching relationships. You can read many books on this topic. It doesn't matter what you call these people—friends, colleagues, partners, your network, or members of your thrive team—any of these names will work. The most important element in these relationships is the strong bond nurtured with consistency, resulting in mutual commitment to one another.

In every fundraising campaign I managed, my first responsibility as manager was to identify for my nonprofit clients those leaders in their community who absolutely had to be involved to assure campaign success. In every town, city, or metropolitan center, there are those who have done so many favors for other people on their way to achieving success that they created a gigantic favor bank they can call on at any time they need help. Every one of these men and women started out in business knowing how critical it would be to call in one or more of the favors they had done for others along the road to building their success.

RED FLAG #63: Human predators love using a tactic known as "The Switcheroo." After they have expressed a strong opinion, they then drop it and adopt the opposite point of view when it's convenient or to embarrass you.

They never set out *only* to be a success in their chosen field of endeavor; they also set out to be of value to other people. Making yourself valuable to others requires getting to know them and what their needs are and then finding a way to help meet those needs. This absolutely must be a daily exercise you create by setting aside a portion of each twenty-four hours as a disciplined routine. The ultimate question you must answer for your own life is, "Am I willing to do that?"

7. FINANCIAL STRENGTH

Many human predators seek out as prey animals for their twisted purposes only those who are financially lost. Other human predators seek only the financially strong as prey animals. So I have to ask, "Which one would you rather be if under attack from one of these beasts of the human jungle? Wealthy or poor?"

If you answered, "wealthy," how do you plan to come by your riches? Wouldn't it be great to find a magic bottle with a genie inside who could grant you three wishes? What would you wish for after releasing the genie from that bottle? Let me guess. Your first wish would be for ten million dollars, right? You might even want more! It's OK to admit you could use a lot more money to make you feel safer and more secure in this rapidly changing world. How much would be enough to give you the feeling of safety and security? More than ten million dollars or less than that? Your answer may be tied to your age. And certainly, your answer will be influenced by your material desires.

Long ago I discovered that genies in bottles are no more real than the tooth fairy, and financial safety and security are defined by every person in a different way. What's crazy, however, is in a nation where free enterprise is the cornerstone of the economy, only a small minority of high schools or colleges offer a course on personal wealth development. This exclusion results in sending young adults into the working world after graduation as prey animals in the same way failing to teach the English language would make young adults prey animals.

How prepared are you to manage your financial life in a way that allows you to thrive in today's financial world? What do you know about personal wealth building and personal financial management? Are you up to speed on how to invest money in a complex financial marketplace, perhaps the most complex financial marketplace the world has ever known? If you answered yes, where did you receive your knowledge and training? Here's betting it wasn't in anyone's college classroom. Once again, the betting is you were never offered or never took a single course on these topics in your life.

Admittedly, financial knowledge doesn't by itself translate into becoming wealthy. Yet financial knowledge is where becoming wealthy begins, and after that comes a great deal of hard work and discipline. This book's pages are not an appropriate place to teach you the principles of wealth building, but wealth-building practices will lead you to being financially strong so that every encounter with a human predator doesn't represent a financial threat you can't handle. I have been poor, and I have enjoyed enormous wealth, and being wealthy has always proven preferrable every time a predator threatened me. Let me give you two examples:

My Encounter with Dr. Heartless. Even though I had three months remaining on my contract that had to be paid by the Heart Institute, I also had six months of living expenses saved in the bank when Dr. Heartless decided to terminate my services without cause. This meant I could go nine months without securing another client and still pay all my bills. Without that cushion, life could have felt seriously out of control.

My Encounter with the High-Conflict Board Member. The advisory role I currently occupy with a nonprofit in Southern California would be intolerable were I not independently wealthy and able to walk away from the organization. The high-conflict predator on the nonprofit's board is not going away, but because my services are not a source of income for me, I have been able to withdraw from the nonprofit, leaving the board to make a hard decision about who they wish to guide them going forward, me or the howling, rage-addicted lady who refuses to back away from her campaign to oust the CEO who has served faithfully for nineteen years.

Volunteering my services as a fundraising consultant has been possible since the year 2000 due to my wealth independence. Being able to pick and choose my charitable clients has been a dream come true for me and allows me to fulfill my desire to serve others on my terms. If I discover I'll be dealing with a human predator who is allowed to eclipse the guidance I bring to the organization, then quietly resigning is an easy option for me. But now our economy is plagued with high inflation, and even I experience this new financial pressure. Inflation threatens everyone's finances, forcing those who thought they might just plateau and coast financially through life to rethink that strategy.

Now, even to stand still in your financial life, you must become a constant student of your financial environment and the world of investing. How will you do that? Where will you learn all you must know to survive and thrive financially over the course of your life? More importantly, how disciplined will you be when it comes to daily management of your financial life? Without the rigorous commitment to living within your means, sacrifice and hard work, constant reading, and study of financial survival and successful investing, you will fall behind financially every day you live.

8. SKILLS IN YOUR CHOSEN FIELD OF ENDEAVOR

Here's a riddle for you. Can you distill from the following parable the key message its authors were attempting to convey?

A turkey was talking to a bull. "I would love to get to the top of that tree," sighed the turkey, "but I haven't got the energy."

"Well, why don't you nibble on my droppings?" replied the bull. "They're packed with nutrients."

The turkey pecked at a lump of dung and found that it gave him enough energy and strength to reach the lowest branches of the tree. The next day, after eating some more dung, he reached some branches a little higher.

Finally, after the fourth night, the turkey proudly reached the very top of the tree. And there he sat for three days.

On the fourth morning of his ascent, he was spotted by a farmer who shot the turkey out of the tree and took him home for dinner.

The moral of this tale is that bullshit may help you get to the top, but it won't keep you there. The turkey got to the top of the tree and then rested on his laurels where he became a sitting target for a human predator with more skills (the farmer with his ability to shoot straight).

Another lesson you can take away from this story is that the purpose of life isn't simply to pour all your energy into a narrowly defined moment of victory and then declare you are the winner. Living for the rewards of a single moment is not living at all. What is living really about?

While the answer you read here is meaningless to human predators, if *you* can embrace this truth, it may change your perspective in profound ways. The purpose of a life well lived is to acquire as many skills as possible in your chosen field of endeavor and then employ those skills to serve others. When you are highly skilled in disciplines you are passionate about and use those skills in service to others, you experience rewarding moments every day of your life. Once again, these discussions would be viewed by human predators as complete insanity. Why? Because they can't imagine serving others for the simple joy of lifting up those who need them. The only question their minds can ever entertain is, "Why help others when they are not ME?"

Furthermore, when you use your skills to make yourself useful and valuable to others, the favor-bank-account concept discussed above becomes a storehouse of value for those times when you need to draw on the help of others to fight by your side when battling human predators. But most important is knowing that with your highly honed skills you are always of great value in your field, even if your current employer proves to be predatory and intolerable.

The turkey in the story above never really learned to fly, did he? The symbolic implication of the turkey's limited success is that advancing his skills by learning to fly could have allowed the turkey to take himself out of harm's way when the farmer came along with his rifle. On your own life's journey, you are going to encounter people hunting you too. Only by constantly acquiring more skills in your chosen field of endeavor will you continue to make yourself valuable to others. If in your working life you have a head-on collision with a human predator as an employer, the only insurance against that predator's abuse is knowing your present set of marketable skills makes you supremely attractive to other employers, those who are not human predators.

9. STRENGTH IN SPOTTING PREDATORS

Until reading this book, the concept of human predators stalking and attacking other humans consistently and without conscience may have been on your radar but likely restricted only to those who commit heinous criminal acts. Because of events during the last twenty-plus years (starting with the 9/11 attacks on the Twin Towers in New York City), you've at least become aware that terrorists are real. Having read this far, of course, you also know that taking lives and taking treasure from other humans are only the two biggest blips on your radar screen as you scan for human predators. What about all those little blips on that screen?

Those smaller blips represent the human predators who may be seeking to use your body for their twisted purposes, to yank you around emotionally, or to become your dominator while taking away your sense of identity and self-belonging. Now, hopefully, you also know about your vulnerabilities to human predators from reading section 2, at least the vulnerabilities you share with every other human. Of course, your idiosyncratic vulnerabilities to human predators will require constant personal assessments and development of greater protections to lower your prey profile and signaling. This is one of the reasons section 4 was written. These ten personal strengthening areas of emphasis will help you become less visible to human predators, assuming you practice them with discipline.

Without doubt, the sixty-five red-flag warnings at the end of this book will also become part of your new defense against ending up in the clutches of people with predatory intentions, but will you memorize all of them in a nice tidy compartment in your brain for instant recall? Very few have that capacity. For this reason, below are five early-warning signs you can easily remember, or even write out on a three-by-five-inch index card and carry with you for quick and ready reference. If any of these five red flags is triggered within you or within your consciousness by someone in your family or your circle of friends or among your colleagues at work or any professionals you have contact with, then return to this book for guidance on what to do next.

1. You always have negative feelings about them.
2. They leave you with negative feelings about yourself or situations.
3. They cause you to say or do things you regret.
4. You are never on the same page and always have conflicting opinions and preferences.
5. They cause more chaos and confusion than order and peace.

Remember, there is no low in behavioral abuses that human predators won't engage in, so the earlier you spot them, the better. Personal slights, verbal offenses, blame for problems you didn't create, guilt trips, twisted dramas that force you to play an unwanted role, nasty psychological games, and direct attacks on your psyche, your reputation, or your person are just a few of the hostile behaviors you can expect from predatory humans. Some human predators will do *all* these things, and some can do them with such subtlety you may not notice until they have you fully defeated. But if you pick up on what they are doing through observation of your own feelings, at least you can pause and come back to this book and check out your suspicions. When you find that being with a particular person makes drudgery of every step you take, it is definitely time to review the lessons in this book and make a plan to remove this person from your life (legally and morally, of course).

If you are going to live happily in this world, you are going to have to become attuned to your gut and identify quickly if someone is abusing you. And then you have to put as much distance between you and your abuser as you possibly can, and you must do this quickly and quietly.

Until you develop the sensitivity required to instantly spot a predatory human, the five points above will serve as corrective lenses when you think your vision may be clouded. Even when in doubt about whether you are being stalked through seeing early warning signs of human predation, simply use the five-point test as a way to check in with yourself and confirm what your gut may be telling you.

You might well ask, "But what if an abuser has something I really want, something I really need?"

If this is true (as you perceive it to be true), then the predatory perpetrator already knows this. This is how that person hooked you, and this is how he or she will keep you hooked. Trust this statement—**your human predator will destroy you before ever giving you what you think he or she has that you can't live without.**

Finally, allow me to remind you that once human predators lock onto you as potential prey, they will always follow through with an attack, even if the first attack is a mock attack to see how you react. They will lie, cheat, bend and break laws or rules of social intercourse, and flout all rules of civility and decency to get what they want from you. They have no empathy or compassion. No conscience or moral compass either. If charm

> **RED FLAG #60:** Human predators will attempt to make you feel guilty for their emotions (especially their displays of anger), accusing your behavior as the reason they became emotionally upset.

doesn't work (and they are often supremely good at charming others), they will use threats of bodily harm, emotional harm, reputational harm, or a combination of those three to get what they want.

Here's a little poem to remind you of the danger these people represent to you:

Of abusers and human predators beware.
They will make of your life
A living nightmare.
You they will annoy.
You they will mistreat.
On you they will gladly wipe their dirty feet.
They never will change.
They have ice in their veins.
So escape from their grasp
By plane, car, or train
Before they can make a big mess of your brain!

10. COUNTERATTACK STRENGTH

The remainder of the material in this section of the book is devoted to teaching you how to counter predatory attacks. You are urged to read and reread the following material until it becomes a part of who you are. Even then, if you are in doubt about how to conduct yourself once you spot a predator on the hunt, come back to these pages and take another deep dive into this material.

There are only three major strategies to counter anyone who has decided you are a prey animal with something he or she wants or a prey animal who stands between your predator and something he or she wants. Those three strategies are:

1. Distance yourself from the predator as quickly and as quietly as possible.
2. Give the predator every reason to believe you don't have what he or she wants as you make your plan for escape.
3. Go to war with the predator.

Each of these three strategies will be presented in as much detail as possible in the following pages. It takes discipline, detachment, cunning, stealth, and determination to survive when dealing with human predators. If you follow the guidance given here to avoid them and learn how to break away from them once they get their claws into you, you will survive and live to fight another day for the good and positive goals of your life.

If you are a person with an open, trusting heart, you may find some of the counsel in this section hard to follow. Yet because you have an open heart, you are extremely vulnerable to the predations of those who have no conscience and therefore no moral compass. Expecting others to be like you and to always urge you to be your best self simply isn't a realistic expectation in a world where human predators are wanting to break your heart. This is the time to grasp fully that your first commitment to anyone on this planet must be to take good care of yourself.

When your compassionate discernment tells you someone may be stalking you, exercise that wonderful compassion you have on yourself first. Recognize that some of the work involved in shedding a human predator may be painful, but for your own sanity, you must listen to yourself and remain true to yourself first and foremost every day you are alive.

Chances are if you are now in the clutches of a human predator, you are already in pain, and that pain must be fully acknowledged and discharged before you can be your best and most caring and loving self. The story of your life is written every day you live by the choices you make. Defeating the dragons as they emerge in your storyline must be done by a hero, and that hero is you. Even if you are surrounded by an army of people devoted to helping you defeat the fire-breathing dragons and tempting snakes of this world, you must see yourself as the vanquishing conqueror. Yes, you will feel fear at times, but by using your mind—your intellect as your superpower, as your bear spray—you will survive and go on to thrive. That's why you have an intellect. It has evolved over hundreds of thousands of years to keep your reptilian brain under control. So use it!

Yes, you are entitled to feel your anger and all your emotions when under attack, but your emotions must not be allowed to interrupt your reasoning. When you use the strategies and tactics you will learn about in the remainder of this book while keeping yourself in a state of dispassionate calm, you will not lose your caring, compassionate nature and turn into a predator yourself. While there is always the temptation within each of us to become our worst selves when under attack, you must not give into that temptation. In fact, letting the lesser angels of your human nature take over your life is exactly what human predators want from you.

Practicing the pause, remaining calm, and following the guidelines of this book will keep you from feeding the regions of your brain designed to act with rage and negativity towards your attacker. If you've stayed with me this far, I know you have what it takes to do this. Allow me to leave you with a short parable, the one I read aloud to myself each time

I find someone trying to get a predatory nose under my tent and stir me to anger and indignation.

One evening, an elderly Cherokee grandmother told her grandchildren about a battle that goes on inside people. She said, "My children, the battle is between two wolves inside us all. One is evil. It is anger, envy, jealousy, sorrow, regret, greed, arrogance, self-pity, guilt, resentment, inferiority, lies, false pride, superiority, and ego. The other is good. It is joy, peace, love, hope, serenity, humility, kindness, benevolence, empathy, generosity, truth, compassion, and faith."

The children thought about it for a while, and then one spoke up and asked, "Grandmother, which wolf wins?"

The old Cherokee simply replied, "The one that you feed."

Every decision you make in your counterattacks to human predators should be examined through the lens of this parable. End of lesson.

ALL THE USUAL SUSPECTS
Predator Attacks and Smart Countermoves

*If you get that gut feeling
that something isn't right about a person,
TRUST IT!*

*You must find the courage to leave the table
if respect is no longer being served.*

Not every attack by human predators is an act of naked aggression. There is a cluster of hostile approaches coated in sugar that most are blind to, at least initially. These sugar-coated approaches are meant to distract their prey from seeing the real agenda(s) of the would-be attacker. Included in this cluster and described below are the following,

which we'll examine at length and for which we provide defensive countermoves for you to employ:

- Grooming
- Love bombing
- Hovering
- Ego stroking
- The honey-pot trap
- Breadcrumbing
- The victim ploy
- Imposter scams
- When predators insult you
- High-conflict predation
- Energy draining
- Sociopathic behavior
- Gaslighting
- Narcissism
- Covert narcissism
- Pathological lying

GROOMING

Grooming is when someone builds a relationship of trust and emotional connection with another person, including a child, in order to
manipulate, exploit, and abuse that person. Grooming behaviors cause
someone to be drawn to that person. When a man does this to a woman,
it is referred to as ***pimping tenderness*** or ***love bombing.*** When it is done
online with children who have few defenses, including no knowledge of
human predation, it is immoral and illegal. Adult-to-adult grooming will
be covered under the discussion of love bombing. In "Grooming," we
focus on predatory grooming of children (which is a particularly despicable type of human predation since it exploits the most innocent and

defenseless in society). Here are seven signs to watch for to see if your child is being groomed. These are not included among the red-flag warnings found at the end of this book as they only apply to parents trying to protect their children from sexual predators.

1. When any adult goes out of his or her way to shower your child with attention, including giving special gifts, that's a red-flag moment.

2. Any attempts by an adult to build a best-friend bond with your child around shared likes and suggesting they share activities around those interests is a red flag. For example, beware if an adult says to your child, "I love that band, too. We should go to one of its concerts together."

3. Typically, the groomer of a child will also groom the parents by becoming extremely helpful to the family. Offering to give your children rides to school, helping with repairs around your home, and providing emotional and financial support are just some of the ways a groomer seeks to become best friends with the entire family.

4. Groomers are constantly seeking opportunities to be alone with your child. Offers to babysit, inviting your child over to play video games, driving the child to meet up with his or her friends are all red flags to watch for.

5. Groomers also use a backdoor approach to stay in touch with your child, sending him or her texts and emails on a regular basis.

6. An adult who frequently touches or hugs your child in front of you is waving a big red flag.

7. An adult asking your child to keep secrets that exclude you as parents is a huge red flag. Usually, groomers begin with harmless secrets in an attempt to create a pattern for having bigger secrets later.

DEFENSIVE COUNTERMOVES

1. Make yourself aware of the signs of grooming.

2. Teach your children about body safety before they are five.

3. Teach your children to report any gifts or treats they receive from teachers, coaches, family members, people at church, and even from their friends' parents.

4. Teach them it is never okay for anyone to show them pornography or tell them dirty jokes.

RED FLAG #64: Because they get bored easily, human predators need constant high-risk stimulation, which causes them to act impulsively and take personal risks that often place them in danger. These behaviors often make them unable to fulfill responsibilities related to family, work, and school.

5. Help your children feel safe with telling you their concerns or asking you questions about anything without fear of being minimized or getting in trouble.

6. If your child comes to you and has a tough time telling you what happened . . . take the HINT! Help them through it with love and encouragement, and don't freak out.

7. Teach your children to report to you anytime they have been alone with an adult that you haven't previously okayed. This counsel also covers extended family members.

8. Children who are educated repeatedly about grooming and sexual predators are also children empowered with the information needed to protect themselves.

LOVE BOMBING

Love bombing happens in romantic relationships when a targeted individual is subjected to excessive displays of affection and grand gestures, which are supposed to convey interest in, appreciation of, and gratitude for the prey target. In most cases, the initial stages of love bombing can be flattering to the receiver, making him or her feel special and even cherished. What could possibly be wrong with being showered with tokens of love and expressions of affection? Love bombing is so in step with our cultural notions of romantic love that it blinds the targeted receiver until the love bomber begins to participate in mental manipulation and attempted monopolization of the target's time and energy. Unlike genuine displays of affection, love bombing occurs purely for the purpose of distracting the target from the predator's character flaws and twisted agendas. The dark, insidious nature behind the love bomber's sweet actions will ultimately reveal itself as time passes.

DEFENSIVE COUNTERMOVES

1. In the beginning stages of a romantic relationship, don't be afraid to slow things down if you feel things are moving too fast.

2. Setting boundaries clearly with your new romantic interest and spending time alone or with other important family members and friends will allow you to remain in touch with your own feelings and to receive clarifying thoughts about your new romance from important affinity groups. Also, if your love bomber has a temper tantrum when you take time for yourself or time to be with other support members of your family and extended family, break off the relationship or at least take a timeout from the relationship. These tactics will give you the pause you require to gain full situational awareness of your romance so you can decide with clear-headedness if you want to permanently break away from the relationship or explore it further.

3. Grow your knowledge of how human predators use manipulation of weaknesses in others to abuse them. Definitely take a timeout before advancing a romantic relationship you may suspect either is moving too fast or is a roller coaster ride emotionally from highs of dramatic, extravagant displays of warmth and affection to lows of loss of temper to punish you when your new romantic interest doesn't get his or her way.

HOVERING

Hovering is a predatory tactic of always showing up in the same places that a love-bombing target shows up, even if the predator has not been invited. Sometimes human predators show themselves openly at the location where their target happens to be, but frequently they don't. Sometimes they will simply remain in their car nearby like they are piloting a helicopter, keeping an eye on their target from above while unobserved by the target. Hovering a target is not to be confused with hoovering, which is basically a way of sucking a person back into an abusive relationship.

DEFENSIVE COUNTERMOVES

1. We all have borders or boundaries we want respected, but those who are predatory either in a romantic relationship or in a friendship like to constantly push the personal boundaries of others. They do this by hovering just below your boundaries or borders and periodically testing them by doing little things you may label as small infringements of that boarder. Your best defense is situational awareness. Make a list of people who are constantly testing your personal boundaries, especially those who do this in ways you label "little" tests. These are almost certainly the same people who will cartwheel or tap dance all over your boundaries one day soon.

2. Once a personal boundary has been fully violated by anyone, watch for how that person handles your confrontation with him or her. If the boundary violator fails to humbly apologize for the discretion, even reminding you of all his or her good qualities, that person is definitely a human predator and someone to never trust again.

3. Some hovering predators are passive aggressive. Such people appear to respect your boundaries but call themselves *rebels* or claim they are *outspoken people* and, in doing so, declare their intent to violate anyone's boundaries and anyone who appears to be telling them what to do. Predators who declare themselves rebels or outspoken are saying they have special rights and privileges to violate your boundaries, and you are expected to comply and give them special latitude and grace for their rebellious or offensive behavior. Cut these people out of your life as fast as you can. Otherwise, they will violate your boundaries constantly and expect you to always forgive them because they are who they are!

4. Having boundaries is knowing yourself and reserving for yourself your own limits. You want to spend time only with people who respect your limits as you respect yourself. Occasionally someone you love very much, perhaps a mother or a father, will be a hoverer who always tests your boundaries or crosses them on occasion. For these people, simply limit the time you spend with them and don't expect them to have changed when you do spend time with them. If you truly love someone but set your expectations low for their respect of your boundaries, the pain of their offenses is less because you have control over how much time you give them.

5. In the event you have an ex-lover or ex-spouse who broke off your relationship (or you broke off the relationship because of boundary issues), be on the lookout for hoovering attempts to woo you back with big promises and grand gestures. These first moves are

typically aimed at your weak spots, but after you reconnect with these predators, they almost always gradually ease right back to whatever they were doing that caused the original issues, even if they had sworn to change.

EGO STROKING

For many people, their ego is who they are. It is the most personal, most self-oriented part of their mind. And this makes them extremely vulnerable to a predator's ego-stroking advances. When human predators truly want something, they can be full of ego compliments, but as you've learned already, not one word that comes out of their mouths is genuine. Predators' use of compliments is one way they endear themselves to a target so they can get close to their potential prey. If your ego is hurting, this approach can be especially effective. For those who have been through the ringer in life (meaning they have been abused, traumatized, neglected, or heavily criticized by others), it's easy to see how this tactic works on them.

DEFENSIVE COUNTERMOVES

1. Understanding you can be easily manipulated by predatory humans with ego-stroking compliments is your first line of defense against entrapment and abuse. It's perfectly fine to be acknowledged for a job well done or to be singled out for rewards and awards for superior performance. This is healthy inspiration and empowerment. But when you find you are being flattered repeatedly by one person and you can't connect the dots to why, don't let the compliments and flattery keep you from asking, "What does this person want from me?"

2. Predatory humans on the hunt are like car salesmen on steroids. They often know just what to say to make you feel good about yourself, but their motives are designed to make you more inclined

to do what they want—even if it isn't in your best interest. One way
to see through the aggression of a predator's flattery is to remain
alert for over-the-top compliments like, "You are the most amazing person I've ever met, and I can't imagine living without you!"
An appropriate compliment would be for someone to say, "I truly
enjoy spending time with you." By knowing this small difference in
the wording of a compliment, you can be more situationally aware
and keep yourself from getting caught in a predator's web.

3. Anyone who approaches you online with flattery as a way to get you
    to open an email should automatically bring on red lights in your
    brain. This is a hard and fast rule, and the foundation for offering
    this counsel as a defense is based on today's massive amount of
    online fraud using phishing. Phishing is accomplished through
    ego-stroking as a form of "click bait" designed to entice you to
    open an email or to open a link attached to an email that then steals
    your personal identification, your pass codes, and even your data.
    Phishing campaigns are the number one source of cybersecurity
    attacks, and ego stroking is a super-successful way to get targets to
    open phishing emails.

4. Give your own ego a checkup. If you find you are a person who con-
    stantly wants more of everything and is never satisfied with what
    you already have, you may be especially vulnerable to ego stroking.
    It's perfectly fine to set goals for your personal self-development,
    but watch out for tendencies to hunger for material gain and over-
    the-top success ambitions. Maybe you are able to achieve anything
    you set your mind to, but if you find yourself declaring to others
    without reservation your material desires and success ambitions,
    you are actually advertising to have your ego stroked. Many who
    hear your declarations will accommodate you but for their own
    selfish purposes. And those selfish purposes, if predatory, could
    involve setting you up to take a hard fall.

5. Consider the source of flattery. Strangely, we often value praise from strangers more than from friends and family. Yet it is often friends or family members who use flattery for less than genuine purposes. It's perfectly OK to question yourself about the motives of anyone who strokes your ego. Simply imagining two file drawers in your brain for compliments and praise from all sources is the best way to sift through "orchids" and "onions." Orchids represent genuine, sincere compliments with no hidden agendas. Onions are offered up as compliments or ego strokes with a potential hidden agenda. Even if you don't know what the agenda is when the compliment or praise is given, it's fine to file all suspicious flattery in the onion file drawer. You can retrieve it and refile it later as an orchid if your initial suspicion proves incorrect.

6. Work on developing your own sense of self-belonging, which is best defined as a self-contained, self-motivated, self-gratified individual who has limited ego needs for stroking from others.

THE HONEY-POT TRAP

The honey-pot trap is very simple and stunningly effective. Simply defined, targets are lured by the offer of sex, drugs, or money into compromising situations. Occasionally, the predators behind this sweet ploy also offer to make your wildest dreams come true, either the dreams you have been chasing without success or a latent dream you put aside years ago for one reason or another. The internet has provided predators with all the data they need to know everything about you from your darkest fantasies and weaknesses to your most positive dreams. They lure the target (prey animals) using anything from promises of shortcuts to make your dreams come true to guilty pleasures they know you seek but are hidden by guilt from the light of day. If they succeed, the predators will document your behavior and then use it to control and manipulate you.

Sometimes scammers will only ask that you sign a contract with them to help you make a dream come true, a contract offer that is so exciting you fail to have an attorney review it. Remember, there is no free lunch (or free anything) in this life. The word *free*, even when used by a grocery store, is designed to get you into the store to spend your money on high-profit items. Whatever is offered free should always be seen as a scam.

DEFENSIVE COUNTERMOVES

1. If there is anything you want to do that you don't want others to know about, don't do it.

2. Assume there are cameras watching everything you do in public . . . because there are.

3. When working on your computer, assume eyes are watching everything you do. Artificial intelligence is real, and every keystroke you make is observed, recorded, and analyzed when on the internet.

4. If you connect with anyone online or are contacted by someone online offering to fulfill a fantasy you have, assume the person is setting a trap. By assuming false identities, people often go online and conduct *catfishing* operations designed to take advantage of the online disinhibition effect, which is the willingness of people to share information more readily in online forums or platforms than in person. Then the information is used against you to blackmail or to compromise you in some way.

5. Be especially cautious about sharing personal information at online dating sites. Online scammers use your personal information to compromise, blackmail, or conduct simple cyberbullying behaviors that give them a feeling of power over others. The best rule to live by is to assume there is no such thing as anonymity once you go online for any purpose.

6. Even your smart TV may be watching you in today's world. Unless you have disabled certain features that are automatically turned on at the factory where the TV is manufactured, your TV is probably gathering data on your likes and dislikes when you tune into certain broadcast or streaming media. Even worse, hackers have learned how to use the cameras on your computer to watch you, and now some TVs have cameras for Zoom calls and conferences. Nothing is sacred to hackers.

7. If someone is using your online activities to control or manipulate you, bully you, or psychologically torture you, contact law enforcement, report the activity, and seek help tracking down the perpetrators. Of course, this counsel will fall on deaf ears if you have been indulging in illegal or illicit activities yourself. However, you will have to decide which is the greater of two evils—exposing yourself to law enforcement officials and putting an end to your suffering or letting your tormentor push you around endlessly.

BREADCRUMBING

Breadcrumbing is the act of leading someone on without any intent of romantic interest in them. Those who are very good at this do just enough and say the right things to disguise their totally selfish purposes (which is to keep you dependent upon them and available for sex). The breadcrumbs are the core of this predatory ploy, and they are designed to make you believe there is a whole loaf of bread waiting at the end of the breadcrumb trail.

When human predators use this nasty strategy, they are abusing you and your needs to feel worthy, loved, and cared for to deceive and dominate you. Breadcrumbing is even more difficult to see in marriage because there are abundant ways for a spouse to disguise breadcrumbing from the other. And you may actually blind yourself to breadcrumbing more readily as a spouse because you don't want the marriage to end for any number of reasons.

What are the signs that someone is leading you on?

1. They are inconsistent. They might keep tabs on you for some weeks, making you believe they are interested in you. Suddenly, they ghost you, and they don't reply to your messages or return your calls. When you've almost forgotten about them, they emerge with the intent of rekindling the flame. They can repeat this pattern several times, certain you will always want to go down that road with them.

2. They don't keep appointments like dates or hangouts. Before the scheduled date, they raise your hopes and make you look forward to the meet. Then, when the date is close, they cancel for some reason. If they repeat this, it's definitely a sign of breadcrumbing, and it is best not to take them seriously next time.

3. They like to play the victim every time, even if they are at fault. For instance, when they go incommunicado for a period, they come back and blame you for not checking on them. Also, if you leave them texts and they answer after a long period, they will fault you for not attempting to call them to check why they didn't answer your texts.

4. They communicate only at odd hours, when their victims are most vulnerable. If you are single and you are spending the night alone, they will contact you. This would be their perfect opportunity to fill your head with lies and sweet words because your loneliness is being felt more at that period. However, they avoid communicating with you during the day because they are busy breadcrumbing other people.

5. When you confront them about breadcrumbing, they deny it and temporarily change. To disprove your point, they will act normally and keep in touch for a while. When they discover you have forgiven them (and you are sucked back in), they return to their old ways. People who breadcrumb others are fully conscious of what they are doing. So if you have asked if you are a victim of breadcrumbing, you almost certainly are.

6. Their messages are ambiguous. One of the reasons why it might be difficult to clearly understand the messages of someone who breadcrumbs is they have mixed feelings—part of them really wants to be with you, but they also feel better just playing around and dating others. They send messages that are hard to decipher because they are unsure of what they want.

7. You start doubting the benefits of your relationship. Even if you have deep conversations with these predators, there is usually no substance in their side of the conversation. Some of them don't feel the need to know more about you because they don't want to be committed. At first, you might think they care about you. However, if you look deeply, you realize all they care about is themselves, and they need you only for temporary companionship.

8. They always wants sex. If things get physical each time you see them, they are interested only in your body. This is one of the signs of breadcrumbing in marriage. They will lie and say they miss you and just want to see you. However, when you meet physically, it ends with sex every time. Such people do not have any long-term plan for you, and they don't want a committed relationship. So they will keep using you to satisfy their sensual needs.

DEFENSIVE COUNTERMOVES

1. Discuss with your lover (spouse) your need for greater awareness of how he or she has been treating you. If there is any hope in changing a breadcrumbing relationship, it has to be because of open and honest communications. Typically, those wanting to please you will apologize and promise to do better. Your job is to watch them and make sure they follow through. If it's rinse and repeat with them going back to their old ways, then you know they were being insincere or they are incapable of giving more to your relationship.

2. Take a timeout from the relationship. If during this time you conclude they have been taking you for a ride, cut ties with them. By severing the relationship, you show you have self-respect and that's the first step toward regaining control of your emotional and mental health. If the person doing this to you is a spouse, a trial separation and marriage counseling are good interim steps. It may not work and often doesn't, but it's an option that sometimes works and is always worth trying.

3. Don't lie to yourself about how you feel about breadcrumbing. Take time to learn the healthy signs of a committed and healthy, rich and fulfilling relationship.

4. Breadcrumbers know what they are doing and are playing by an entirely different set of rules than you are. But they also have an Achilles heel. If you completely ignore them and behave as if they don't exist by giving them no audience whatsoever, they can't stand this. If they really want to change their ways, this will wake them up. But if they are truly human predators, they will only come at you again to get revenge. Be very careful.

5. Date other people. Find people who love being with you and know how to show it.

6. Always send yourself the message that you deserve the best, that you don't have to beg for love or attention. It's far better to be alone than to be abused. If you have a history of falling for unavailable people, it's time for you to get help with that from a qualified therapist.

THE VICTIM PLOY

Probably the most invisible entrapment play is known as the *victim card* to get sympathy first and then convert that sympathy into money, sex, food, or something else of value that you have and the "victim" doesn't have. One of the biggest reasons we fail to see this entrapment play is because of the Christian value expressed best by the parable of the good Samaritan. That story was meant to teach what an act of mercy between humans looks like. A main character in that story is a real victim lying beside the road who had been beaten, robbed, and left to die from his wounds. The Samaritan, not hesitating, stopped

> **RED FLAG #62:** Human predators will make you feel like a hero when doing their bidding and will present your heroism as fighting the barbaric enemy who threatens everyone.

his journey and treated the man's wounds, then placed the beaten man on his own donkey, took him to the nearest town, and paid from his own pocket to have that man attended to, fed, and boarded. The Samaritan never expected anything in return, showing he understood the act of unconditional love, even though the victim (the wounded man lying beside the road) was not a member of his tribe.

Unconditional love is a real phenomenon and should never be discouraged. On the other hand, conditional love is an entirely different phenomenon that is often confused with unconditional love.

A dear friend recently took in a woman living on the streets of a town here in Idaho and helped her by providing free room and board, odd jobs, and encouragement. She did this for five months. The homeless woman presented as a victim of a horrific childhood, filled with trauma caused by her parents. My friend did not understand that the homeless woman was addicted to her role as victim, and for this reason, all attempts by my friend (and others) to encourage employment and bootstrapping her way up and out of the homeless lifestyle were rebuffed. What my friend also did not understand was that she harbored a hidden agenda to see her acts of kindness pay off through a change of lifestyle and hard work by the homeless woman. This hoped-for result did not materialize. In the end, the homeless woman left to resume her life on the streets as she was fully addicted to playing the victim and had no desire to change. When we give of our own treasure to help others expecting change in them, this is known as philanthropy. Philanthropy works only when the giver and the receiver agree from the outset to reach for a shared goal with clear consequences spelled out if either party reneges. Accountabilities and agreed-on measures of progress are always part of the philanthropic contract. Therefore, a philanthropic contract is something entirely different from unconditional love and mercy.

Human predators love to take advantage of the confusion most people have about the difference between unconditional love and philanthropy. They do this by playing the victim card in a variety of ways (scams).

The often-used way of playing the victim card is during a simple exchange where the predator has been accused of doing something wrong. When under fire, predators will immediately play the victim card to switch the emotions in the room, claiming they were set up or accusing their accusers of launching a witch hunt against them.

Another way for predators to play the victim card is to send an email claiming their inheritance has been stolen but also claiming, with your help, they (the victims) can get the money back. While there are many variations on this scam, these ploys work because prey animals have powerful empathy and compassion for anyone claiming they have been victimized. When the victim card is played, it's as if an on switch has been hit, and the empathy and compassion for the victim flow like a river.

DEFENSIVE COUNTERMOVES

1. Listen carefully to anyone claiming a need for help but remain situationally aware that you may be looking at a setup.

2. If the proclaimed victims declare a law has been broken, offer to call or take them to the police. If they refuse, then you have done your best. If they ask you for help, say no.

3. If the proclaimed victim is homeless, offer to take the person to a homeless shelter or any agency that serves the homeless. You can't address the needs of homeless people without the proper resources and training.

4. When you receive any appeals online in the form of emails or texts claiming a desperate need for help, discard them immediately. Do not open them, and if you do open them, do not reply.

5. If you love helping others, you are encouraged to meet that need by working as a volunteer for a reputable nonprofit. If you wish to give money to help the needy, give responsibly by working closely with nonprofits that can help you surface and satisfy your desired outcome from giving.

6. Beware of fake nonprofits that spring up whenever there is a national disaster. While writing this, Louisiana and Texas are getting hammered by a tropical storm only two weeks after hurricane Ida devastated Louisiana. Many scams are springing up around assisting the victims of these tragic events. If you want to give in ways that will truly help in times of national disasters, stick with the Red Cross and The Salvation Army. These organizations take good care of the funds they are given, spend as little as possible on overhead costs, and responsibly deliver the services promised to the suffering.

IMPOSTER SCAMS

Whenever societies enter turbulent times, imposter scams multiply. While imposter scams are always occurring in society, since the COVID-19 pandemic, imposter scams have been on the rise. In 2019 when the pandemic was still considered an epidemic restricted to China, the Federal Trade Commission received 647,000 complaints about imposter scams—a 23 percent increase over the previous year. Reported losses topped $667 million.

Imposter scammers lie about who they are, always pretending to be someone you know (and therefore trust) or representing themselves as a well-known business or government agency. Imposter scammers are willing to spend hours on the phone with their victims because the payoff is so big.

Imposter scammers are also referred to as con artists, and con artists fit perfectly into this book's definition of human predators. Let's review that definition again:

Human Predator: Anyone who consistently acts without conscience to dominate others using fear, psychological manipulation, trickery, or violence.

Masquerading as someone you know (including a friend or a family member), as a reputable business, or as a government agency creates instant trust or respect in the minds of many people (believe it or not). And the telephone is still con artists' weapon of choice, although more recently they use a combination of email and telephone to ensnare their victims. Taxpayers and good, honest customers of reputable businesses don't expect to be scammed when they receive an email like this one from Best Buy:

Dear Ms. Smith,
We have renewed your warranty on the television you purchased from BEST BUY three years ago. Your card has been charged $257,

and this extended warranty will give you another three years of protection, including free shipping and repair of your television in the event you have a warranty issue. If you have any questions, please call using the number below.

When this email arrived in the mailbox of our former personal assistant (officially retired), she immediately placed a call to us asking if we had authorized the charge. At that moment, we were in Colorado with our grandchildren high in the Rocky Mountains on horseback, but we still had cell-phone reception. Our former personal assistant was told no, the charge had not been authorized, and we instructed her to make the call and have the charge reversed.

When the call was made, the con artists told our retired personal assistant they could not simply reverse the charge, but they could transfer the funds directly to one of our bank accounts. For some reason I will never understand, our former personal assistant agreed to give them one of our bank account numbers where they could wire the funds, but she did this only after spending hours on the telephone in an effort to explain how easy it was to reverse a credit card charge. Worn down and frazzled, with tons of other commitments that day, our good friend and former employee caved to the lies she heard from the highly trained con artist on the other end of the call.

Having one of our account numbers is not a real help to con artists because they can't access our accounts online without the PIN, a fact they, of course, explained very carefully to our former employee. And here is where everything turned ugly. The woman we knew and trusted for twenty years as a top-gun professional and a woman with an iron will to get things right gave the con artists our PIN number.

The next call she received from the con artists informed her that Best Buy had made an error in wiring the $257 refund to our account and had, in fact, transferred $25,700 to my wife's account. To correct the error, we would have to wire the $25,700 BACK TO THEM, and we were instructed to wire those funds to a bank in Thailand. It was now late in the afternoon when out in the Rocky Mountains my wife and I received this updated information. Shocked and in disbelief, fully aware that a scam was in play, we instructed our former employee to call the bank and shut down all our accounts, working only with a specific banker and close friend, then stop all communications with the scammers, and call the FBI.

There is a happy ending to this story, believe it or not. Our banker immediately froze our accounts. Then he looked at the transfers made between accounts on that day and found the con artists had never transferred any money into our accounts at all. But they had transferred $25,700 from one of our accounts to another, hoping we wouldn't notice. The PIN number did not give these thieves an ability to wire money from our bank to their bank. They could see all our accounts and transfer money between accounts, but that's all they could do, unless we authorized a wire transfer out of our bank to their bank in Thailand. This means they had spent an entire day on the telephone working to get a big payoff. Instead, they received

> **RED FLAG #51:** Con artists are human predators. The telephone is still the favorite tool of con artists, but some scams are accomplished through face-to-face contact. Be aware of debt collector scams, computer performance scams, student loan and financial aid scams, fake bills and invoices received by mail, arrest warrant scams, scam text messages, and affordable care scams aimed at seniors. Avoid all; don't respond to them in any way.

nothing, we received new PIN numbers from the bank instantly, and new account numbers were assigned when we arrived home. Yes, this caused some minor headaches for us with authorized automatic payments to approved vendors, but not one dime was lost.

How slick are human predators when they play imposter scams on human prey animals? Good enough so they generate hundreds of millions of dollars from their efforts. If you don't want to be scammed, follow these guidelines:

Defensive Countermoves

1. When anyone calls you saying he or she is with a government agency such as Social Security, Medicare, or the IRS, hang up immediately. Government agencies never call. They do send out written notices, but even written notices should be carefully investigated for authenticity. If you are asked to make a phone call in response to a written notice, go to the government agency's website and see if the telephone number is authentically listed.

2. If you receive an emergency phone call from a purported family member claiming to have been arrested in a foreign country and in need of bail money right away, hang up immediately. After hanging up, call other family members and alert them about the call you received. Almost everyone traveling overseas carries a cell phone, but occasionally the devices are stolen by pickpockets, and that's when the troubling calls start coming.

3. If you ever receive a call from a tech support representative of Apple or Microsoft claiming to have found a problem with your computer that needs fixing, hang up. Even if you receive an email with such a claim, simply go to the software firm's website to check on alerts and software fixes. Only download software fixes from the website of the software developer's authorized, secure web page.

4. If you use dating sites and believe you have fallen in love with someone you met online, any requests for money from your newfound love interest should be met with a resounding NO! This is true even if you have had several dates with the person. Most times romance scammers avoid in-person connections, but not always.

5. In the event you are persuaded by a caller that he or she is really as claimed to be and demands payment immediately in the form of wire transfer or a gift card, hang up the phone. No government

agency will ever demand immediate payment, and certainly none would ever accept payment in the form of a gift card. Scammers can threaten with everything from arrest and jail time to attaching your wages from an employer. These are lies. Don't let fear shut down your reasoning power. Just hang up on anyone who threatens you in any way.

6. Defending against identity theft should be your biggest concern when, over the phone or through email or texts, you are asked to give anyone any information like your Social Security number, PIN, account number, credit card number, etc. To suggest you should just say no to such requests seems so obvious, but people give out this information every day to complete strangers. Please, whenever you are asked, imagine a huge STOP sign, take a deep breath, and just hang up.

WHEN PREDATORS INSULT YOU

Let's face it, insults are hurtful. And if someone insults you in front of other people, you can be certain the aim is to hurt you. Why? Why on God's Earth would anyone choose to use an insult to harm you? There is only one answer to this question: the act of hurting you brings pleasure to the one making the insult. Further, watching you squirm and struggle to handle the insult brings that person more pleasure.

While you can't control what other people say to you, you can control how you react. Human predators have in mind a specific reaction they want from you, and when you are prepared for insulting words from one of these sultans of insults, you can defuse a hot situation by how you choose to respond. By being prepared to defuse the insult, you can deny the predator the hoped-for pleasure and buy yourself time—to plan with extreme care the steps you will take to extract yourself from the predator's soul-sucking behavior. So what are the ways to disarm an insult hand grenade?

DEFENSIVE COUNTERMOVES

1. Initially, when you hear an insult directed your way, say nothing. Even though the natural response is to protect yourself when insulted, all your energy needs to be directed to avoiding the blow that has come from the naked aggression of the attacker. Snapping back at the insult or defensiveness validates accusations and insults. By remaining calm, the insult misses its target. But if you lash out at the person making the insult, you may make that person look like the victim to everyone else.

2. To make sure the intended attack misses its target, you can't allow the insult to fester inside you either. All you really know is that someone (your would-be offender) will be studying you to see if your non-response is betrayed by boiling emotions inside you. If the predator detects emotional turmoil, communicated by your body language, micro-expressions, and even the dilation of your pupils, he or she will know that, despite your non-response, the blow has hit home.

3. In your moment of silence, ask yourself if there is any truth in the insult, but even if there is, imagine you are looking down on the situation from fifty thousand feet above it. If the truth in the insult is an area you have self-identified as a weakness, you can pull the person aside and have a private talk about his or her best suggestions on how to improve. But if the insult is intended to embarrass or shame you in a hurtful way, after a micro-moment of silence, simply say, "OK," and then pause again before taking the next step. By saying OK, you acknowledge you have heard your attacker's insult, but it doesn't mean you accept it. In its own way, the response of OK tells your attacker that you see him or her, but it doesn't broadcast your next move. Saying OK is part of practicing the pause, and it buys you time.

4. The next words from your mouth should be "thank you." Saying these two words is completely counterintuitive and non-aggressive. As in the martial arts where each student is taught to "never be where your enemy expects you to be," the words *thank you* announce you are prepared and strong, but these words also signal you are able to turn a potentially explosive situation into a peaceful one if you are allowed. This is extremely important if others are witnesses to the insult, as it immediately lowers their emotional temperature and is your first step to bringing them along as allies. Witnesses to an insulting comment can be very important to helping avert mortal combat in a highly charged situation like this.

5. Saying "thank you" doesn't mean you are accepting the insult. It means you are deflecting the insult so you can say these words next: "That's an interesting take on things." Remember, people who hurl insults are not interested in your opinion when they throw an insult grenade at you. They come prepared for war, but you are not giving them what they want. The words, "Thank you. That's an interesting take on things," are really saying, "While you can see me and I can see you, today I will not fight you." Besides, predators who insult you have revealed something very important to you. They have revealed themselves as an enemy, maybe even a mortal enemy. Even if you decide to retreat permanently from the attacker, you now know where an enemy is located, which is something you always need to know and must never forget.

6. What you do next depends on whether you plan to continue relating to the offender. If the offender is your employer, for example, simply ask if he or she has time for a private meeting with you to answer the questions implied in his or her comments. The point of this request is to defuse a hot situation. And

because there is no constructive way to respond to an insult, especially one hurled at you in front of witnesses, your best strategy is to convert the insult to a question. For example:

"You are way too old to be doing this work, Susan!"

"I know, right! Maybe you can spare some private time and we can discuss a transition strategy to bring in new and younger talent to run this agency. Are you up for that?"

This insult was actually leveled at a CEO I work with in front of her entire staff by a board member. It was totally uncalled for and a real shock to the CEO and her staff. Instead of taking offense, the CEO deftly invited the offender to discuss the matter in private. When the time came for a private meeting, the offending board member failed to show up, thus making it clear she was trying to insult the CEO and pick a fight. The CEO's staff members who were very loyal to her became even more devoted to her because of her professionalism. And the CEO knew she now had an enemy on her board who had to be dealt with in a different manner.

Of course, it doesn't always go this way. Some people have momentary outbursts of anger, and by inviting them to discuss their concerns in private, you may gain some consensus around two different interpretations of the same data or facts. On the other hand, if your employer is intent on yanking your emotional chain only for the twisted joy from embarrassing you in front of others, trying to defuse the insult by acting professionally is always better than lowering your standards and engaging in combat. Acting as peacemaker and inviting private discussions will always be noticed by any witnesses to the insult. On the other hand, and perhaps more importantly, by changing the venue for continued dialogue to a private meeting at a future point in time, you have bought time to plan your next move with a potentially very dangerous predator.

7. If the person who insults you is someone you meet casually and you don't intend to relate to them after this first edgy encounter, you have several options. The first is to say something self-deprecatingly humorous like, "You know, I resemble that remark!" Or you might say, "Let me check with my wife to see if she agrees with you because she alone decides whom I should listen to on these topics." These are goofy enough responses that any witnesses to the insult will find them humorous and the humor will deny a predator of the angry, get-ready-to-rumble reaction hoped for. Then you can spend the rest of your life ignoring the vile creature who hurled the insult at you. Humor is the most powerful way I know of to disarm an insult from a person who doesn't know you and has no standing in your life. Why be humorous? Because in the event fate brings this insulting person to cross your path at some future date, your self-deprecating humor will not have insulted him or her. Life will give you enough enemies, so there is no need to go around trying to make more, including people intent on yanking on your emotional chain.

8. If the one who insults you fits the definition of a human predator as defined in this book, a person without conscience and who consistently insults people for personal pleasure (even extreme pleasure), then you need to know this and plan your life to have no future contact with that person. Remember, you can't change these people, and you will only drive yourself crazy if you try to change them. Telling you this may not be what you want to read, but soul-sucking insults hurled at you daily will make your life a living hell. So when one of these specific types of predatory humans crosses your path, unless you are ready to commit homicidal acts, make plans to permanently cut that person out of your life.

HIGH-CONFLICT PREDATION

Some predators are addicted to high conflict. You may cross paths with these people at work and in volunteer organizations (including church and nonprofit leadership groups). Often, they become politicians. Some show up in your affinity groups as friends, family members, and even in marriage. All these predators are addicted to the emotional payoff they experience from creating conflict and using it to dominate others. And sometimes just getting others to fight with one another as the predator stands by fanning the flames of conflict gives them their payoff (referred to by therapists as their *supply*).

One way you can identify them is by noticing how everything is a crisis for them. They will often deliver several strongly worded concerns as darts at a dart board (with individuals or small groups) to see which dart hits a bullseye and gets a hot reaction. When they see one of the darts stirs emotion in you or others in the small group, they will expand on the theme and explain (with emotional heat) how the crisis is terrifying. At this point they are stoking the fire to see if your emotional flames (or if the emotional flames of the group) will burn hotter. If this works, they will identify the hideous villain who is behind this terrifying crisis, a villain who must be destroyed at all costs. They will simultaneously identify the hero who has the power to vanquish the villain and quickly solve the crisis (and frequently they identify themselves if they are narcissists who want to rule).

> **RED FLAG #31:** Human predators make promises they never keep. Then when you get upset, they try to make you look crazy for being so rattled. Then they make another promise they won't keep. Any apologies you hear from them are false, and the unkept promises will just keep coming.

The crisis itself can be entirely real, a fantasy created by the imagination of the conflict addict, or somewhere in between these two extremes. All that matters to the high-conflict addict is to whip you (or the group) into an emotional frenzy with sides taken by different members of the audience. This is the divide-and-conquer strategy of these addicts, and it works brilliantly to get people fighting with one another.

Even after you spot one of these conflict addicts, knowing how to deal with them is totally counterintuitive. Most want to call them out, rip them apart, and fight them in hand-to-hand combat. That is a huge trap because they will purposely change their demeanor when challenged and proclaim they are the victims. Suddenly, everyone will feel sorry for them and turn on you. How do you win with these people if you can't just slip away from them?

Defensive Countermoves

1. Give them respect, empathy, and attention (which are the exact opposite of what they expect or want from you).

2. Turn every crisis declaration into an opportunity to learn more and convert every element of the declared crisis into a question to be asked and answered by the group as a team. Those who master this strategy always stay away from personal attacks and focus on how the group might create a winning strategy. As long as you help the group focus on their need to solve a problem as a team, or as a group of humans with a shared challenge, the conflict addict's hoped-for eruption of conflict can be held at bay.

3. At the first sign you have a hot reactor in the group, remind the individual that the group is at its strongest as long as all energy goes into constructive problem solving, rather than taking up arms against one another. Urge all to remember that nothing gets solved when tempted to go down the rabbit hole of us against them.

4. Let everyone know you are willing to fight with all your might once all agree on a winning solution to the problem to be solved.

5. Present always (and in all ways) that you are a crusader for wisdom and are strong. To beat the conflict addict at this game, you must match his or her rhetoric for hysteria with calm and strength. Never engaging in high emotional warfare is strength. Confidence in the power of the group to make wise decisions is strength. Listening to others without judging them (no matter how far-out their thoughts may be) is strength. Graciously admitting someone has come up with a better idea than yours is strength. But the minute you lose it emotionally, you are giving the signal you are not strong.

ENERGY DRAINING

Energy vampires literally suck all the energy out of you and leave you feeling drained after every encounter with them. You may have them in your life as family members, friends, or co-workers.

There are many types of energy-draining vampires, and all are human predators by the definition used in this book. They seek to dominate you (and others) without any regard for you as an individual with needs of your own. Some of them are narcissistic drama queens who are always dealing with some crisis they insist you listen to and help with. Often, they are co-workers who don't care whom they step on to get ahead. Or they may be a spouse or a friend who wants your nonstop attention. Sometimes these people are very entertaining and charismatic with charming personalities, but they demand to be the center of attention all the time. Some of them are liars and cheaters who constantly let you down. There is a wide range of types of energy vampires, but for you the only important consideration is how you feel after you've been around them—exhausted, disappointed, or let down. Do you know anyone who makes you feel like this?

If you answered yes, at some level you probably believe these people need you. You are definitely wrong about this. From the perspective of energy vampires, they behave this way because it fulfills their needs in some twisted way, and their thinking and continued behavior is only about getting their needs met. You are to them merely a tool or a source of supply for the payoff they get from zapping your time and energy.

Over time, if you don't shed these energy-sucking people, you will pay a huge price. In the same way your internal organs slowly shut down from depleting your red blood cells, the chronic stress of an energy vampire in your life has a deleterious effect on your immune system, your cardio-vascular system, and your central nervous system. Energy vampires are a health threat that can definitely kill you. Unloading them from your life is not a selfish act and will help you avoid getting overwhelmed, anxious, and seriously ill.

Defensive Countermoves

1. If energy vampires are someone you can avoid, cut off all contact with them immediately.

2. If they are someone you can't avoid (like a spouse, a family member, or someone you work with), communicate with them as little as possible, using texting and emails to your advantage until you can make new plans (including divorce or finding new employment).

3. Set boundaries with those you can't avoid. When you must meet with these people, set specific start times and ending times, and stick to these boundaries.

4. Now that you know energy vampires can never meet your needs, lower your expectations for them. Don't continue trying to share your life with these people, hoping they will miraculously change. They won't!

5. Always be prepared with an excuse to avoid spending time with the energy vampires who have been sucking you dry. Tell them you are feeling under the weather and have to go lie down and get some rest. Remember, they are looking for high-energy people

who can give them intense attention and encouragement. If you're not that person, they will immediately find someone else.

6. If you can't get away from them, stop giving off energy so they become bored with you. Just stare at them with a puzzled look on your face. They may get a little angry and even offensive, but that's OK. Your new goal with them is to make sure they find you boring.

7. After they vent on you for a while about all their problems and annoyances, ask them, "Are you just venting or is there a problem you are trying to solve?" This often brings them up short, and they will pause. During the pause, tell them politely you don't have time to be a good listener right now to venting, but if they can identify a problem they are trying to solve in twenty-five words or less, you will give them your best suggestions.

8. Remain cool, calm, and collected. Don't do what empaths so often do and start mirroring an energy vampire's energy. Most importantly, don't get angry or display your anger if you feel it. Emotional vampires will match any anger you display and then exceed your anger while trying to make you feel guilty for being angry. Imagine yourself as a huge boulder that has no energy and is immovable.

9. Say no as nicely as you can when an emotional vampire comes seeking your time and attention. The word *no* should not be followed by an explanation. You, like everyone, gets to decide how you will spend your time. You don't owe others your time or attention, and you can trust with your entire being that others can figure out by themselves how to find someone else to listen to them, solve their own problems, or both.

SOCIOPATHIC BEHAVIOR

Sociopaths fit perfectly into the definition of human predator. They also are hard to spot as they look like everyone else, and it's their intent to blend in with human prey animals. Further for consideration is that addictions and traumas, brain injuries and extremely harsh life challenges can turn people sociopathic, making them impossible to distinguish from the natural-born sociopath.

Just for drill, let's review the core traits of sociopathic behavior:

1. No conscience

2. Zero empathy for others

3. No compassion

4. No moral compass (essentially no inner sense of right and wrong)

5. No genuine feelings or emotions, although they can imitate emotional affect to help them get close to those they have targeted for their twisted agendas

6. No fear and, therefore, no hesitation to take actions that would make anyone else pause and ask, "Is this the right way to treat others?"

7. Always cold and calculating

8. Never any sense of guilt, remorse, or shame for any action taken

9. Infinite range of the ambitions expressed, some having grandiose megalomaniacal agendas, others simply desiring to live off the kindness and generosity of others, and many simply perceived as annoyingly eccentric

10. Zero respect for laws, rules, and social conventions that other humans embrace as the glue holding society and social order together

Complicating this confounding constellation of sociopathic characteristics is that sociopathy often expresses in combination with many other mental health pathologies and deviant behaviors, including (but not limited to) narcissism, psychopathy, high-conflict personality disorder, drug and alcohol addiction, and bullying. You as a human prey animal must spot these predatory humans early and find ways to avoid them or spend countless months and years of your life enduring their use and abuse of you. Early avoidance will save your mental and physical health so use the red-flag warning signs in this book and the counsel below to save yourself.

> **RED FLAG #52:** Human predators have extremely low emotional intelligence. As a result, they are highly likely to fail to pick up on subtly expressed emotional needs you have, often challenge or belittle you on directly expressed emotional needs, and mostly ignore your emotional well-being entirely.

DEFENSIVE COUNTERMOVES

1. The moment you come to an awareness you may be involved with or about to be involved with a sociopath, get a therapist to help you sort out what you are seeing and to help you make a plan to save yourself from the predator's clutches.

2. Sociopaths are looking to control or manipulate others, and the payoff for them is to witness oversized emotional distress in their targets. If you are involved with one (whether at work, in your family, through marriage, or in a professional relationship), do all in your power to mute, put on pause, or turn down the volume of your emotional reactions to his or her outrageous behaviors or

comments. The less attention you give sociopaths, the more boring they will find you. The terrible things they say or do are meant to amuse themselves with your over-the-top emotional reactions. Don't give them what they want.

3. If the sociopath is trying to involve you in illegal or unethical behavior, resist, resist, resist. Once you take one step in the direction of illegal or unethical activities, the sociopath will use this against you to leverage more of the same from you.

4. Keep a handwritten journal of everything you observe happening, and record your feelings about what you have witnessed. Keep this journal at home, make sure it is handwritten, and place it under lock and key. Never create a computer file with your journal entries.

5. Do not panic. From personal experience, I can say that discovering you are in the clutches of a sociopath elicits total panic in normal people and is the universal default for empaths. My very first experience with a sociopath taught me how destructive and dangerous—to you and others—it is if you do panic. Yes, you are going to have to adjust your personal goals to steer your way out of a sociopath's grip, but flexibility and adjusting your plans and your dreams are signs of higher intelligence and the survivor's first rules for continued survival. If you panic, you may become obsessed with what has happened and lose all perspective on leading a happy, enriching life in the present and going forward. If the sociopath has already taken away some of your peace of mind, why give that person the rest of your life and the joys of living that can be yours once you move on?

6. Don't even think about getting revenge! The best revenge is to disentangle, ignore, and then go forward and live a good life. Besides, those who seek revenge are giving sociopaths exactly what

they want. Denying them what they want is your best revenge. Remember, they don't feel anything anyway, but when they feel powerless over the people they have messed with, they become furious and vengeful.

7. No matter how traumatized, angry, and vengeful you feel, don't go around telling others and expect them to understand or to feel the way you feel toward the one who has abused you. Of course, if you've read this book, you should feel less traumatized because you are fully informed about what these people are capable of.

8. If you are still in danger—physically, of sexual abuse, emotionally, or financially—go to the police. They will listen and either take action or guide you in how to take immediate action to protect yourself. Your health and safety are supremely important, and if you believe your sociopathic abuser is capable of physical harm, you must surround yourself with people whose sworn duty is to protect life.

9. Once you get free from your sociopathic abuser, don't allow that person back into your life for any reason. Even if he or she begs you with promises never to harm you in any way, you must never give in to his or her pleas. This attempt to draw you back is known as *hoovering*, and the goal of the sociopath is to suck you back in for more abuse.

GASLIGHTING

Gaslighting is loosely defined as making someone question his or her reality (and, therefore, sanity). The term is also used to describe those who persistently put forth a false narrative (known as fake news, in current times). The purpose of a false narrative (an intentionally manufactured untruth) is to lead people to doubt their own perceptions to the point that they become disoriented or distressed. Gaslighting is always intentional and has a predatory purpose. When men and women in positions of power over others (elected leaders, for example) create false narratives, they are abusing their power and committing predatory acts. Frequently, those who gaslight others are engaged in the very acts they are accusing others of committing. More common, however, are the following gaslighting tricks and deceptions:

- **Withholding** is when the predator feigns a lack of understanding, refuses to listen, and declines to share his or her emotions by saying things similar to this—"I'm not listening to that crap again!" or "You're just trying to confuse me."

- **Countering** is when a predator constantly calls into question another's memory, even though the person has remembered things perfectly. Typically, the predator will say, "Think about when you didn't remember things correctly last time," or, "You had a similar interpretation last time, and that turned out to be wrong."

- **Blocking and Diverting** is when a predator shifts the conversation from discussing the subject matter at hand to attacking the victim's thoughts and, thereby, controlling the conversation. Questions or statements like "Where did you get a crazy idea like that?" or "I'm not going to have a discussion like that again" or "You're just trying to hurt me on purpose" are verbal ploys designed to put the victim on the defensive.

- **Trivializing and Minimizing** are hostile tactics for making you believe your thoughts or feelings are not important. There are various ways to achieve this, and some of them are extremely subtle. Treating an adult like a child, giving any adult the silent treatment when appealing for support, failing to keep promises, ignoring birthdays or anniversaries, and even accusing another person of being crazy all qualify as trivializing or minimizing acts. When the victims of these acts begin to internally and externally make excuses for their abusers' minimizing tactics, the damage done to them is obvious. When you constantly hear from your partner or boss or even parent statements that mock your memory of events like the following, you are being minimized:

- "What are you talking about? Nothing like that ever happened."
- "I don't have to take this."
- "You're making that up."

Acts of trivializing or minimizing should be huge red flags that you're dealing with a predatory human. And a series of these behaviors from anyone you see and regularly interact with means you need to get help right away. Begin by checking in with yourself to see if you are experiencing any of the following:

- Constantly second-guessing yourself
- Asking yourself, "Am I too sensitive?" a dozen times a day
- Feeling confused and even crazy
- Always apologizing to your mother, father, friends, boss
- Frequently making excuses for your partner's behavior to friends and family
- Lying to avoid put-downs and reality twists

Defensive Countermoves

1. Pay attention to the signs, the red-flag warnings that you are being declared crazy, forgetful, and minimized.

2. People who gaslight lie about nearly everything. They spread false gossip, they are committed to always being right, and they lack a sense of personal responsibility. If you haven't become a target of

gaslighting yet by someone who lies about many other things, you may soon become one if this person is your boss, your life partner or spouse, or a member of your extended family. Trying to defend yourself after you become a target is impossible because once such a person locks onto you, he or she is wretchedly hard to shake. Your best defense is to spot gaslighters early and escape before they see you as their next target.

3. At the first indication you are being gaslighted, be assertive. You can show no weakness to these people. Tell them straight away you are strong and won't be mistreated by anyone questioning your memory, your understanding of your own feelings, or your intentions.

4. If being assertive doesn't work, cut your ties to people who gaslight you. They won't change, but you can. Rather than staying in a friendship, a marriage, or a job where you are being abused, choose yourself first and go find better people to spend your life with. No matter how hard this is, you are better off fighting for your sanity than staying involved with someone who will kill you with a thousand small cuts.

NARCISSISM

In the broadest sense of the word, narcissism is an excessive interest in or admiration of oneself or one's personal appearance. Narcissist predators can be anything from boring to agonizingly abusive, especially if the person is an intimate other. Any psychologist or psychiatrist will tell you that excessive self-interest exists among humans on a spectrum from overly self-confident to a constant need to be the center of attention and admiration. While a narcissist's self-esteem can be off the charts, ironically, it can also be super fragile, dependent on external validation or self-deception. Yet basically, those on the spectrum of narcissistic self-centeredness believe they are smarter, more attractive, and more successful than everyone they know. These people easily put other people down and hijack any conversation/situation to make themselves feel superior by acting as if they are superior to everyone else.

Frequently, people who are on the extremely high end of the narcissistic spectrum come to the attention of professional therapists and are diagnosed clinically as having narcissistic personality disorder (NPR). These clients almost never gain insight into their deviancy. They begin therapy believing any problems they have with others is the fault of those others, and they leave therapy still believing this. All narcissists are human predators, whether or not they have narcissistic personality disorder.

If your life becomes entangled with a narcissist, it will be agonizing for you and remain that way until you completely shed the narcissist. The worst entanglement with a narcissist happens when someone deeply empathic and compassionate becomes a significant other who is devoted to helping change this incurable self-aggrandizing soul. Empaths like to think they are helping the narcissists, while narcissists are using the empaths to fill up their self-esteem. Empaths see themselves as pulling narcissists out of a swamp, while the narcissist is pulling the empath into the swamp as a flotation device. Neither one of these two actors has any insight into how he or she is propping up his or her self-esteem by using the other, but only one of them is getting what he or she wants from the relationship. The empath basically gets nothing except feeling deeply depressed.

Defensive Countermoves

1. Your first line of defense is to be aware of the mind games played by narcissists.

2. Narcissists are always looking for your weaknesses so they can get you to do their bidding. Since they are supremely good at identifying the weaknesses of others, you must be supremely good at not displaying your weaknesses and at spotting these manipulators quickly so as not to be caught in their predatory grasp.

3. Narcissists need you to trust them so they will create early signals that they are trustworthy. For example, they will typically come on as very charming, deeply interested in you, and very supportive. This charm and the show of interest are designed to persuade you to reveal your weaknesses, and it is never about being into you. Please note that if you ask penetrating questions about them, they will not open up. You will receive, instead, superficial responses to your intimate inquiries about who they are and what's really going on inside them. That is your first red-flag warning, and you absolutely must look for this in those showing interest in you.

4. After securing your trust, narcissists will begin to assert their power over you by small criticisms. You may hear, "Why did you do it that way?" or "No, you need to listen to me because this is my area of expertise, and I'm right and you are wrong." You will never receive an invitation from a narcissist to brainstorm a problem or to lay out a series of options you can choose from to solve a problem. This is a second red flag, and this particular pattern is what you will always see from someone trying to take control of your life. After hitting this wall of resistance even twice with anyone, you must begin to retreat because you are under attack. Even though the claim of superior knowledge may not look like naked aggression, it is naked aggression. So fall back, and go into immediate invisible mode with this person.

5. If you lie low and the person you are now avoiding is a true narcissist, he or she will become very angry with you. His or her anger will slowly grow in an attempt to make you fear him or her. Narcissists love being feared. For that reason, if you show fear of them, they will remember what worked to make you fearful and repeat that behavior again and again. This is the biggest tipoff yet about who they are, and now you have an enemy who is determined to make you compliant. At this point, you have no choice but to shed this

predator from your life. No matter what you must do to disappear completely from their grasp, you are in survival mode once they know how to push your fear buttons.

6. In the event you don't withdraw completely from narcissists after they learn how to trigger your fear response, they will next attempt to isolate you from all other affinity connections, including all your family and friends. Their goal here is to take away all supportive contacts so they can control you even more fully. One way they do this is by sabotaging you behind your back with friends, family members, colleagues, and professional connections. Once they successfully isolate you from supportive connections and loved ones, they finally have you completely in their power. Can you still escape? Yes, of course, but at this point you must plan very carefully with the help of professionals to make your break and go it alone. This defensive move on your part requires total secrecy and the creation of a supportive army of men and women who have helped others make the break from narcissists. Plus, because such narcissists will be losing a former soldier in their army of admirers, they will stalk you and do all in their power to get you back while undermining you with everyone in their reach.

COVERT NARCISSISM

Covert narcissists are those who thrive on pretending to be something they are not. They achieve this by attempting to be altruistic, kind, and even empathetic. By creating this false self, they become the center of attention, and this feeds their need for admiration by others, but the presenting self they manufacture is merely a façade. Much of what they really want from others, in addition to adulation and admiration, is easy to obtain offstage and out of sight. They easily score sexual conquests, make connections with people they want to rub shoulders with, or business deals, and this gets them money. Human prey animals easily fall under their spell and see them as great men and women. Seeing them as great human beings with kind hearts and great empathy for others opens all kinds of doors among human prey animals. But it's all BS. Fooling others with this fake philanthropist façade gives them enormous pleasure. Often they become religious leaders, even pastors, in stand-alone churches. They see themselves as chosen by God to lead, and they definitely see themselves as superior to all other aspiring Christians. In conversations with others, covert narcissists dominate with their ability to quote the Bible and are eager to share with others what they must do to be saved. Frequently these covert narcissists are self-effacing and even withdrawn in their approach to sharing their special status as saved and among the chosen, making them even more difficult to spot. What you can trust is that they always see themselves as superior to everyone and their distaste of all lesser beings is carefully camouflaged by their seeming humility and soft-spoken persona. Never doubt, however, that the inner life of a covert narcissist is the same as that of an overt narcissist. Both navigate the world with a sense of self-importance and fantasizing about success and grandeur. But the covert narcissist gets the greatest pleasure by blaming and shaming others.

Defensive Countermoves

1. In a romantic relationship, covert narcissists are often late to your dates or never ready to go when you come to pick them up. They also display stinginess with compliments and encouragement. This is all because they want you to feel small so they can feel big and more important than you in the relationship. It's a form of control for them, and while this works for them, it almost certainly won't work long for you. If you are dating someone like this, the smart move is to break off the relationship ASAP. This behavior on their part won't ever change.

2. Because covert narcissists have no sense of boundaries, have a strong sense of entitlement, and exploit others, you must set strong

boundaries with them if they are members of your family or you are involved with one at work. Remember that boundaries are just a way for you to let someone else know what your values are. They will test you again and again, so each time you tell them to back off, you are encouraged to explain what the boundary means to you. Be consistent because that's the only way to stop covert narcissists.

3. Since covert narcissists will never voluntarily take an interest in you and what is important to you, then you must always be your own advocate with them. Doing so may not come naturally to you, but it's the only way to maintain your own voice with a covert narcissist.

4. Try to put distance between you and the narcissist. If a family member, limit your personal interaction time with the person. If you find you are working with one, ask to be moved to a different location in the office, take breaks at different times, or cut off contact with the individual. These steps are designed not to insult covert narcissists but to protect your sanity by keeping them from bringing your emotions to the boiling point.

5. If you find these suggestions don't give you the relief you need from hurtful encounters with a covert narcissist, get coaching from a qualified therapist. The therapist may have a number of suggestions not provided here. Remember, taking good care of yourself is always of paramount importance.

PATHOLOGICAL LYING

The largest cohort of predators on the planet are predatory liars. In fact, deceit is a universally embraced strategy of all human predators. Lying and deception are what allow human predators to get close enough to human prey animals to strike and cripple or devour them. Yet truth and honesty in all matters are the glue that holds a society together in any cooperative enterprise. Deception and lying are anti-social by their very nature, and like termites, lies eat away at the framework of trust supporting shared human endeavors of any kind. For this reason, all lying has trust-destroying power. Intentional lying is especially destructive to relationships, business ventures, national interests, and national security.

In America, after World War II, there was such a disgust for dishonesty and deception that grade school through high school students were required to take a course on propaganda techniques used by the German Third Reich as a way of helping children grow to adulthood with full awareness about how to defend against and disarm the strategies and tactics of lying and deception. But the disgust and intolerance society felt towards dishonesty after 1944 has been steadily evaporating over the last sixty years. Why?

> **RED FLAG #57:** Human predators will dramatically threaten to leave an intimate relationship if they sense you are thinking of separating and attack your ego to keep you reactive and off-balance.

Today we have reached a point where the employment of lying as a strategy either to harm others or to defeat and destroy competitors has created a culture of lying in America that is highly tolerated and even accepted as the norm in politics. And the expansion of lying as a weapon acceptable for attacking and destroying perceived competitors or opponents has now reached a level that looks like it wants to give the lies and deceptions created by Hitler's Germany a run for its money.

What follows are our best thoughts for you to consider in protecting yourself from lies and deceptions:

DEFENSIVE COUNTERMOVES

1. Since rumors and lies often take on a life of their own, make sure you do not participate in spreading them yourself. Everything you say or write should be carefully fact checked by you before

you share information with others. This applies to all social media platforms, as well as face-to-face communications.

2. Embrace the discipline of approaching all incoming information with enlightened skepticism, which is the practice of assessing truth through fact finding and questioning. You gain in three ways by filtering all incoming information this way: (1) you hone your critical thinking skills, (2) you learn whom to trust and in what degree, and (3) you discover who seeks to benefit at your expense.

3. Here are eleven questions to protect yourself from falling into someone's deceptive trap:

- What do I know for sure about the speaker's truthfulness?
- What assumptions are explicit or carefully concealed by the speaker's claims, and what are my personal assumptions and biases that might allow me to respond positively to those claims?
- Is the statement consistent with reality?
- Can I verify the statement?
- What do I stand to gain by accepting and acting on the statement?
- What do I stand to lose by accepting and acting on the statement?
- What does the speaker gain if I accept and buy into his or her statement?
- What is exaggerated or possibly downplayed in the speaker's statement?
- Does the idea seem too good to be true or too awful to be true?
- Would I advise my best friend to accept the statement without any doubt whatsoever?
- What does my gut tell me? Is there something in the statement that doesn't quite compute, or is the tone off somehow? (Perhaps the speaker is too strident or too pushy in asking me to act on the statement.)

4. If you are harmed by a hostile, predatory lie, the damage can range from minor disappointment in the offender to seriously tangible and measurable wounds, as in loss of money, reputation, and even emotional stability. Take these steps to help you recover and get back on track with your life.

     Assess the damage done to you with help of a professional therapist. Some losses due to predatory lying can be recoverable in a court of law, while others can only allow you to lick your wounds and move on. The course of action you choose to recover from a betrayal of trust is supremely important for rebuilding your self-confidence.

     Confront the truth about what has occurred to you. Notice, please, that you are not being counseled to confront the person who lied (other than legal action if it's appropriate as determined by legal counsel). Forget about getting revenge or cornering the liar to demand an apology. Those who intentionally harm others with lies will never see how their behavior is wrong. Just naming what has transpired by calling betrayal out as the behavior that set in motion destructive consequences for you gives you a sense of power that is required to make your own psyche feel honored and important.

     Avoid knee-jerk reactions after the insult has occurred. Slow yourself down and plan a course of action that is commensurate with the insult caused by the lie. The action you take *may* include court action to recover damages. However, taking legal action doesn't mean you will get what you ask for. If your request for appropriate reparations is rebuffed in a court of law, then at least you have confirmed you are important. If nothing else, this action on your part clears the air of doubt about the intent of the offender and sets the stage for you to begin healing.

     Move on with your life. When we've been wronged, it's easy to fixate on the offense and the offender and find ourselves emotionally stuck. I'm not saying it's easy, but you don't want to be spinning your wheels emotionally, so move ahead with living as soon as possible. Staying angry is the worst thing you can do and means the offender (the liar) has won. Put the offense and the offender in your rearview mirror. A dear friend reminds me every time she sends an email, "forgiveness ends all suffering and loss." Those who offend with lying and betrayal should not be forgotten, but you can take away their power to keep hurting you. My favorite way to do this is to imagine the offenders shrinking in size every time my mind drifts in their direction. Eventually they become the size of a cockroach, and when I see their face in my mind's eye, I simply squash the little roach under my foot.

5. Start living by the Two Lies Limit Rule. When you catch people in a lie of any kind, you should see this as a huge red-flag warning. But the second time someone is caught lying to you, even if not a pathological lie that brings harm to you or to others, cut that person out of your life. By making this a hard-and-fast rule, you can save yourself a ton of pain and suffering.

    Lies are the most effective way I know to destroy human trust and important relationships. Yet lying is a universal behavioral trait. As discussed in section 3, people lie for different reasons, and one of those reasons is to control others and situations with the intent of getting one's way with no regard for the hurt caused to others. This is what human predators do all the time, and they feel no shame or embarrassment about doing this, even when caught. These kinds of lies are pathological, and they are both antisocial and often harmful to others in ways that are irrevocable, illegal, and financially and emotionally costly. For this reason, whenever you catch someone in a pathological lie, you must make it a hard and fast rule to isolate them from any future contact with you.

    There are legions of ways to murder the human spirit, but lying is one of the most painful ways to do this. So the question to consider is, "Why would you ever extend a relationship with someone you have caught lying to you twice?"

HUMAN PREDATOR VENUES

While it's easy to assume you already know this truth, it is valuable to repeat it—human predators are searching for human prey animals in places where prey animals spend most of their time. Just as ancient hunter-gatherers sought out four-legged prey animals at watering holes because they gathered there in large numbers, you will be targeted by predatory humans where you hang out in large numbers with other human prey animals. The three places where human prey animals gather in large concentrations today are places of employment, on the internet, and in our homes with marriage partners and family members. Let's look at the predatory behaviors you should expect when at these three venues.

THE WORKPLACE AS A HUNTING GROUND FOR PREDATORS

All nonpredatory humans who work for a living try every day to be, do, and give their best to make themselves valuable to their employer. Yet the workplace is often the biggest killing field where human predators seek out their prey. What should be a place of business where you are encouraged and duly rewarded for giving your best to make sure everyone succeeds can quickly turn into a war zone where epic confrontations by human predators who dominate the working environment (either predator versus predator in gladiatorial combat or psychological attacks on prey subordinates). These confrontations can play out in the form of sexual predation, high dramas that get enacted through office politics, bullying, criminal behaviors, and sociopaths ruling over the peasant employees as masters over slaves. These bad actors in the workplace are serving an unstated, twisted, or even psyche-destroying mission of their own invention, instead of the corporate entity's publicly stated mission. Below are five of the most common, everyday types of minor predators.

- **Green-Eyed Monster.** This is about jealousy. The predator seeks to make you feel guilty about your good luck in the workplace, at the same time wanting your sympathy.

- **Control Freak.** This predator steamrolls everyone as the know-it-all leader and simply barks orders while ignoring ideas suggested by subordinates or even suggestions from co-workers with equal status.

- **Idea Thief.** You came up with a brilliant idea to advance an office project, but your manager found it only interesting. Later you discovered she ran with the idea, took it to top management as her own, and received huge support and a raise for increasing productivity.

- **Constant Critic.** This predator sees everything you do as just wrong or slightly less than your best, with something negative to say about everything you do.

- **Non-recognition Aggressor.** This is any at-work colleague who ignores you, is unwilling to answer totally reasonable questions, and basically acts as if you don't exist.

Frequently, these minor aggressors can be turned into friends through doing your job competently and displaying a pleasant, kind, and encouraging persona. You will never know the back stories and struggles of your fellow employees, and getting to know their backstories is not why you are at work, anyway. You are going to work to make yourself valuable to your employer in exchange for well-earned payment so you can support yourself and your family. Do not react emotionally to these minor predatory actors. While it's normal to want to fight fire with fire, that's the worst thing you can do.

Also, do not take your own emotional life and your emotional needs to work! At all times, be a professional. Don't go to work thinking this is the place to make close, supportive friends. Be in every way a total supporter of your employer's corporate mission by bringing your gifts, talents, training, and experience to help fulfill that mission. That's it!

Because you know the at-work environment can expose you to minor and major predatory actors seeking to use the workplace as a battleground, it's also recommended you spot these bad actors early and ignore or avoid them if possible. Find people at work who are better than you, and spend time with them while learning from them.

Hopefully, before taking your job, you asked, "Do I want to become more like the people here?" If you didn't address this question before taking the job, you may find yourself just going through the motions of doing your job and bored out of your mind or worse. In this case, *worse* means you are tormented in some way by just being around your co-workers. If you came to your present employment aspiring to change the corporate culture, that won't happen unless you accepted the CEO position. Few of us are immune to how a corporate culture will change us if we made a poor choice. And if you decide you did make a poor choice, don't compound that decision by staying in a toxic corporate environment.

What about major predatory actors? What should you be alert to as a way of protecting yourself from their soul-sucking, vampire-like behaviors? Here's a good starter list:

Sexual Predators. Headlines these days are filled with the perverse sexual behaviors that take place in employment venues. How would you feel about being mentioned in one of these headlines, either as a victim or as a perpetrator? There's simply no way for a healthy sexual connection to happen in the workplace unless one of the two people resigns so dating can proceed without the possibility of manipulation or quid pro quo victimization. If the one being pursued sees any sexual or romantic advance as unwelcome, then lawsuits can become the endgame.

Are sexual harassment lawsuits good for your employer? They certainly are not. Essentially, adopting a personal, zero-tolerance policy for office romances is your best way to avoid what can become a nuclear bomb at the office, with the timer already triggered and set to go off at the worst possible moment for everyone involved.

The worst sexual advances happen when an executive member of the firm is a sexual predator and uses his or her power position to demand quid pro quo exchanges for sexual favors. That means men and women at the firm are not safe from being approached and harassed when a sexual predator with power over them looks at them as sexual objects, believing he or she has special privileges. In the event you become the target for any of the following behaviors, immediately begin keeping a formal journal and document daily the harassing you experience.

1. Asking for a date, just out of the blue by any colleague
2. Uninvited remarks about your body
3. Inappropriate gifts, like underwear, from a co-worker
4. Sexual overtures at holiday parties
5. Telling of sexually loaded stories and jokes at any office venue

Your mantra when you feel emotionally uncomfortable with any sexual advances in the workplace must be, "DOCUMENT, DOCUMENT, DOCUMENT." If the unwelcome advances keep coming, take your documentation to the Human Resources Department and ask them to intervene and put a stop to the offender's behavior in a way that keeps your complaint confidential. Show them your documentation of the offender's behaviors, but don't give the human resources team your journal. The less they know what is in your journal the better. Not knowing how big of a problem they have will motivate them to do something. And if they don't do something and the sexual advances continue, contact a lawyer who specializes in defending victims of sexual harassment. Then take your guidance from your lawyer.

Law Breakers. Violations of the law by your employer or by any employee at work can pose a real dilemma. Most who witness illegal activities are reluctant to report what they see out of fear of reprisals, especially loss of employment. Anything from money-laundering to altering employment records to drug related crimes happen in the workplace, and if you witness any of this, you must know those involved will attempt to implicate you in their crimes after you report them. What are your choices when you know crimes are being committed? You have only one choice—to leave your employer and then go directly to the appropriate law enforcement authorities to report the crimes you witnessed. When you go to the authorities, always be accompanied by an attorney. In fact, contact an attorney before you resign so he or she can work with you on exactly how to handle your exit strategy. Keeping a personal journal and documenting in detail all you have witnessed is also supremely important. And be sure to create this journal at home, in private, on paper in your own handwriting. Don't ever document criminal activity on a computer because computers can easily be hacked.

Entrapment Predators. You must be wondering what it means to be entrapped in the workplace. *Entrapment* is a term usually reserved for strategies used by law enforcement to encourage a suspected criminal to commit a crime he or she might not have otherwise committed. The idea is to catch the suspect in a criminal act and take him or her off the street.

At work, employers and members of the employee group may also entrap (or attempt to entrap) you in anything from a psychological drama being acted out to unwittingly participating in crimes. Additionally, employers now use emails to test their new hires and see if they can be lured into making mistakes that are illegal, immoral, or lacking in good judgment. For example, you may receive an email that is a phishing exercise by your employer. The email might indicate your password on the company email system is about to expire and to click a link provided to update. Upon clicking the link, you are sent to a page saying essentially this was a test, you failed, and the result has been forwarded to IT. Tests like this one can be used as training exercises or even to terminate people who show poor judgment that could lead to devastating consequences for the firm. All employers have the right to control activities in the workplace to ensure security and to protect the company from theft, drug and alcohol use by employees, poor work performance, and unsafe practices.

When employees use entrapment to entice an unwitting fellow employee to do something that entangles the person in illegal or immoral acts, this is truly predatory and meant to create evidence of collusion in immoral or illegal acts. Or, as pointed out earlier, the entrapment snare may be aimed at forcing you to play a role in a psycho drama that is being acted out by other players for twisted reasons. When entrapment is designed to ensnare an innocent employee to play a part in something as low as getting another employee terminated, this is a form of blackmail. Sadly, clever predatory humans can use entrapment and coercion to make you do things you would never consider doing because the predators have information on you that you never want exposed to the light of day.

> **RED FLAG #65:** Sexual coercion is using emotional extortion; withholding love, affection, or conversation; or even threatening to end the relationship if you do not engage in sex acts that you find personally offensive.

The most pervasive type of entrapment at work is emotional entrapment. When predators go hunting for ways to yank your emotional chain, they will try several ways to attack while watching closely to see which one pushes your hot button. Trust me, we all have tender emotional spots that can trigger a hot response. As you've been warned, it's your job to build your emotional strength so when you first feel someone pressing in on one of your tender places, practice the pause and refrain from a hot reaction in the event the person triggering you is a human predator. In those moments when you are unable to resist a hot reaction to something said or done at work, predators will take note and repeat the offense to see if they can get you to have an even hotter reaction. If they succeed, it will be rinse and repeat ad infinitum. Here is a list of triggering behaviors emotional entrappers frequently use to rile up others and get their predatory supply.

- Misplaced blame for errors
- Sabotage of work done
- Unreasonable work demands
- Stealing credit for work done
- Discounting accomplishments
- Intimidation
- Insults and put-downs
- Humiliation
- Threats to a person's job, seniority, or assignments

These offenses are always about power. And the consciously repeated effort to wound an employee emotionally is a form of harassment. Psychologically, harassment is not about hurt feelings. Over time, daily harassment by a fellow employee can cause stress, depression, and even posttraumatic stress disorder. These emotional wounds can't be easily healed. Even worse for the employer, emotional entrapment and abuse can result in reduced productivity, increased absenteeism, and sometimes extended leaves of absence. For these reasons, you should look for an employer who has a stated human resources policy of zero tolerance for emotional abuse.

The theme of Robert Sutton's *The No Asshole Rule: Building a Civilized Workplace and Surviving One That Isn't* is that bullying behavior in the workplace worsens morale and productivity. Sutton believes there is a difference between temporary assholes and certified assholes. The first of these are people having a bad day. As pointed out earlier in this book, having a bad day periodically can happen to any of us. But certified assholes are persistently nasty to be with and target only people less powerful than themselves. Sutton urges private businesses to embrace a written policy of zero tolerance for certified assholes and recommends a zero tolerance for hiring spineless wimps.

It's easy to see parallels between Sutton's certified assholes and human predators and his similar intolerance of spineless wimps and prey animals. Yet my assessment of Sutton's assholes is that they are the minor players on the human predator spectrum. The human predator spectrum begins with Sutton's assholes and ranges upwards to malignant predatory beasts who are willing to bring down the entire corporation, if they must, in order to win the war against anyone opposing them (and that includes members of the board of directors). And while Sutton's spineless wimps are not good at combat with either assholes or malignant human predators, they may bring a fabulous talent to the business world and make a superior contribution to a project under management of an empathic, encouraging manager who brings out the best in them.

Where Sutton gets it right is his encouragement of human resources departments to embrace a corporate policy that anyone acting like a certified asshole will be terminated. My recommendation builds on Sutton's "no asshole policy." I urge all human resources departments to adopt a written corporate policy against harassment in the workplace. Such a policy should be presented in writing, and all employees should be asked to sign the policy before being placed on the payroll. Why? Because while there are no laws against being an asshole, there are laws against harassment in the workplace, and allowing harassment to occur on the job often results in major lawsuits costing corporate America hundreds of millions annually just to defend themselves.

THE INTERNET AS THE WILD, WILD WEST FOR ONLINE PREDATORS

With all due respect for the brilliant minds involved in creating the internet, these people may have made one slight miscalculation. Clearly there was an assumption by these geniuses that the human race had evolved sufficiently to use this new communications tool responsibly, rationally, and free from human predation. Right now, in the middle of the COVID-19 pandemic, we are inundated with overwhelming evidence to the contrary.

In the United States, for example, we are witnessing a civil war of information over getting vaccinated against the COVID-19 virus (and its many variants). On one side of this war are those believing mandated vaccinations are an attack on their constitutionally guaranteed freedoms. On the other side are those who see vaccination against COVID-19 as a way for each citizen to protect himself or herself and neighbors from getting this virus. Not meaning to pick a position of support for either side of this war, I will point out that those who see mandating vaccinations as an attack on their constitutionally guaranteed freedoms are losing the war. The outbreak of the delta and omicron variants of COVID-19 is literally costing the lives of those refusing to get vaccinated. Thousands of unvaccinated freedom fighters are dying every day in our overstressed healthcare system from COVID-19, as well as clogging up hospital beds (because they are deathly sick with COVID-19). Those hospitalized, unvaccinated patients are causing many others to die who need a hospital bed due to other illnesses or injuries from accidents. What is the point of these observations?

There is now powerful proof that humans who presently exist on planet Earth are not yet ready for the World Wide Web. And the disinformation campaigns over COVID-19 vaccinations are prime examples of what can happen to social order and community when human-against-human information wars are waged on the internet. Of course, you may disagree and find the bitterness and vitriol of these information wars a sign of healthy debate. In that case, let's see if we can agree on another topic relating to the internet.

Lawlessness and Its Consequences. Those who are reading this book to discover how to protect themselves from human predators must see the internet (or the Web, if you prefer) as an ungoverned venue where human predators thrive because it is truly a lawless, morally uninhibited, wild frontier where anything goes, just like on the wild plains of the African savannah. There is almost no accountability on the internet as everything happening there is based on the honor system. Companies face no penalties for changing or violating their own policies. And they can make up any policies they want. Anyone with an internet connection can create a website that looks every bit as legit as a big company's. And the internet is where our privacy is most under attack. That means you are under attack every time you use the internet.

When humans engage in an activity they believe will incur little or no consequences to them, they have no incentive to guard against risk; their action is known as *moral hazard*. In truth, there's no such thing as consequence free. This truth especially applies on the internet.

Supposedly cost-free and consequence-free online services like Facebook and YouTube make you pay for everything you do there with your data. Is that really free? You might think Microsoft's Do Not Track or Google's Incognito settings keep you safe, but that's not true. There are no federal regulations requiring websites to honor a "do not track" request. Is that consequence free? And don't even ask about internet pornography. Every keystroke you click is being recorded and watched by supercomputers that learn your secret desires and feed those desires in ways that create addictions and grow those addictions with mind-control strategies and tactics designed to separate you from your money as the ultimate goal. But wait, are there worse consequences awaiting you when you use the internet? Let's look and see what spooky monsters are lurking on the World Wide Web, carefully concealed behind the opaque veil of internet anonymity that you think is so wonderful.

Types of Online Predators. There are many types of online predators. They include financial predators who run a myriad of twisted scams for money, sexual predators who target adults and children, and internet trolls, a type of sadistic predator who posts inflammatory, insincere, off-topic messages in online communities simply to provoke readers or to manipulate a political process through causing confusion or even harm. Most of these predators are high-conflict people, and they get their psychological payoff from watching people fight with one another or by goading people into fighting them.

There are also online human predators known as stalkers. The word *stalking* is a hunting expression, and an online stalker is, for sure, a type of hunter. Stalking is never a random act. Stalkers don't just go online and start targeting the first person they meet. They have a type of person in mind, someone vulnerable and easy to exploit. They also choose their online environment carefully. They know that certain online platforms offer more opportunities to meet human prey animals than others. Social media sites, like online dating platforms, are excellent places to find lonely individuals who are looking to meet people. These sites also offer a lot of personal information, so stalkers (predators) can get to know their target before the first online contact. And you should know that many stalkers simply get their joy from yanking their victims around emotionally. Are you signing up for that when you register with an online dating platform? Yes, you are!

Another type of online predator is the confidence scammer who loves building a relationship and then asking for money for a personal emergency. But the more profitable online version of confidence scamming is known as the webcam extortion ploy, a type of extortion to get the victim to engage in cybersex on a webcam or by simply claiming to have a webcam video of the victim watching porn online. Then the predators blackmail the victim. If the victim is young, they threaten to tell the parents or friends unless money is sent to pay off the scammer. This is what happened in the sad, highly publicized case of Scottish teenager Daniel Perry and resulted in his suicide. In fact, many teen suicides are caused by these human predators.

RED FLAG #59: Online stalkers of adults are human predators. Online stalking is unwanted, obsessive attention given to a specific person. This form of predation is different from regular stalking because, in this case, stalkers primarily use digital technology to torment their victims. Many cases of online stalking escalate into real-life stalking.

Some of these predators make over one hundred thousand dollars a month. If the victim is in a relationship, they will threaten to send the photos to the victim's partner. The predator may also threaten to discredit or embarrass the victim by sending compromising photos to the victim's employer or clients, too. Occasionally, the threat is simply to post these humiliating pictures online, tagging them so those searching the victim's name will find the photos. These predators also search for victims they can manipulate into providing sexually explicit pictures or to meet up with them for sex. Frequently, such predators are serial rapists who target women or men, engage with them online, arrange a date, and then rape them. The victims are often too embarrassed to report it. They feel others will judge them less sympathetically for having engaged in risky behavior.

Confidence scammers know a lot about the people they target. Pedophiles know where they can find their target age range online, how to sound and act like a young person, and how to groom. They have the skills to identify either kids or adults that are vulnerable by what they say and how they act in online chat rooms. Once they zero in on those who are lonely, are sexually confused, lack confidence, or are experiencing some form of emotional pain, neglect, or loss in their life, the predators befriend the target, and then the manipulation begins.

It is difficult to track down online predators of any type because they know how to camouflage themselves. They hide behind fake identifies, fake profiles, and fake photos. They also access sites via proxy servers so they can be more anonymous and untraceable. These predators are usually very experienced. It takes patience and time to develop a successful online victim for the scams they are running, but the payoff for the predator is often thousands of dollars. For this reason, these bad actors will spend an inordinate amount of time and energy developing their online relationship with potential victims. Typically, these monsters are grooming multiple targets simultaneously, and over time, they will drop some of the victims because they see more potential in others. Getting dropped, however, doesn't mean the torture ends because these predators are extremely well-networked and will often pass on a dropped victim to other predators. If a stalking victim is being methodically targeted by online predators, the abuser typically contacts the victim's friends and family members, then hacks the accounts of these affinity connections, and begins stalking *them* for money or sex, as well.

Please, have no doubt that online predators are smart, experienced, effective, master manipulators, and very focused. They gain enormous satisfaction finding new prey and achieving their goals. That is why they are so dangerous. Warning signs of an online predator include:

- Agreeing with everything you say as if you were soul mates or someone who just really gets you.

- Anxious to move from online site engagements to dating or to private methods of communication, email, instant messaging, Skype, texting, or telephone calls.

- Asking for personal information—where you work, where you went to school, etc.

- Wanting to know about your emotional state, getting you to pour your heart out to them.

- Starting to say how much they like you after only a few chats—too interested, too soon.

- Trying to disrupt existing relationships suggesting that your friends and family don't understand, appreciate, or love you—in contrast to the predator who can always understand, appreciate, and love you.

- Knowing things about you that you didn't tell them (they've done their research).

- Knowing when and where you are online, saying "I know you were online because I saw your posts" or always showing up in the same chatroom.

If you are being harassed or stalked online, you will find advice on how to protect yourself on www.digital-stalking.com.

Internet fraudsters use internet services or software to defraud victims or to otherwise take advantage of them, resulting in victims losing hundreds of millions of dollars each year. Online scams are often deployed from unexpected regions of the world, where justice can't easily reach out to catch the perpetrators. According to a report from the Federal Trade Commission, Millennials are particularly vulnerable to online scams, even more so than seniors, as shocking as that may seem. The research finds that 40 percent of adults aged twenty to twenty-nine who have reported fraud ended up losing money in a fraud case.

Online Safety for Kids. Just as parents teach kids to be safe at home by locking the doors at night, parents must now learn how to keep kids safe online. Children are spending more time online for school, clubs, and playdates. Parents don't know all the apps or how to use them, but sexual predators do. They know where the kids are and how to reach them. While it's not necessarily likely your child will be contacted by a predator, the danger does exist.

Cyberbullying is so pervasive and destructive that there really should be jail time required for cyberbullies. Cyberbully predation includes embarrassing or cruel online posts or digital pictures; online threats, harassment, and negative comments; and stalking through emails, websites, social media platforms, text messages, and deepfake videos. Every age group is vulnerable to cyberbullying, but pre-teens and teenagers, as well as young adults, are especially vulnerable targets. Cyberbullying is a growing problem in schools and has become an issue because the internet is anonymous enough to give bullies cover, making their intimidation difficult (but not impossible) to trace. Unfortunately, rumors, threats, and photos can be disseminated online very quickly.

Keeping children safe online starts with the realization that (1) they're going to be online interacting with the entire world, and (2) they're going to be using the social networks, apps, and services that their friends are using and the human predators stalking kids are using. All this will be happening, whether you like it or not.

Parents should also become familiar with parental controls for online devices and use age-appropriate settings to filter, monitor, or block their children's activities. However, if the focus is on monitoring and limiting where their children go online, they may begin to hide their activity from parents, which can put children at greater risk. Safe online behavior is largely about good decision-making and keeping the lines of communication open with your children. Are you prepared to do that?

Defensive Countermoves

Every predatory actor on the World Wide Web is a threat to human prey animals, and it's largely up to the users to take actions to self-defend when using the internet. Most challenging is that technology changes rapidly, and steps you take today designed to defend yourself may be meaningless tomorrow. The smartest countermoves you can make right now are offered by the FBI, other government agencies, and nonprofit organizations at the websites listed below. You are urged to check them out and update at least once a month your knowledge of what to do to protect yourself and your loved ones.

CYBERCRIME INFORMATION

READY

- **https://www.ready.gov/cybersecurity** – This US government website has information about cybersecurity—how to protect yourself, steps to take during and after a cyberattack, and more.

CISA

- **https://www.cisa.gov/cisa-cybersecurity-awareness-program** – The website of the US government's Cybersecurity and Infrastructure Security Agency (CISA) has topics for the public, such as cyber safety, detection and prevention, bad practices, and how to shop safely.

- **https://www.cisa.gov/publication/cisa-cybersecurity-awareness-program-toolkit** – The CISA Cybersecurity Awareness Program Toolkit provides resources for education and awareness regarding internet safety for all segments of the community.

FTC

- **https://www.consumer.ftc.gov/topics/privacy-identity-on-line-security** – Federal Trade Commission (FTC) website has consumer information related to online practices. Topics include limiting unwanted calls and emails, online security, identity theft, coronavirus scams, and how to report fraud to the FTC.

FBI

- **https://www.fbi.gov/investigate/cyber** – The FBI's website has information about cyber threats—how to protect yourself and understanding common cybercrimes and risks online.

NCA

- **https://staysafeonline.org/** – National Cybersecurity Alliance is a nonprofit organization dedicated to online safety with information for individuals, families, and businesses with a robust selection of up-to-date advice.

CYBERCRIME REPORTING

FTC.gov

If you think your computer or mobile device has been infected with malware, report it to the Federal Trade Commission at:

- **https://reportfraud.ftc.gov** – to report fraud
- **https://www.identitytheft.gov** – to report identity theft

SSA.gov

If you believe someone is using your Social Security number, contact the Social Security Administration's fraud hotline at 1-800-269-0271. For additional resources, visit https://oig.ssa.gov/report/.

IC3.gov

If you have been the victim of an online crime, file a complaint with the Internet Crime Compliant Center (IC3), a partnership between the FBI and the National White Collar Crime Center (NW3C), at https://www.ic3.gov/. The website also contains alerts about scams.

MARRIAGE, THE NUCLEAR FAMILY, AND YOUR EXTENDED FAMILY MEMBERS AS VENUES FOR HUMAN PREDATORS

At home among family members is where much of human predatory behavior plays out, and statistics strongly support this claim. On average, nearly twenty people per minute are physically abused by an intimate partner in the United States. In the course of their marriages, one in four women and one in nine men experience severe intimate partner physical violence, intimate partner sexual violence, or intimate partner stalking with impacts such as injury, fearfulness, post-traumatic stress disorder, and contraction of sexually transmitted diseases. Do I have your attention yet?

Why does this happen? What is there about home, marriage, and family life making them venues where predators act out with fierce emotional abuse and violence?

One explanation is that the problems of drug and alcohol abuse are highly correlated with domestic abuse. Let's face it, the drug addicts and alcoholics go home nearly every day, high on drugs or inebriated, or they get high or inebriated at home. The connection between drug and alcohol addiction and violent behavior to gain control over (dominate) others is very high. But this isn't the only driving force behind controlling behaviors in marriage and family life. Much of the abuse that shows up between marriage partners is mate retention behavior. What does that mean?

RED FLAG #47: Human predators oscillate between warm, approving behavior and cold, angry behavior in a pattern that keeps you emotionally off balance. This effect causes you to repeatedly question yourself.

Only in recent times did being a loving, affectionate, kind, considerate, supportive, and encouraging marriage partner become a culturally accepted strategy for retaining a wife or a husband. Historically, iron-fisted domination was the most embraced strategy for a man to retain a woman once married. And only in the last sixty years did married women have any rights at all. Take a look at this list of the rights women didn't have even as recently as 1970 in the United States:

- Women could not own credit cards under their own names.
- Women could not lease property in their own names.
- Women could be fired for becoming pregnant.
- Women could not be admitted to an Ivy League university.
- Women could not attend military academies.
- Women could not be astronauts.
- Women could not serve on juries in all states.
- Women could not serve as a judge.
- Single women struggled to get birth control pills.
- Women could not charge their husbands with spousal rape.
- Women could not receive direct consultation about their physical or mental health.
- Women did not receive any maternity leave.
- Women could not protect themselves from sexual harassment.
- Women could not be the CEO of a Fortune 500 company.
- Women could not adopt a baby as a single person.
- Women could not get abortions throughout the country.

So when you read that women have been retained as marriage partners through control and domination until recent times, you can easily do the math and see what the expression *recent times* means. Societies throughout the world have treated a married woman as property going back to the days of living in caves. But there are many other contributing factors leading to emotional abuse and battering in marriage. Let's look at a common check list of causes:

- Mental illness
- Poverty
- Young parents
- Poor education
- Infidelity
- Cultural/religious differences
- Sexual coercion
- Emotional blackmail
- Money management differences

Are abusers and batterers human predators? The answer is complicated. What's clear is that once the abuser's brain delivers any of the five feel-good brain chemicals for abusive behavior, the offender can quickly become addicted to using abuse, especially if the abuser is also rewarded for his or her abusive behavior. When an abused spouse cowers, gives in, or presents the abuser with behavior(s) deemed in line with what the abuser wants, there is a double reward for the abuser. That can quickly lead to a positive feedback loop encouraging the abuser to repeat abusive behaviors to get his or her way.

Of course, many abusers (and batterers) come to marriage already hard-wired for the role of human predator. This includes all the usual suspects mentioned in this book and many not exposed by this book. Many abusers with personality leanings to be abusive have clinically diagnosable conditions (sociopathy, narcissism, psychopathy, borderline personality, etc.), and many are just shitty humans. The most confounding phenomenon for the outsider looking at abusive marriages is trauma bonding.

Trauma bonding is when the one abused in marriage or family life (including extended family members) comes to see the abuse as normal. Many abusers invest heavily in selling their victims that their abusive behavior *is* normal *and* acceptable. This also occurs where there is sexual abuse of children by relatives or even parents. Fear and actual violence against the abused can also create trauma bonding to the extent that the one being abused will go to great lengths to protect the abuser. It's common to see these abuse victims lie for their abuser, make excuses for the acts committed against them, and threaten anyone who offers to intervene to stop the abuser by going to the authorities.

What are the best defenses against abusers in a marriage or within a nuclear or extended family?

Defensive Countermoves

1. All defensive action against domestic abuse begins with seeing yourself as worthy of defending. If you have been abused, your self-worth has been wounded. That means it's likely you will not take immediate action but, rather, will attempt to sort things out on your own. Do not make this mistake. At the first signs of emotional or physical abuse, take action to at least talk with a professional therapist and sort things out in his or her office where you can let your feelings out and make a plan together.

2. If you experience battering and there are just the two of you (no children in the marriage), get out of the house and stay with a friend or family member you trust. You are now one step away from the level of danger where your life may be at risk. If the marriage has any chance of surviving, you have to make a powerful statement by leaving immediately. Your batterer must know that under no conditions will you remain in a marriage relationship where you are physically at risk.

3. If your abuser becomes more threatening in response to your leaving, you now require a team of protecting specialists, and the players on that team must include a local domestic violence agency, the police, your physician, legal counsel, a domestic violence therapist, and family members and friends who you know to be strong advocates of your mental and physical health.

4. If your abuser is contrite and willing to enter couples therapy while giving you distance (and, therefore, a sense of safety), understand that while couples therapy may work, it can also reveal truths about your abuser that you didn't know and which can torpedo a marriage. Never go into couples therapy without signing a written agreement prohibiting any physical abuse or violence by either party. A verbal commitment prohibiting physical abuse is not sufficient.

5. If it turns out your abuser is a human predator prone to stalking, threats, psychological torture, and violence, you will need training in self-defense. For these people, being rejected is a justifiable reason to commit extreme violence and even murder. Every form of self-defense and protection from these extreme predators should be considered.

6. If you have children and only you are being abused, your children are, nevertheless, being affected by the conflict in your family, even if they aren't directly exposed to the abuse. If there is direct exposure to the abuse, or worse, if your children are also being abused, then you must take their welfare into consideration immediately. Providing therapy for your children is one strategy to consider if you can afford it. Most can't afford therapy for their children, but an emergency plan can be created by anyone wanting to protect his or her children from the damage created by marital abuse and violence. The National Domestic Violence Hotline for victims is 1-800-799-SAFE (7233); or for TTY, 1-800-787-3224; or www. thehotline.org. Information about local programs or resources is also available through this service.

THE DIFFICULTY OF SPOTTING PREDATORS AND PROTECTING YOURSELF

Seeing sharp lines delineating those with predatory behavior patterns is not easy. Life is extremely untidy, and this is no less true when it comes to spotting predatory humans and defining exactly what you are looking at. This means all the preceding effort to help you create understanding of the usual predatory suspects who may cross your path won't be as useful as you hope it will be.

Some people are only situationally predatory, meaning they become predatory only under certain circumstances. Think of the military veteran who hears a loud noise while out to dinner with friends. The noise sounds like a rifle discharge to his ears, but in fact the loud noise was caused by a waiter accidentally dropping another patron's meal. Instantly, the military veteran goes into fight mode as if he were back in Afghanistan. He grabs a knife from the table and immediately stabs several people, one of whom is mortally wounded. In the veteran's mind, he is saving the lives of his buddies seated around his table. Looking at his behavior through the eyes of everyone else in the restaurant, he has become a stone-cold killer. This is only one example of how hard it can be to see predatory behavior in advance and change course to avoid becoming a target.

RED FLAG #49: All those behind online scams and offline scams are human predators. The largest cohort of scam artists are conducting their cons as investment opportunities. The largest, most profitable investment scams are cryptocurrency scams and unsolicited contacts by phone about investing. Right behind these two huge threats are Ponzi schemes, celebrity endorsement scams, and investment seminar scams.

Another case in point comes from when I was in graduate school, working on a master's degree in social work (which I did not ultimately complete). A professor presented our class with a case study of a homeless person who presented as a narcissistic sociopath with an attendant persecution complex. After a two-hour presentation and discussion with the class, she revealed the subject to be Jesus of Nazareth. Some in the class went ballistic. Others laughed at their own inner conflict caused by religious beliefs and the discussion they had just participated in. Perspective is *huge* when it comes to defining what we think we see. Yet the overarching message of this book is that you must be able to discern when you are personally under attack by human predators. How to do this accurately isn't ever going to be easy.

Sometimes you will observe patterns of predatory behavior that look like a wolf, walk like a wolf, and talk like a wolf, but what you are seeing isn't a wolf at all. Sometimes you are looking at people with shadow syndrome behaviors—mild patterns of behaviors we typically assign to human predators. These can be the result of stage-of-life issues, difficult people with emotional or mental health problems who occasionally annoy others, or people just being assholes. All these individuals fall at the lower end of the human predator bell curve, representing about 5 percent of the total. They are not soul-sucking human predators or malignant human predators who populate the higher end, also about 5 percent, of the human predator bell curve. (The massive middle, representing about 90 percent of human predators are not as bad as the worst 5 percent, but they are still capable of doing material harm to you and to people you care about.)

The point is your new knowledge of what to look for to protect yourself must *always* be weighed carefully before acting on your observations. But what should you weigh your observations against?

The word DEFCON, a combination of *defense ready condition*, is embraced by the military as referring to five progressive levels of threat to security where DEFCON 5 is the lowest threat condition and signifies a current state of peace and DEFCON 1 is the highest level and, therefore, should trigger the highest defense-readiness status. I have come up with my own DEFCON status scale for assessing human predator threats, which I highly recommend as a way of answering these three questions:

1. Does someone I deeply care about need to take defensive action?
2. Do I need to take defensive action?
3. How rapidly do I need to take defensive action?

- DEFCON 5. No one I am aware of and care about is being stalked by a human predator, and presently I am not being stalked by one. I am good to go about my daily life with only my lookout antenna scanning for new predatory humans who may cross my path.

- DEFCON 4. I have seen red-flag warnings a new human predator is in my territory looking for fresh meat. Because he or she has the potential to engage with me or someone I deeply care about, I am on alert. There is still ample time to notify my friend(s) and to personally review the lessons taught in this book to confirm my suspicions. I am now officially on predator-watch and will do all in my power to avoid this person (or his or her predatory wolf pack) while I continue my observations and evaluate the threat level.

- DEFCON 3. I am (or someone I deeply care about is) now in the sights of a confirmed human predator. This predator has engaged with me (or someone I care about) and is already causing upset, confusion, and fear. Every move I make has to be carefully thought out, and at no time must I show the predator fear or take action that will cause an escalation of his or her interest in me. It's time to gather my support team and begin carefully preparing my strategic battle plan because soon enough this predator will, at the very least, test me and see how I react to a mock attack. If a friend, colleague, or family member is the one under threat, it's time to give the targeted prey a copy of this book to read, as well as have a heart-to-heart talk with him or her.

- DEFCON 2. I have become the target of a confirmed human predator who has locked on to me and is ready to make a full, frontal attack or already has begun the attack. Making myself invisible or untouchable is my only option now. This is my last off-ramp opportunity. If I am going to escape this predator's clutches, I must move beyond his or her grasp NOW.

- DEFCON 1. I am committed to all-out, thermonuclear war with a human predator. The fight is on, and I will win only if my army of friends, colleagues, and family are as committed as I am to my battle plan. I must be wily, cunning, and clever and never play by this predator's rules and expectations in the battle ahead. I will employ every deceptive strategy and tactic to defeat my enemy. Surprise, shock, and awe are my most deadly weapons against this person. Only one of us will walk away from this fight.

Never expect a smooth transition from one threat level to another. Sometimes you can go from DEFCON 4 all the way to DEFCON 2 in a matter of minutes. Talk about feeling blindsided! Yet you don't ever have to be completely blindsided if you've read this far. And having read this far, you will always be able to find your way back to DEFCON 5 because of the lessons taught in this book.

Please also remember this: we all have chinks in our armor that make us look like predatory people at times, so be slow to judge because the human eye and the way the human mind connects dots are often flawed.

Finally, no one falls at 0 on the predatory behavior rating scale from 1 to 10. Even you, dear reader, have the potential to become predatory (something that has been brought to your attention more than once in this book). If you think you know someone who has zero potential to display predatory behavior—BE AFRAID! BE VERY AFRAID! You are only fooling yourself.

RECOVERING FROM HUMAN PREDATOR ENCOUNTERS

No one likes the aftereffects of having been terrorized or traumatized by a human predator. If you have been married to a predator, dated one, worked for one, been conned by one, or had to deal with one of these monsters on the internet, you know exactly what I'm talking about. But do you have to get stuck emotionally and wallow in the pain of what's happened to you the rest of your life?

Resilience describes the ability to bounce back from any defeat or failure, mistake or setback caused by any number of life's crackups. And resilience is what is required to move on from entanglement with any type of human predator.

Resilience begins with accepting your thoughts and feelings about what has happened to you and looking at them with deep curiosity and a willingness to learn how and why you got caught in a human predator's trap(s). But moving on from the hurts and scars from your ordeal requires something else. And that something else is what I want to discuss with you now.

Moving on with your life begins when you take time to consciously think about what you really care about in life and commit to writing the goals and objectives you think will truly allow you to believe and to feel your life matters in this world. Additionally, moving on means looking at the values you believe in with all your heart and rededicating yourself to organizing your behavior towards others around those values.

Practically speaking, I've found the following strategies to be the most helpful ones for managing your emotions and bouncing back from a human predator's negative impact on your life. These suggestions will help only once you have redocumented your goals and objectives and recommitted to your relationship values.

1. Do an honest self-appraisal

Do you still feel threatened? Then what would it take for you to *not* feel that way? Imagine there existed no restrictions on you to get the burden of feeling fearful off your back (legally, of course). How can you eliminate any further threats from your tormentor? How can you improve your personal sense of safety? Write down all the ideas that come to your mind, then go back, and circle the most practical ideas. Finally, start implementing those steps immediately. If something unresolved about your former entanglement with a human predator still lingers, nip it in the bud. If you don't, you'll feel perpetually frustrated and angry.

2. Reframe

Resilient people bounce back faster when they eliminate the drama they have in their heads. I learned about reframing initially from the greatest hypnotherapist who ever lived, a man named Milton H. Erickson. By deeply relaxing in a quiet room with no distractions, I was asked to tell myself a different story about a highly traumatic experience that had nearly paralyzed me emotionally. After doing this, I was instructed to write the new story down in great detail. Then every morning when I awoke, I read the new story before getting out of bed, and I repeated this discipline each night before falling asleep. Soon, this new story became the only way of thinking about the events that had transpired. The old story I had been obsessing on slowly became completely replaced by the new story. Anyone can do this by following these same steps.

3. Set new boundaries

Something blinded you to the predator who got claws into you, and it's time to look at the cause of this blindness. Why? Because there will be others, and to avoid them next time you must set new boundaries that will keep predatory people at arm's length. The most resilient people recover from predatory encounters by learning what weaknesses in themselves drew them to their tormentors and then saying no to anyone who interferes with their goals, schedules, personal values, and beliefs. You don't have to let anyone into your inner circle who isn't invited there. Those in that select group believe in you, respect what you are trying to accomplish, and can help you reach your goals and objectives. Draw a line in the sand against anyone who insults you, offends you, or belittles you or your goals and values. Firmly (but not harshly) push back against all would-be critics, nay-sayers, and those who want to take you on detours.

4. Don't take responsibility for the actions of your tormentor

Once you are disentangled from a human predator, it's important to recognize you aren't responsible for who they are, how they mistreated you, or if they will continue harming others. Having read this book, you understand that just surviving entanglement with a predatory human is a huge accomplishment. Don't ever play the blame-game with yourself for what they are (which is the epitome of darkness). Don't lay a guilt trip on yourself. Predators are supremely good at setting traps and making themselves difficult to see for what they are. You are not stupid, a sucker, or irresponsible. Whatever drama they sucked you into is not your fault. Take responsibility only for yourself, and don't go through life beating yourself up for the destructive behaviors of others.

5. Cut all ties to toxic people

When you have been wronged by a human predator, not only do you have to cut all connections to them, but you also need to thoughtfully assess your entire network to see if there are others who may be lurking close by, just waiting to pounce. The purpose of this final suggestion is to clear your network of all toxic people. Getting yourself free of anyone who is poisoning your life is the best way to lighten your load and begin the rest of your journey unburdened. Once you weed out the control freaks, the manipulators, and the takers who are leeching from you, it's like a rebirth. Resilient people are those who periodically weed their garden of friends and professional connections who are sucking up the nutrients from the soil that are vital to their own growth and development. Yes, weeding out your network is hard work, but as any farmer will tell you, those weeds are worse than toxic; they will kill off your dreams and end up putting you in the ground.

DO YOU NEED HELP?

Some reading this book may be suffering from clinical depression as the result of an encounter with a human predator. Clinical depression from emotional trauma is treatable only with prescribed medications from a competent physician or psychiatrist. If you are hesitant to find the medical help you need, that's perfectly understandable but not at all help-ful. Here is a list of signs you may be suffering from depression:

- Feeling sad, empty, or tearful
- Feeling worthless or guilty with self-blame
- Loss of interest or pleasure gained from activities
- Agitation or irritability
- Decreased energy, fatigue, sleep disturbances (too few or too many hours)
- Changes in appetite with weight loss or weight gain
- Difficulty concentrating, thinking, speaking, or making decisions
- Frequent thoughts of death or suicide

Depression may also be experienced more physically, with some indi-viduals reporting back pain, headaches, or body aches that cannot be otherwise explained. If any combination of the symptoms listed above is interfering with your daily life, it may be time to seek help from a medical or behavioral health professional. Do not wait another day. Reach out and get the help you need and deserve.

A FINAL WARNING

Since forever, humans have been attempting to answer this question about life, "What is really going on here?" Some of the most intelligent people who ever walked the Earth have taken their best shot at this question. From Plato, Socrates, Karl Marx, Charles Darwin, and many others have come some of the most thoughtful theories on the meaning and purpose of life, community, and social organization as expressed by the human mind. Each theory offered up by these brainiacs was an attempt to explain every human interaction we witness. Problematically, they all made the same assumption (whether explic-itly or implicitly)—that humans are all similarly rational and similarly capable of forming warm, caring, even loving bonds with their fellow humans.

We, as authors of this book, set our sights much lower than the great philosophers and economists who wanted to provide humankind with a grand theory explaining the meaning and purpose of human existence and the natural order of things. By focusing only on a small part of the truth about human beings and human existence, that is, the threats and real dangers of human predators, our book was designed from the beginning to protect rational humans from those predators. What does it mean to us to provide you protection from predatory humans? Simply stated, we set out to give you a new set of lenses so you can at least see these dangerous people, avoid them if you can, or free yourself from those who are using and abusing you.

> **RED FLAG #61:** Human predators use scarcity of supply, phony deadlines, and other classic sales tricks to manipulate you.

The assumption we made is that relatively intelligent readers will easily connect the dots to the deviant behaviors they have witnessed, that we described in these pages, and that are reported on news services daily. Reading this book will, at least, have given you a deeper understanding about human predators and their actions—scammers, con artists, financial crimes committed against unsophisticated investors, and cruel and twisted behaviors witnessed at work, in the home, or on the internet—and the armor needed to protect yourself from them.

Now, however, what you do with this information is your decision to make, and the consequences of your decision are yours to deal with. If you go around calling people names like *human predator* or *asshole* (or worse), you won't like (or find any sympathy for) the hostility that is swiftly heaped upon you. However, if you use the red-flag warnings and your new in-depth knowledge to dodge the sugar-coated ploys, tricks, manipulations, bullying tactics, and threats of human predators hunting for you and others, you will find your life's journey a lot more pleasant.

KEY POINTS

1. You can't change human predators! But you can make yourself less attractive to them by coming across to everyone you meet as physically strong and confident, calm and observant, emotionally solid, highly skilled in your chosen field of endeavor, and fully aware that everyone in the human jungle is not a potential new friend.

2. Section 4 has covered all the usual suspects to raise your awareness of how they operate and the smart countermoves you can make to avoid them when you spot one of these deviants. Yet there are many predatory humans who have only shadow syndromes of the classic predators described here. Still, these shadow syndrome predators can often be spotted using the red-flag warnings found at the end of this section.

3. *Resilience* is the ability to bounce back from any defeat, failure, mistake, or setback caused by any number of life's crackups. And resilience is required to move on from entanglement with any type of human predator. If you are presently in the clutches of someone who is sucking the emotional life out of you, reach out and get the help you need and deserve. If you recently escaped abuse at the hands of anyone who fits this book's definition of a predatory human, you also may need guidance, coaching, and treatment for trauma in order to find and be your most resilient self. Do not hesitate to seek the guidance required to learn fully why you were targeted, trapped, and abused. Then use your new knowledge to protect yourself in the future and cut all ties to toxic people in your life.

RED-FLAG WARNINGS OF HUMAN PREDATORS

"

*In the following pages, sixty-five RED-FLAG WARNINGS
are presented to help with early identification
of human predators.
As long as you continue to believe and treat
predatory humans as normal people,
avoiding entanglement with them is impossible.
Trying to continually explain your feelings to them,
as if human predators don't understand, is a mistake.
They know what they are doing,
and they know it is painful to you.
They just don't care.
The sooner you accept this fact, the sooner you will
escape their grasp, and the sooner you will heal.*

"

BEWARE!

RED FLAG #1 – Human predators will try to isolate you from friends and loved ones. Their purpose is to be the only voice you ever hear so they can better control you.

RED FLAG #2 – Human predators will try to keep you away from anyone from their past who knows them intimately and may try to warn you about them. Their goal is never to reveal anything about their real lives, letting you fill in the blanks on your own.

RED FLAG #3 – Human predators become extremely jealous if they see you enjoying yourself with other people.

RED FLAG #4 – Human predators have little to no empathy for anyone or any living creature. Occasionally they can appear to have empathy for family members (especially their own children), but this is actually an expression of their ego as they see their offspring as mere extensions of themselves.

RED FLAG #5 – Because they have no empathy, human predators do not catch a yawn when you yawn. You can be in a room with five people and yawn, and everyone will start yawning except the one who has no empathy.

RED FLAG #6 – Flattery will often be used by human predators to get close to their prey. The line between compliments and flattery is often indistinguishable to human prey animals who are needy for attention. But there is an essential difference between the two. Flattery is a form of seduction and is used to get you to lower your defenses and surrender your trust and loyalty. A genuine compliment never seduces; it builds you up. A human predator's compliments may be true but have no sincerity, making flattery one of the hardest manipulations to see.

RED FLAG #7 – Human predators will repeatedly test your boundaries. If you try to mark boundaries, they will label you reactive and narcissistic, and they will constantly attempt to push past them or get you to loosen your standards.

RED FLAG #8 – Human predators love bomb during courtship, snowing their victims with a whirlwind of attention and validation and showering the person they are courting with gifts, love letters, texts, emails, and constant, over-the-top pronouncements of their love with statements like "Ours is a real connection," "I never met anyone like you," and "You are a true soulmate." All this behavior is presented too much and too fast with courting predators but may go unnoticed by anyone suffering from a broken heart or deeply needy. This practice is designed to make you feel like you can't complain.

RED FLAG #9 – Human predators use emotional blackmail—a technique that makes you believe if you do X, you are a great friend, girlfriend, daughter, wife, colleague, etc. But if you do Y, you are unattractive, bad, dumb, etc.

RED FLAG #10 – Human predators will say things to friends and colleagues like "If you were a true friend, you would do (BLANK) for me." This is called friendship shaming.

RED FLAG #11 – Human predators build you up and praise you everlastingly when you are loyal, but they tear you to pieces if you ever disagree with them. Creating this contrast of emotional highs and lows makes you desperate to win back their favor when they are displeased with you.

RED FLAG #12 – Human predators love to use self-esteem sabotage. Whatever you accomplish, they will always make it sound like it's nothing important. Downgrading your accomplishments and belittling you are all part of this same predatory behavior.

RED FLAG #13 – Human predators manipulate human prey animals by attacking a person's character. For example, a dear friend was once told she would make a horrible mother because her pet cat whined constantly. She was dating a man who wanted the cat out of her life, perhaps because the cat was receiving more attention than he was. Human predators will stoop to anything to get what they want.

RED FLAG #14 – Human predators constantly give back-handed compliments—negative feedback offered as a compliment, a hostile question, a comparison of you to others, or comments about the way you dress or even about your body in an attempt to lower your self-esteem. For instance, "Your sister looks fantastic! You should take a cue from her and start working out." Or, "Well don't you look fabulous! I would never be brave enough to wear that hairstyle with your face shape."

RED FLAG #15 – At all costs, human predators set up their lives so they aren't directly accountable to anyone at work, at home, or in any way that might bring down criticism on them.

RED FLAG #16 – Human predators offer evasive answers when confronted or even probed casually for information about themselves. If they feel you are accusing them, they will respond with counterattacks, putting

YOU on the defensive. Behind this ploy to distract you or change the subject, look for a denial of anything they are accused of doing.

RED FLAG #17 – Human predators always blame others when things go wrong—a way of deflecting responsibility for bad outcomes of all types. They always accuse others of being the reason for their bad luck, their failed relationships, or the problems they have with fellow workers or their boss. Frequently they will engage in preemptive reputation trashing of others as a way of setting these people up to be the fall guy for their own failures.

RED FLAG #18 – Some human predators love to create conflict and will often blurt out inappropriately negative comments about someone who is in the room or part of a shared conversation. This is designed to force everyone else in the room to choose sides of either the person whose feelings have been hurt by the negative comment or the predator who has made the negative comment. With just the utterance of a small follow-on negative comment by the predator, the two sides can find themselves at each other's throats. The predator gets a reward from watching the conflict unfold.

RED FLAG #19 – Human predators frequently engage in truth bullying. They will beat you up with their version of the truth until you acquiesce. If you attempt to argue or defend your version of the truth, they will belittle your argument or dismiss it.

RED FLAG #20 – Bullies are human predators. Bullying is any intentional and aggressive behavior causing another person stress, duress, or anxiety. It's used to make a target feel inferior, small, unimportant, and unloved. Bullying gives the human predator a false sense of power and a temporary feeling of superiority. It can include yelling, cursing, threats or other forms of intimidation, physical assaults, laughing, mocking, name calling, giving orders, shaming, belittling, negative and hurtful comments or criticisms, ignoring, gossiping, false accusations, leaving others out on purpose, acting disrespectfully, minimization and invalidation, and having no regard for how cruel behaviors are affecting the other person.

RED FLAG #21 – Human predators are masters of bringing in another to make you and the other fight for the human predator's attention. This is known as triangulation. One way triangulation is achieved by predators is forcing you to relay all your communications to them through a third party, and they then send all their communications to you through a third party.

RED FLAG #22 – Human predators often use guilt trips on their intimate partners to dominate them. The point of laying guilt trips on intimate others is to flood their minds with feelings of taking responsibility for everything that happens in the relationship, which is a form of imprisoning them.

RED FLAG #23 – Anyone with whom you must work, live, or have a professional relationship and who is constantly self-referential is a warning you are dealing with a human predator. Being self-referential means frequently using *I*, *me*, *my*, and *mine* and always steering the conversation back to himself or herself in whatever way possible.

RED FLAG #24 – Human predators tell very impressive stories about themselves and dominate conversations with you and others to maintain control of the narrative they want to promote as a way of maintaining their dominance. Human predators may hear you tell a story about something important that happened to you, but instead of actively listening and encouraging you to talk more about your feelings, the details of your experience, and how those details contributed to your feelings, they follow your story with a story of their own that they think is very similar, but it will always top yours in dramatic ways, inviting you to make them the center of attention. This is known as conversational narcissism.

RED FLAG #25 – Human predators are superior at playing the victim when others confront them with behaving badly. A person with real confidence never needs to be in the victim position.

RED FLAG #26 – A pervasive pattern of grandiosity in someone's storytelling, or the need for admiration demonstrated by exaggerating achievements and talents, is also a sign you are with a human predator.

RED FLAG #27 – Human predators often take credit for the achievements of others, thereby making themselves look like the hero when they are, in fact, the chaos-maker.

RED FLAG #28 – Human predators have an exaggerated view of their abilities. They consider themselves to be the best to handle or manage any situation, even if they have to rewrite history.

RED FLAG #29 – Human predators can't take constructive criticism. If you try to correct them or confront them with their own issues, they become offended and even angry. Often, they will turn your most constructive suggestions into an attack on you.

RED FLAG #30 – Human predators always say no to invitations you extend to them that are important to you but from their point of view not useful to them and their highly focused agenda.

RED FLAG #31 – Human predators make promises they never keep. Then when you get upset, they try to make you look crazy for being so rattled. Then they make another promise they won't keep. Any apologies you hear from them are false, and the unkept promises will just keep coming.

RED FLAG #32 – Human predators can't speak the words "I'm sorry." The closest they ever come to expressing empathy for others is to say, "I'm sorry you feel that way." This is usually followed by some subtle criticism like, "If you were more mature . . ." No circumstances will ever move them to express guilt or remorse for letting you down.

RED FLAG #33 – Rules and ethics do not apply to human predators! This includes little social rules, dating rules, and parking rules, or it could mean breaking laws, embezzlement, fraud, or murder. If human predators want something and conventions, rules, or laws prevent it, justifications will be invented as to why in their case none of these proscriptions apply. Look for patterns or a sense of entitlement with unrealistic expectations of special treatment or compliance with their expectations.

RED FLAG #34 – Many human predators see themselves as superior to everyone, and if they don't receive treatment reflecting their superiority, they often become rude or even abusive.

RED FLAG #35 – Human predators frequently come across as cold and punishing, overly punitive, and vengeful in both thoughts and actions.

RED FLAG #36 – Whenever you find yourself with someone who speaks in all-or-nothing terms, you are highly likely with a human predator. These people see others as all good or all bad. When they get into disagreements with others, the human predators rapidly escalate the conflict into much larger judgments of the whole relationship. For example, you might hear them declare, "If you won't agree (on this minor issue), let's just dissolve our business partnership. Besides, you are the worst partner I've ever had."

RED FLAG #37 – Human predators often display no emotion in their conversations with you.

RED FLAG #38 – Lying, misdirection, and tricking others are human predators' ways of dominating human prey animals and among their few
sources of personal satisfaction. Be quick to distance yourself from
anyone you catch lying or using misdirection and obfuscation. Even if
someone only boasts about how he or she tricked others, you should
sit up and take notice.

RED FLAG #39 – When human predators engage in lying, they can do so without any of the tells of people who have a conscience.

RED FLAG #40 – Because human predators don't have empathy and an emotional life as you experience emotions, they have to guess and act out
what they think are appropriate emotions. But they often get it all
wrong and express (act out) inappropriate emotions. They get emotional at the wrong things. Emotional responses that are out of sync
with the situation should be a huge red flag for you. Human predators
don't understand why everyone else cries at the end of the movie and
will actually say so. Be sure to notice what they DO react to.

RED FLAG #41 – Human predators take risks that endanger others. They have
a reckless disregard for safety of self or the safety of others as indicated
by being indifferent to or rationalizing having hurt, mistreated, or stolen from another. This trait is called shamelessness.

RED FLAG #42 – Human predators are often addicted to drugs.

RED FLAG #43 – Human predators often engage in trolling activities on the
internet (a form of cyberbullying). Online forums, Facebook pages,
and newspaper comment forms are bombarded with insults, provo-
cations, or threats by trollers. Supporters argue it's about humor, mischief, and freedom of speech. But for many, the ferocity and personal
nature of the abuse verges on hate speech. In its most extreme form, it
is a criminal offence. It is usually carried out by young adult males for

amusement, boredom, and revenge, but the targets of these predators are left feeling abused and emotionally harmed. Some of their victims have even committed suicide.

RED FLAG #44 – Human predators often offer evasive answers when confronted, especially if they are hiding something from you. Be especially watchful for evasive answers that do not actually deny what you accuse them of doing. And be aware that if you don't settle for their evasive answers, they will become extremely angry at you and turn on you with violent outbursts.

RED FLAG #45 – Human predators often present in sports activities as players who care only about the game, not about the other players. For them, winning is all-important, and they will employ any tactic to make sure they win (including cheating), no matter how irrational or inconsistent they may appear to others.

RED FLAG #46 – Human predators love to gaslight their victims. Gaslighting is a form of abuse and manipulation focused on making someone doubt his or her own reality. How do they do that? They deny they said or did something, even with proof. They accuse you of doing things you know they have done. They turn others against you to take away your support system. They tell you that you're crazy. If you find you are never right when around someone, you constantly feel like you have to defend reality, your self-trust erodes, you feel confused about whether you are on good terms with the person gaslighting you, or you are collecting proof things happened with a particular person, you are almost certainly a victim of gaslighting.

RED FLAG #47 – Human predators oscillate between warm, approving behavior and cold, angry behavior in a pattern that keeps you emotionally off balance. This effect causes you to repeatedly question yourself.

RED FLAG #48 – A willingness for someone to use violence or threats of violence to achieve his or her ends, even when unnecessary, are warning signs you are with a human predator. This trait is often seen in abusive spouses.

RED FLAG #49 – All those behind online scams and offline scams are human predators. The largest cohort of scam artists are conducting their cons as investment opportunities. The largest, most profitable investment scams are cryptocurrency scams and unsolicited contacts by phone about investing. Right behind these two huge threats are Ponzi schemes, celebrity endorsement scams, and investment seminar scams.

RED FLAG #50 – Online dating sites are a favorite hunting ground of human predators looking for human prey animals. Because their potential targets on dating sites are people who openly declare they have lonely hearts, those who use these platforms make easy pickings.

RED FLAG #51 – Con artists are human predators. The telephone is still the favorite tool of con artists, but some scams are accomplished through face-to-face contact. Be aware of debt collector scams, computer performance scams, student loan and financial aid scams, fake bills and invoices received by mail, arrest warrant scams, scam text messages, and affordable care scams aimed at seniors. Avoid all; don't respond to them in any way.

RED FLAG #52 – Human predators have extremely low emotional intelligence. As a result, they are highly likely to fail to pick up on subtly expressed emotional needs you have, often challenge or belittle you on directly expressed emotional needs, and mostly ignore your emotional well-being entirely.

RED FLAG #53 – Human predators listen to your hopes and dreams and concerns to make you feel understood, but then they tell you the only way forward to make your dreams come true is through them.

RED FLAG #54 – Human predators are masterful at getting those around them to keep secrets.

RED FLAG #55 – Human predators who are capable of violence frequently express indifference or violence toward animals.

RED FLAG #56 – Human predators can't tolerate hearing any perspective that threatens their self-perception, and if you or any audience is nearby when this occurs, they will tell their version of the story loudly and with great vigor to erase the cognitive dissonance of your differing account. This is called identity-protective cognition.

RED FLAG #57 – Human predators will dramatically threaten to leave an intimate relationship if they sense you are thinking of separating and attack your ego to keep you reactive and off-balance.

RED FLAG #58 – Online sexual stalkers of children are human predators that you can't see and you can't trace, but they are working seven days a week to make contact with vulnerable teens, and that means children in your family are always at risk when they are online. It's unthinkable, but every year, thousands of children become victims of these predators through kidnappings, violent attacks, rape, or sex trafficking.

RED FLAG #59 – Online stalkers of adults are human predators. Online stalking is unwanted, obsessive attention given to a specific person. This form of predation is different from regular stalking because, in this case, stalkers primarily use digital technology to torment their victims. Many cases of online stalking escalate into real-life stalking.

RED FLAG #60 – Human predators will attempt to make you feel guilty for their emotions (especially their displays of anger), accusing your behavior as the reason they became emotionally upset.

RED FLAG #61 – Human predators use scarcity of supply, phony deadlines, and other classic sales tricks to manipulate you.

RED FLAG #62 – Human predators will make you feel like a hero when doing their bidding and will present your heroism as fighting the barbaric enemy who threatens everyone.

RED FLAG #63 – Human predators love using a tactic known as "The Switcheroo." After they have expressed a strong opinion, they then drop it and adopt the opposite point of view when it's convenient or to embarrass you.

RED FLAG #64 – Because they get bored easily, human predators need constant high-risk stimulation, which causes them to act impulsively and take personal risks that often place them in danger. These behaviors often make them unable to fulfill responsibilities related to family, work, and school.

RED FLAG #65 – Sexual coercion is using emotional extortion; withholding love, affection, or conversation; or even threatening to end the relationship if you do not engage in sex acts that you find personally offensive.

ABOUT THE AUTHORS

JOHN SHIMER

As co-author of *Human Predators*, John Shimer calls on his lifetime of experience as a high-profile consultant to explain the dark and dangerous side of human beings.

"Predatory humans are everywhere among us, yet no one prepares us. Unprepared, we are nothing more than prey animals in the eyes of human predators, people who receive their greatest pleasure from tormenting us with their lies, their head games, their manipulations and abuse."

John is the author of many books including, *Turn Right at the Dancing Cow*, *Secrets to BIG MONEY Fundraising*, *Secrets to Financial Success in Marriage*, *Bubblegum for the Soul*, and *Be Someone's Miracle*. Now retired, John has over fifty years experience managing fundraising campaigns for nonprofit organizations.

CHRISTIAN SHIMER

As a digital filmmaker over the last twenty years who specialized in telling the stories of nonprofit organizations, Christian Shimer has been exposed to the goodness and evil of human nature.

"Why has no one written a book that prepares us for the everyday sociopaths we all come into contact with? We wanted to resolve that in a way that was easy to access and offers real, practical advice we can use in our daily lives."

Christian also has experience as a cruise director for Royal Caribbean International, a radio personality, and a comedy writer. He has been a student of human behavior and psychology throughout his life. He is author of the book, *Secrets to Big Money Using Video: The Art of the Video Case Statement*.

CPSIA information can be obtained
at www.ICGtesting.com
Printed in the USA
BVHW061329070622
639081BV00001B/1